Jon Gruden

All It Takes is All Ya Got

Take This Job and Love It

by Rich Wolfe

Published by Lone Wolfe Press and Legends Publishing

ISBN: 0-9729249-3-0

Cover Photographs: Michael O'Neill and Corbis; Associated Press
Cover Design: Dick Fox
Cover Copywriter: Dick Fox
Photo Editor: Dick Fox
Interior Design: The Printed Page, Phoenix, AZ

You can contact the author directly at (602) 738-5889.

Dedication

To Gary Froid

The Scourge of Burlington, Iowa
The BMOC at Harvard Square
The Towering Figure in St. Petersburg
The King of Rockland, Maine

Acknowledgments

The people who helped me put this book together could probably be sorted into three groups. I don't know what the three groups are or why I would want to sort them, but since everything else in this book is sorted into groups, I thought this would be an appropriate place to start. I'm sure I could figure out the three groups if I had to.

I am personally responsible for all errors, misstatements, inaccuracies, omissions, commissions, comminglings, communisms, and fallacies.... If it's wrong and it's in this book, it's my fault.

What a fun book this has been to put together. But make no mistake, it would never have happened without the help of many people starting with Bill Chastain, Publicist Jack Glasure and the talented team at the Glasure Group PR firm in St. Pete including Beth Bohnsack, Alesia Stevenson, Gail White, and Becca the Beauty, along with Tony Simpson, and Jim Hayley.

A tip of the hatlo hat to the good guys at Wolfegang Marketing Ltd.— BUT NOT VERY! Also Ron Kolwak at the *Tampa Tribune*, John O' Loughlin at Fox 13 in Tampa, Lisa Nelson at the Associated Press, Bob Passwaters at Provident, Jamal Curry at Corbis in New York City and particularly to Barbara Jane Bookman of Louisville, Kentucky, and Celebration, Florida...also, to Andy Pongracz, Tiger Trivia, Karl Miller, John Cunavelis and Paul Hughes. Thanks to Ellen Brewer, the most beautiful, talented and nicest woman in Edmond, Oklahoma, if not the entire state, and clearly the best typist any Sooner has seen since Troy Aikman of Henryetta (OK) High School won the state high school boy's typing championship in 1983.

Thanks also must go to Lisa Liddy, The Printed Page, for her hard work at all hours of the day and night and her patience and professionalism in pulling the many pieces of this book together. Thanks also to Joe Liddy for editing and proofing.

But most of all, thanks to the incredible Gruden family. The way people describe them in this book is exactly the way all of them treated me with kindness, a smile and laughter. Why can't everyone be like them?

Go now.

Preface

Just fifteen months ago, I was more likely to be struck by lightning while honeymooning with Christie Brinkley than to be watching Jon Gruden coaching the Tampa Bay Buccaneers in 2002. You were more likely to see a left-handed female golfer before you would ever see that Tampa Bay offense score 48 points in a Super Bowl.

For so many years, so many Bucs fans had so many hopes, so many expectations...so much for that.

But then Jon Gruden came marching home again with a tint of a tan, a touch of regret, and a ton of intensity. Less than a year later, Gruden and the Bucs had hung the moon and scattered the stars over Tampa Bay. If he was a wise man, he would quit right now 'cause it ain't ever gonna be better than Super Bowl XXXVII. But that's as likely as expecting Refrigerator Perry to stay out of the kitchen.

Meanwhile, he who would trade money for Bill Parcells deserves neither.

Growing up on a farm in Iowa, I avidly read all the Horatio Alger-style books of John R. Tunis, the Frank Merriwell collection and Clair Bee's Chip Hilton series. All preached the virtues of hard work, perseverance, obedience, and sportsmanship, where, sooner or later, one way or another, some forlorn underweight, underdog would succeed beyond his wildest dreams in the arenas of sport. Frank Merriwell, thy name is Jon Gruden.

But Jon Gruden is better than Frank Merriwell. He is real life, more natural than Roy Hobbs, a Rudy with talent. Gruden is manna from heaven to the NFL and every other beleaguered professional sports league. When the Washington Redskins sold for $800 million, perhaps three other teams had a higher street value. More and more players were widowers by choice, Wilt Chamberlain had boasted of having been with 20,000 women (I'm not sure that I've even peed that many times), NFL general managers were hoping that bail money didn't count against the salary cap, Ravens fans didn't know whether to root for the defense or the prosecution, and O.J. was down to about six commandments. (In June of 1994, I was in a restaurant in Branson, Missouri, when I heard someone say that a famous, retired football player had murdered his wife. I said a silent prayer it was **Frank Gifford**.) And, along come the A-Rods, Grant Hills, Kurt Warners, Tom Bradys and Jon Grudens of the world—young people who warm the cockles of an old man's heart. Maybe sports will survive the quagmire of idiots who are dominating the SportsCenters of the day.

I only do books on people who I admire from a distance. The fear, once you start a project, is that the subject will turn out to be a jerk. With Gruden's intensity it could easily follow that he could be a self-absorbed, arrogant, rude boor. As you will soon find out, you would want your son, your brother, your husband or your friends to possess the qualities of humbleness, thoughtfulness, joy for living, the passion for his job, and the love of football and football fans that Jon Gruden has.

There are many stories in this book, but three best sum up Jon Gruden in a nutshell: in high school, Gruden—the star quarterback and Homecoming King—treated a middle-aged retarded follower of the team—a man many of his peers were making fun of—with the same dignity as if he were the principal of the school; Gruden once said he loves football so much that he could get just as much joy from coaching a Pop Warner youth football team as coaching a Super Bowl team; and when defensive coordinator/genius Monte Kiffin

O. J. Simpson's cousin is Ernie Banks. Their grandfathers were twin brothers.

Frank and Kathie Lee Gifford have the same birthday, except they're twenty-three years apart age-wise. They were married in 1986. Frank Gifford was a grandfather at the time. Cody and Cassidy are Uncle and Aunt to Frank Gifford's grandchildren. When told that Kathie Lee was pregnant, Don Meredith said, "I'll hunt the guy down, Frank, and I'll kill him."

was offered other NFL head coaching jobs, Gruden offered to step aside, make Monte Kiffin the Buccaneers head coach and Jon would become his offensive coordinator. Jon Gruden is a man and a coach the way men and coaches once were in an America that is not the way it once was. Tampa Bay is lucky to have him as a coach, Tampa Bay is luckier to have him as a native son and resident. The looming question is: How long before they forget? After all, the composite record of all coaches in NFL history is .500.

From the age of ten I've been a serious collector of sports books. During that time—for the sake of argument let's call it thirty years— my favorite book style is the "eavesdropping" type, where the subject talks in his own words. In his own words, without the "then he said" or "the air was so thick you could cut it with a butter knife" waste of verbiage which makes it hard to get to the meat of the matter. Books like Lawrence Ritter's *The Glory of Their Times*, Donald Honig's *Baseball When the Grass was Real*, or any of my friend Pete Golenbock's books like *Go Gators* or *Amazin' (Mets)*. Thus I adopted that style when I started compiling oral histories of the Mike Ditkas and Harry Carays of the world.

There is a big difference between doing a book on Mike Ditka or Harry Caray and doing one on Gruden. Ditka and Caray were much older than Gruden, thus they had many more years to create their stories and build on their legends. Furthermore, they both liked to enjoy liquid fortification against the unknown, which leads to even more and wilder tales… and multiple wives. So the bad news is when you have someone as young as Gruden, who rarely drinks, who is not a skirt-chaser, who works so many hours a day, he doesn't have time to create "stories."

I'm a sports fan first and foremost. I don't even pretend to be an author. This book, with this unusual format, is designed solely for other fans like myself. I really don't care what the publisher, editors or critics think but I'm vitally concerned that my fellow fan has an enjoyable read and gets his money's worth. Sometimes the person being interviewed will drift off the subject but, if the feeling is that sports fans would enjoy their digression, it stays in the book. So if you feel there is too much on Arena Football, or Steve "Sudden

Death" Sabol, don't complain to the publisher...just jot your thoughts down on the back of a twenty dollar bill and send it directly to me.

In an effort to get more material into the book, the editor decided to merge some of the paragraphs and omit some of the commas which will allow for the reader to receive an additional twenty thousand words, the equivalent of fifty pages. More bang for your buck...more fodder for English teachers...fewer dead trees.

I gotta go now. The phone is ringing. Maybe it's Christie Brinkley. Hey, it could happen. After all, just ask Jon Gruden if there is an expiration date on dreams.

Rich Wolfe
Celebration, Florida

Chat Rooms

Chapter 1

There's No Expiration Date on Dreams

Growin' Up Gruden

WHY CAN'T SUGAR BE AS SWEET AS BOBBY KNIGHT?

TIM KNIGHT

Tim Knight, 38, is the son of famed basketball coach Bobby Knight. He was a childhood friend of Gruden; they served as ball boys for the 1976 national champion Indiana University basketball team. Knight now works as the assistant athletic director in charge of special projects for **Texas Tech**. *He lives in* **Lubbock, Texas**.

In 1976, Jon Gruden and I were thirteen years old, and his dad was assistant football coach at Indiana when my dad was head basketball coach. Jon and I played Little League football together for one year, which is how I first got to know him. After that, I can remember him calling me. I used to go to my mom's and she used to take my brother, Patrick, and me over to Jon's house early on the Saturday mornings that Indiana had home football games. I would play with Jon; and my brother, Patrick would play with Jay. We would head over to the Indiana football games, and then we would play after the games. During IU's basketball games, Jon used to sit on the bench with me and help either mop the floor, or get the towels, the water, whatever, for the players.

Each year my dad would let me take Jon on one or two of the trips we had. Back then, the colleges were allowed to play what they called

> The Texas Tech basketball arena—The Spirit Center—is on Indiana Avenue. Texas Tech has the same nickname as Bobby Knight's high school in Orrville, Ohio—the Red Raiders.

> When Hayden Fry was a high school teacher and coach in Lubbock, Texas, one of his home room students was Roy Orbison.

exhibition games. Each year my dad's team would go play in three or four high school gyms in the state, and the majority of the Indiana high school gyms seat anywhere from five to eight thousand. So, we would go and play an inter-squad game—just split the team up, and play in front of packed high school gyms. Jon would sit on the one bench, and I would sit on the other bench. That meant we got to travel with the team on the bus and have dinner with the team afterwards.

I hadn't talked to Jon for a long time until a couple of years ago—you know how it is when people move—but I have talked to him occasionally since and I have always followed his career. I know he has been quoted as saying that being able to come to practice and sit on the bench has helped influence his career. I just look back to all of the fond memories I have of spending time with Jon and Jay and with my brother. It was kind of interesting. Their brother Jimmy was older, and I think I'm six months younger than Jon. We had a good time. My mom stayed in touch with Jon's mom, Kathy, and I know she talks to Kathy every several months.

Jon and I would be hanging out with guys like Quinn Buckner, Scott May, Bobby Wilkerson and Kent Benson. We would have been sitting on the bench with those guys, sitting on the bus with them, having dinner whenever they had dinner on the trips, and we would have sat with some of those guys at the table. It was a fun interaction. Those guys were really good because they always took care of me. I used to stay with some of those players on the road.

We would leave early in the afternoon and have a couple hour bus ride and then have an inter-squad game, have dinner, and then get back home well after our bedtime. It was a special treat for us to go. Obviously, we would be staying out past our usual bedtimes, but the nice thing was that Jon's parents had no problem with him going with us, because they knew that with dad over his team and the program, there was good supervision. We would just hang around watching my dad work.

I was terrible with Little League sports. I can remember that I didn't like it, and Jon was always the one who would urge me on. We had a coach who made us run, and I just hated it. Jon was always there, "Alright, let's go." He would try to help me get through that. I only played Little League football a couple of years. I remember my last year was on a team with Jon, so I can remember back then that he was the guy that would keep encouraging me to keep going because he knew I did not like it. I think he was the quarterback back then.

I respected the job his dad did, and I respect the job my dad did, and I think the two of us were brought up that way. Hey, we know how to act, and we always did that, so I don't think that was ever an issue. I think for the most part, both of us had the reputation of doing what we were supposed to do, or what our parents wanted us to do.

I hadn't talked to Jon in probably twenty years, and then I've probably talked to him half dozen times in the last couple of years. I called and we talked for a while and then I went by to see him. Three or four summers ago, I had to go to a wedding in California, and I stopped by his office and probably spent one and a half or two hours with Jon. It says a lot when you can just sit there for two hours and visit with somebody you haven't seen for twenty-two years. That is why I kind of regret that I hadn't stayed in touch with him, but as you know, when you're in sixth grade and move on, it's kind of hard. I went to Stanford and Jon went to Dayton, so we were at opposite ends of the country for college.

Even though we hadn't had contact for a while, I always followed where he was in the NFL, when he was assistant and then head coach, both in Oakland and then at Tampa Bay. I have been fortunate in that, here is a guy who was a childhood friend that I was able to follow. Then even further back, I have known Coach Parcells since I was two years old at West Point, so I have always followed his teams. I was ecstatic for Jon to get the Super Bowl this year.

LITTLE LEAGUE GAMES BIG LEAGUE GOALS

ARNOLD SHUSTER

A former administrator at the University of Indiana, Arnold Shuster was among the first to notice Jon Gruden's great potential. He was Jon Gruden's Little League coach.

In '74, my oldest son turned nine and was eligible to play **Little League**. I had a baseball background and wanted to get my kids involved in sports so I began coaching there in Bloomington. We lived in the university environment area, and the Grudens were there. This was Jim Gruden's first year there as assistant to Lee Corso. There were thirty-two teams, four leagues, eight teams per league, and I took the team, Westside Lions, that had the worst record in the city.

About 125 kids would come to try out. They would basically throw the ball back and forth to each other, take a couple of swings, do some pitching and do some defensive work, fielding and catching flies. Before we even started, it was obvious that this little blond kid was very well coordinated and had a really, really intense attitude. I had the number one pick, so I said, "Gee, I think that's going to be my number one pick." Sure enough, when Jon started to hit and started to play defense in practice, it was obvious that this was the kid around which I could build a team. I had five draft picks.

The team was 1 and 13 the previous year and had been knocked out in the first round of their tournament. The first year I had this team, Jon was both pitcher and shortstop. He was the key player. It was such a joy to have Jon as an eleven-year old. He was a "coach in the

> At the Little League World Series, for $16 total, a family of four can each get a ticket, program, hot dog and soda.

making." Half the other kids were not as gifted or talented as he was. He was a real team player and very supportive of the other kids. He was a very bright kid. He got along well with people. He was very intense. He worked hard. He practiced hard. Most important, he wanted to win very, very much.

The first year I had that team, they went 8 and 6 and got to the third round of the tournament. We played three exhibition games before the season, and Jon pitched and played shortstop. We lost a very close game, and the kids were disheartened. Of course these were just youngsters between nine and twelve, not professionals, so being the teacher I said, "Hey, there's always tomorrow. You guys did well. We'll learn from our mistakes and be better the next time." Everybody's spirits seemed a little bit more buoyant except for Jon, who had his chin down. I took my own kids home and went over to see Jon Gruden because he seemed very dejected.

I went to the back of the Gruden house, and Kathy let me in. Jon was sitting on the front steps with his head down. I sat with him for about twenty minutes. We talked about learning. We talked about sports being a thing that helps you cope with life—the successes and the failures. As I left him, his head had come up a little, and he smiled a little bit. I felt very good about the many interactions I had with kids, but I felt particularly good at that point.

At one point, Kathy came out with some milk and chocolate cake, and I waved her back so I could continue the discussion with Jon. Kathy has since told me that was a very, very important time for Jon. It was the beginning of a new kind of thing: competing. We won the city championship the following year. This was unusual for a bunch of professors' kids. This was the league where stonecutters predominated in Bloomington, and their kids were tough and were the good athletes. The University professors' kids were not really the athletes. Jon was the trigger for the Westside Lions. He was the spark plug. He was such a joy to coach.

His brother, Jim who was thirteen, was too old for Little League. Jimmy wasn't that interested in sports, but he was at all the games. He would help out periodically and was a very bright kid and understood the game of baseball very well. Jay was too young at that point, but later I coached Jay for two years, and he was an extremely good athlete, a lot quieter than the two older brothers. He, too, was very intense, and it was fairly obvious that he was going to be a great athlete, too. He was also a very bright kid. They all have different personalities of course.

Jon was an extremely good player. In my opinion, he was the outstanding player in the Little League both years he played. His parents were always very supportive. They were at all his games; although, it was tough for Jim because football interfered periodically. Kathy was more the "team mother" kind of person. She was always there and was very supportive of her kids and of the other kids as well. They were just good people, great people to know and wonderful people to have had in the community, unfortunately, far too briefly. The two who played baseball for me were just wonderful to have because they were such gifted athletes. They were very disciplined, and they are good people. They never downplayed any of the other kids.

My memories of Jon are of him helping other kids. He was like a little coach, as an eleven-year old. He was far more polished in many ways and had innate abilities that the other kids didn't have. He was always very helpful and very patient with the other kids. When they did dumb things, Jon was always there to show them what to do—that kind of thing. Sort of like a little assistant coach.

I saw Jon and his dad in '77 when they were just ready to move up to South Bend. His dad made it to the finals of the City Golf Championship. My boys were just getting into golf, and we went out and followed them around. Jon was **caddying** for him and was very intense, and he wouldn't talk to anybody. He was always just a great kid and always seemed to do things right, both academically at school and certainly in sports. He is what he is because of Kathy and Jim. They're both just super people. Kathy was the ideal mom.

> The Professional Caddies Association (PCA) has 2,800 members and is headquartered in Palm Coast, Florida. Until 2002, the PCA's Hall of Fame was located in founder Dennis Cone's Winnebago.

GRUDEN REALLY PLAYED HARD. HE BROKE HIS NECK FOR ME

BILL FUERBRINGER

Bill Fuerbringer, 62, was the junior varsity football coach when Gruden played at South Bend Clay High School. Fuerbringer is retired and lives in South Bend, Indiana.

I was the Junior **Varsity** coach when Jon Gruden was at South Bend Clay High School and he played quarterback. I liked Jon. He had a little bit of an ornery streak, I guess, which you like to have. You have to have that in your quarterbacks anyway. He's a competitor. There's no doubt about that.

At least in his sophomore year, he was just an average high school quarterback. In his sophomore and junior years he played JV so you know the kids ahead of him were a little stronger and bigger and a little more skilled. I had Jon in the classroom too. I taught History, Social Studies and a little bit of everything. Oh, I guess I could say that grades weren't his priority. He just sort of just "coasted" in the classroom. Every once in a while I'd have to say, "Hey. You have to quit screwin' around." But he was very likeable. He had a good personality. You could just see him in the pros. The way he's coaching now, you seen him get that little look on his face when he's irritated. He hasn't changed in that respect.

He was totally different in the classroom and on the football field. The old intensity barometer went way up to the top when he put on a uniform and his motor was in high gear. You could tell he was passionate about football. When you're around a coaching environment from the time you're seven or eight years old, it just kind of gets ingrained in you. Sons of coaches become very knowledgeable by

> The word "varsity" is the British short form of the word "university."

the time they get into the high school level because they've seen so much and been exposed to the terminology. They really have an in-depth understanding of the game.

Elkhart was a good sized school and pretty tough in football. During his sophomore year, we went over there. During the game, they were just taking pot shots at him. He had one late hit and then another late hit and it was so obviously way after the play was over. I walked out on the football field and called a time-out right to the officials face. One official recognized it and called time-out, the other one came over and gave me a warning for walking out on the field but, basically, I was telling them, "Hey, you guys need to get this game under control or someone is going to get seriously hurt." They didn't really do much about it.

The next year, they came to our field. That's when Jon got hurt. They started out the same way again. In the first half, Elkhart had two players kicked right out of the game. They were taking cheap shots and hitting him late all over again.

Back then in the South Bend area, usually the JV games were not played under the lights. It was late in the season so when we got into the fourth quarter, it was getting a little harder to see out there.

He got another late hit and that's when he went down. That's how he got hurt. He had one of those vertebrae in his **neck injured** badly. I can't remember if it was a crack or a clean break. I know the head coach real, real well and he had some new guys down there trying to help him out on the JV and staffers and these guys just didn't know how to control their players.

It almost turned into a fight after that. Tom King, who was working with me on the JV, and I basically grabbed three or four of the kids and just ran the whole team right towards the locker room so there couldn't be a fight. They shortened the last quarter because it was getting so dark. Fortunately the injury wasn't quite that bad but it was still something scary. By the next season he was okay.

Lost time due to injury in high school football is six days. Lost time due to injury to a high school cheerleader is 29 days.

DOWN AT THE CORNER
OF WHAT AND IF

Photo from 1982

LISA WEBBER KAHLER

Lisa Webber Kahler, 39, was Jon Gruden's high school girlfriend. Today, Lisa is a stay-at-home mom who lives in West Bloomfield, Michigan with her husband and two children. She is a graduate of Ball State.

Jon moved into town in ninth grade, our freshman year. He was a great guy. At that time he was a great kid! He had freckles all over. That is the first thing that comes to my mind. He stood out with the blond hair and blue eyes. The beach boy look is not that prominent in South Bend. He came from Bloomington, Indiana so it wasn't there either.

I met him my freshman year. We hung out with the same group, and with Steve Radde, and they played football. We went to the football games, and we just kind of met through that.

We started dating during freshman year and dated all through high school and for almost two years in college. That is a long time. He was different. After a regular football game on a Friday night, everybody seemed to go to a party. Jon would go home, he would change, and he would come to our house, and we would sit down in our basement and watch TV. It wasn't like he was a big partier, and that's what I liked about him. It took a confident person to go against the grain. I remember we would listen to John Denver.

I have nine brothers and sisters and he was overwhelmed when he would come to the house and everybody would be there—you know, six brothers and three sisters. In talking to my brothers now, they all say it's amazing what he has done. If you would look back on what he was like in high school—he stood up against a wall, and he was very quiet. In high school, you think you're in love, and we talked about marriage.

He always took care of the underdog. There were a couple of kids, especially in high school, who might have had a learning disability or something, and Jon was always for them. Jim Derbin was a neighbor—they used to call him "Derb." Jon was real good to him. A lot of people made fun of Derb because he had a learning disability. Jon didn't make fun, and he was right there for Derb.

Jon was President of our senior class. None of this ever went to his head. He just wasn't that kind of guy. I remember Jon turning red when the school voted him "King of the Prom." It was out of character for him. That's why, when I look at him now, he is very much out of character from what I remember. People ask me, "Was he like that in high school?" I say, "Not around me, he wasn't."

I had brothers who played football and having six brothers in my house, I absolutely never felt I competed against football. Football never got in the way. I loved sports. I remember him telling me early on that he wanted to be a coach. I felt at that age, go for it, do what you want. I didn't really think he was going to do it. I remember his father saying that he didn't want him to major in physical education, because coaching was hard to get into. He wanted him to have another background, whether it was business or whatever—but coaching is what Jon wanted to do.

A typical date for us would be to go out to dinner, go to a movie. When his dad was at camp, I flew out one time to see Jon, and he was working in a restaurant, flipping burgers or something.

He was a caring person. We couldn't afford romantic things like roses and candy while we were in high school. It didn't matter where we went to dinner. We went to Red Lobster a couple of times. It's funny because when we would go to dinner, very rarely would he use his real last name, because no one could pronounce it.

I remember my grandmother loving him. We would go over to see my grandma sometimes and she just thought he was the "cat's meow."

Having my grandmother approve of someone I dated always made me feel good.

When he was at **Muskingum** in Ohio, his first year, he had a great group of friends. I would drive six hours to see him. I was at Holy Cross Junior College in South Bend, going to school part-time and working part-time. My mom would give me her little Mazda and away I'd go for the weekend. We'd go up to Ohio State and see the guys that he hung out with. He knew some people at Ohio State and that's what we would do. When he went to Dayton is when it kind of went downhill. I remember sending him back two rings in the mail. I got married in 1989, and I don't know when he got married. Our breaking up had nothing to do with his personality. It was hard. He was at one school and I was at another school. You read back on some of the things, like what he wrote in my yearbook, and you think, "Wow, I thought we would really try to get married." But, in high school, how many people say that? Probably a lot!

My husband gets harassed. My brothers call him, and they say things like "Oh, you know, we could have got Super Bowl tickets, but instead we're getting golf balls with your logo on them." Poor guy, he hears it from everybody. He's a great sport. When the Bucs came out to play the Lions, one of my brothers tried to get close down to the field, but, of course, you can't do that.

I did talk to Jon when he was a graduate assistant at Tennessee, and I think that was our last conversation. I absolutely have good memories of Jon. I wish him well. I always have. I have two girls now, and we were all rooting for the Bucs. They're like, "Mom, he's your old boyfriend, mom, mom, mom." I have a nine- and a seven-year-old, and they were excited. My family was too. My family was rooting for him. How could you not? He was almost like one of the family. My mom says, "I don't remember him saying a lot."

One out of 40 high school basketball players play college basketball. One out of 15 play football.

JOE MONTANA WAS HURT, SO COACH DEVINE PULLED JON AND I OUT OF THE STANDS TO WIN THE GAME FOR NOTRE DAME. PLAY ALONG, OKAY?

STEVE RADDE

Steve Radde, 39, was a high school teammate and friend of Gruden. Today, Steve runs a security company and lives in South Bend, IN.

Photo from 1982

My earliest memory of Jon is probably going into our freshman year at South Bend Clay High School, mostly when we were playing baseball. We hit it off right away. Jon was an athlete in every sport, baseball, basketball, intramural basketball, the whole works. He is a great guy.

As we moved up to our sophomore year, we got more and more involved in football, and were a little bit tighter as well. I was a wide receiver, and Jon was a quarterback. We spent some time together on and off the field. We used to go fishing every once in a while and just hang around. We were closest in our junior and senior years. One time, we left school a little bit early with two other buddies of ours to go fishing up in **Michigan**. It was not during football season or anything. It was kind of a laid-back trip. We rented a rowboat and went out where it was quiet with maybe only one other boat on the lake. We would go from bluegill to bass. Jon went there a couple of times with our football coach. He loved to fish.

> The state of Michigan has more golf courses than any other state in the Union.

As a kid, he was the same way he is now. Back then, we played a lot of sports and just had a lot of fun. We would go to a party together and have a couple of beers. When Jon was in his junior and senior years, he was with a girlfriend, Lisa Webber, for a lot of the time. In school he was like everybody else—you stand in the hallway, you talk, you walk your girlfriend to class.

But football was the fun and the joy of it all. It wasn't until senior year or so that we really got intense about football. We tried to find out what we wanted to do, try to go to schools, try to look for scholarships, different things like that. That's where he and I were off the beaten track, and we just started throwing. Before our senior year, we went over to Penn High School—a rival school—and worked out with the guys there. We would throw against them. We practiced our patterns, and we just did a ton of stuff together.

I played in the game against Elkhart when Jon broke his neck. That was the end of our sophomore. It was a "B" team game at the high school, and he got speared right in the back. Back in those days, you didn't have the doctors around right away, especially for "B" team games. Coach said, "You're all right." But then a couple of other people were saying, "No, hey, don't move him, don't touch him. Wait and see what's happening." He had a neck brace on for quite a while, and it's in our yearbook.

That summer before our senior year, we went to the **soccer** field by his house and practiced every day. We'd go up there and stretch a little bit. We ran wind sprints, and then we did pass patterns. We did everything from down-and-outs to short slants and post patterns… everything. We practiced Jon scrambling out, me going deep, Jon going back, and me coming up. We just practiced every scenario that might happen to a quarterback. Every once in a while his father, Jim, stopped by. Jon just knew it all. He knew what he wanted to do, and we had a pretty good season our senior year. We were running the veer, but it really didn't work in with the passing. We didn't throw

> More U. S. kids today play soccer than any organized sport, including youth football. The reason so many kids play soccer is so they don't have to watch it.

until our third or fourth game, and once they realized that it was working, we started connecting. A lot of times there were broken plays, and that's where we got most of our touchdowns—from broken routes. We knew what we were going to do.

The Penn High School game was our big rivalry game. I scored once on a slant pattern that went about seventy yards. We turned around and did a broken route play to go for two, because we were down 16-0. We ran the broken route play and got a two-point conversion on that. We did a couple more pass patterns and then ended up hitting our buddy, Ty Monroe, for a touchdown. And then it was 16-14, with not much time left. They called the play while Jon and I planned on working a broken route as we did before. Sometimes, when we ran a play, people got in the way, so with the broken route I knew where I was going, and Jon knew where he is throwing as well. It was going to work, but one of our other guys didn't know what was going on and knocked Jon down. Jon was real happy about that.

Our last game was against Mishawaka High School. Our 1976 team beat them and this was 1981, so it was five years since a South Bend team had beaten them. Jon and I hooked up for four touchdowns to beat them, 28-24. He had a couple of long passes—one was seventy yards, another one was about thirty-four. Then he threw two corner passes, one-on-one. Jon knew exactly where I was going, and he was throwing it up. It was going to be a dogfight—either I got it down, or no one was going to catch it. It worked, and I caught both of them.

After South Bend Clay High School, we went to Muskingum College together about 300 miles away in Ohio. It was kind of neat because he and I were roommates there. We played in the opening game. We had a senior **quarterback** and a senior wide-receiver who didn't move the ball very much. They put us in for the first time in the second quarter, and we scored two plays later. It was kind of neat—two freshmen coming in together. Unfortunately, I screwed up on my scholarship and I ended up at Holy Cross, a junior college here in South Bend. Jon said it was probably a good thing because he stayed

> A quarterback needs seven seconds to call an audible and to make sure his teammates heard him.

that one year and then transferred. He did not get along at Muskingum. He didn't see eye to eye on some of the things that were being done. From Holy Cross Junior College here, I transferred to Ball State, but I didn't play any more sports. I tried baseball at Ball State, and that didn't work out. I saw Jon during his first year down at Dayton and also went to visit him there.

After Dayton, I saw Jon less and less, and we didn't keep in touch as much. He was married. When he was coaching at the University of Pittsburgh, they played Notre Dame and we hooked up briefly. He has not changed at all over the years. He still wears his sweat pants, untied tennis shoes, baseball hat, the whole thing—same Jon.

His family is a genuine bunch. Jay, his younger brother who plays Arena Football, is just like Jon, laid-back and quiet. When Jon was in his last year with Oakland, I went out there to watch a game and I went to his office. We were all standing there. Jay looked at Jon and asked, "Did you guys ever miss any passes?" Jay was a quarterback, too. I said, "Yeah, we missed some." That is what everybody talks about—the two of us hooking up a lot, but we missed our share of them, too.

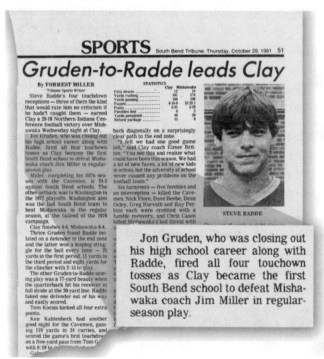

SPORTS South Bend Tribune, Thursday, October 29, 1981 51

Gruden-to-Radde leads Clay

By FORREST MILLER
Tribune Sports Writer

Steve Radde's four touchdown receptions — three of them the kind that would rate him no criticism if he hadn't caught them — earned Clay a 28-19 Northern Indiana Conference football victory over Mishawaka Wednesday night at Clay.

Jon Gruden, who was closing out his high school career along with Radde, fired all four touchdown tosses as Clay became the first South Bend school to defeat Mishawaka coach Jim Miller in regular-season play.

Miller, completing his fifth season with the Cavemen, is 24-2 against South Bend schools. The other setback was to Washington in the 1977 playoffs. Washington also was the last South Bend team to beat Mishawaka in the regular season, at the tailend of the 1976 campaign.

Clay finishes 4-6, Mishawaka 6-4.

Thrice Gruden found Radde isolated on a defender in the end zone and the latter won a leaping struggle for the ball every time — 25 yards in the first period, 11 yards in the third period and eight yards for the clincher with 2:15 to play.

The other Gruden-to-Radde scoring play was a 77-yard beauty when the quarterback hit his receiver in full stride at the 30-yard line. Radde faked one defender out of his way and easily scored.

Tom Kocsis kicked all four extra points.

Ken Kahlenbeck had another good night for the Cavemen, gaining 119 yards in 24 carries, and scored the game's first touchdown on a five-yard pass from Tom G with 8:19 to

STATISTICS

	Clay	Mishawaka
First downs	12	18
Yards rushing	101	174
Yards passing	194	196
Passes	8-16-0	12-22-1
Punts	3-31	3-32
Fumbles lost	2	5
Yards penalized	40	30
Return yardage	15	0

back diagonally on a surprisingly clear path to the end zone.

"I felt we had one good game left," said Clay coach Elmer Britton. "You see this and realize what could have been this season. We had a lot of new faces, a lot of new kids in school, but the adversity at school never caused any problems on the football team."

Six turnovers — five fumbles and an interception — killed the Cavemen. Nick Fiore, Dave Beebe, Dean Oxley, Greg Horvath and Ray Perkins each were credited with a fumble recovery, and Chris Cason killed Mishawaka's last threat with

STEVE RADDE

Jon Gruden, who was closing out his high school career along with Radde, fired all four touchown tosses as Clay became the first South Bend school to defeat Mishawaka coach Jim Miller in regular-season play.

GRUDEN STANDS TO MAKE A BUNDLE ON HIS STOCKBROKER'S CATTLE AND OIL DEAL...
IF THE CATTLE EVER GIVE OIL

BRIAN TRANT

Brian Trant, 39, was one of Gruden's high school friends. Brian now works as a stockbroker in Chicago, Illinois.

photo from 1982

Jon and I met in eighth grade when I moved to South Bend. That is about the same time Jon moved there, and we lived in the same neighborhood. We met early on during the school year, and we played on an intramural basketball team together. Jon was the captain and picked the colors and made us all buy the same colors in tennis shoes and shoe strings and all that stuff. He was starting off early with his leadership abilities. He was real meticulous.

We used to always play the Turkey Bowl every Thanksgiving. Jon would make sure that we had the towels, and he would cut the towels out and draw little turkey guys on the towels. We could all hang them in front of our pants so that we all looked like we had towels like the quarterbacks would wear. Everybody on our team had one of those to wear. That's the kind of stuff he would do, because he was into everything and he was pretty detailed about what he was doing. He was a **Houston Oilers** fan so we had light blue, high-topped Chuck Taylors with red shoe laces and powder blue jerseys with red numbers. He loved the Houston Oilers back when they had those powder blue and red uniforms, and he was a big Dan Pastorini fan.

> The "name" of the Houston Oilers logo was Derrick... Dan Pastorini was drafted by the New York Mets but opted for football at Santa Clara.

Jon is just a normal guy. He is quick witted and has a great sense of humor. He's just a regular kid, that's how I know him. We were buddies, and we played ball, and we hung out. We went fishing once in a while. We would sit around his place, my place, and talk about girls and look at magazines. He loved _**Rolling Stone**_ magazine. He always said he was going to be a coach, but I also said I was going to play in the major leagues in baseball, too. Kids talk that stuff when they're young. He consistently said he was going to be a coach since he was a sophomore in high school. His dad was a coach, so he grew up with that. He loved the game. He loved football way more than he loved baseball. He was a good baseball player, a better baseball player, in my opinion, than he was a football player. He wasn't big enough. He was a little small to be playing quarterback.

The one home run I remember that Jon hit that sticks with me the most was probably about a four-hundred foot homer he hit in Michigan City, Indiana. The baseball diamond was actually situated in a football field. He hit this home run out of the football stadium, about four-hundred feet, which at that time was the first home run I had ever seen hit by a high school kid. That might have been the home run that gave Coach Jim Reinebold his 400th win.

Jon used to always dance to _YMCA_ by the Village People. A couple years ago when I was out in Oakland, I told him, "Because of all these people who have started calling me, I am going to tell them about you dancing around in your room to _YMCA_ by the Village People before games. I think people would get a kick out of that." He was like, "Well, I've got that CD in my car right now." He just laughed. That's how he is.

We went to Notre Dame games together quite often. I wasn't with him at the game when he got in a fight. A fan was mouthing off about the play calls and saying that the coaching staff wasn't doing very good, but not in those nice words. Jon told the guy to shut up because his dad was a coach. The guy kept mouthing off, and then Jon ended up hitting him. In the winter, we used to go to Notre Dame all the time. We could

> In 1976, Detroit Tigers pitcher Mark Fidrych became the first athlete to be featured on the cover of _Rolling Stone._

get in because his dad coached there. We used to go there and work out, and play baseball inside in the winter, before our team would start practicing at high school. He and I would go over there and throw, and they would drop the cages down, and we would find a couple of college kids to pitch to us and stuff. We did that pretty much every day during the winter when his dad was coaching there. His dad pretty much liked him doing that but we didn't see his dad much. He would pop his head in if he was there, and say, "Hey, how ya doing?" And then, "See you guys later." I think his dad enjoyed that Jon was around and into athletics and was taking advantage of what was there for him.

Jon would get —— off and lose his temper if something would happen in the baseball game. If things didn't go his way he would get angry and cuss and swear and kick the dirt and sail some things around in the dugout, but it wasn't like he was a hothead.

At our school, the tennis season happened to be the same time as football, where in a lot of schools it's at different times of the year. Those guys would all be running out to the football field and it was right by the tennis courts and I would be playing tennis. Jon and his football buddies would say "Don't get hurt, don't hurt yourself playing tennis." So I would fire tennis balls at them and hit them off their heads when they would run by.

Being "King of the Prom" wasn't out of character for him. What is he now, one of the 50 most beautiful people of the world? So I guess he should have been the Prom King, right? I was on that court with Jon and Steve Radde. It didn't surprise me that he won. He was a pretty boy, and the quarterback, so I guess that was all fitting.

I stay in touch with him all the time. I got my little Day-Timer book in front of me here and I have the phone numbers of his last seven jobs in my book. Guys at work say, "You don't know him," and I say, "Here's his Green Bay number, his Philadelphia number, his Oakland number…."

As he progressed, I noticed his drive. I didn't know how much he worked in the early years. When I first talked to him at Green Bay, I didn't know he worked as much as he did and how driven he was and how much he was into studying the game and mastering it. I found out how much he dedicated his life to it, and learned that he only sleeps three or four hours a day. That used to bug him, but then a doctor finally said, "Hey, if it's something you love and you can't sleep, there is nothing wrong with it, just keep going at it." That was the most impressive thing to me is the dedication and the hours he puts in. He has his three young boys and his wife, Cindy, and a great little family, but he just is so dedicated to that game that he doesn't even get to see his kids and wife very much. I know that tears him up inside. But that's the life of a football coach. Growing up with his dad being a coach maybe makes it a little bit easier on him. I don't think a lot of people could deal with not seeing their kids or their wife like he does. I just read an article the other day that said, "Well, at least now when I get home at 11:30 or 12:00 at night, and Cindy gives me a look, at least I know I've got the Super Bowl trophy."

He has always been full speed ahead, never looked back. I have never seen any other side to him except work, work, work, and try to get better. He's funny. I'll talk to him and say, "Hey, Jon, what are you doing now?" He would say he was watching film and say something like "trying to figure out how to score a touchdown in this league" —stuff like that. I would say, "You got Arizona this week?" or whatever, and he would say, "Hey, every game in this league is a tough one and any time you get a win you're lucky and you gotta be prepared and I'm just trying to figure out how to stop this guy." And he will always name somebody from the other team. "You know, we need to stop this guy, and I got this guy hurt, daa, daa, daa." When he was with Oakland, one of his guys ran up on a punt and ended up fumbling. He probably should have just let the thing bounce and let it be down, but he ran up and tried to dive and catch it like it was almost a pass. He fumbled it and the other team recovered the ball and they ended up losing the game over that. When I talked to Jon the next day and said, "Well, what was that guy doing?" He goes, "I don't know, but he's not going to do it anymore. You see what I did to him? Cut his ass." He doesn't take any ——. He goes, "Yeah, he won't be doing that anymore."

He really likes rock music. He loved Bob Seger and the Silver Bullet Band and any other type of 80s music like Def Leppard and the Village People, too. He had a wide array of what he would listen to.

He's a fun guy to go out and have a beer with. You see these young guys and older guys responding to him the way you have in the NFL and you talk to Jerry Rice or those guys, they will tell you the reason they went to Oakland was to play for Jon. That's how he ended up signing Rich Gannon. The first time they met, he took Rich Gannon to some pub somewhere and they got a hot dog and a beer, and they sat down and shot the breeze and talked about Rich Gannon being a quarterback. He's just as down to earth as you can get. He'd like to sit back and have a couple of beers with you, like ordinary guys do. He's funny. I look forward to it when I have the opportunity to get together with him. He just clicks. Off the top of his head, if somebody says something he will have an answer for them. He doesn't get quite as crazy as Bobby Knight, but you know how Bobby is. As soon as somebody says something he's got some kind of smart aleck or funny reply to it, and I sort of look at Jon in that way too—he always has a pretty good answer.

When he appeared on Letterman, he handled himself real well and I didn't ever catch him saying anything stupid. It seems like he is always politically correct with what he says. He's pretty intelligent and does a good job when he is interviewed.

I never went to Muskingum, but I went to Dayton a few times. We would watch a few of his football games and then go out with him and a couple of his goofy football buddies afterwards. He was probably discouraged with what was going on there football-wise. Anybody who was an athlete in high school and a star on the football team, or baseball team, who then goes to a situation where he wasn't playing much is gonna feel let down. Just being competitive in nature, you want to play. He handled it, and he got his playing time, but I think he also knew that he was five feet, ten, and he wasn't playing high school football anymore, and Division III, Dayton, was a pretty darn good football program. He was glad to be on the team, but he wanted to play.

He was always into fitness ever since I've known him. He played in every sport—football, baseball and basketball, and he was always doing something athletic. I don't remember if he was always eating real healthy when we were younger, maybe he started that later on in life, but I don't remember what his actual eating habits are.

He was crazy at the Notre Dame games. We'd usually be up in the seats, in the stands somewhere. He was totally into the game and half the time he was questioning the plays that were being called. "What are they running that for? Why don't they do this? Look at this opening here." He was up in the stands coaching like all the other guys, but he probably knew more than those other guys in the stands, and probably more than some of the coaches down there on the field at that time.

SPORTS South Bend Tribune.

Broken neck ends season for Gruden

Jon Gruden, Clay High School junior quarterback, is resting at home after suffering a broken neck (fifth cervical vertebra) at the conclusion of a B team game between Clay and Elkhart Central on the Clay field Monday afternoon.

Gruden had executed a handoff on the final play of the game and, according to witnesses, was injured after the play ended and as the officials were walking off the field. He will be in a neck brace from four to six weeks. He is also a pitcher-outfielder on the baseball team.

Gruden had been punting for the varsity and was a backup to No. 1 quarterback Todd Troeger. He is the son of Notre Dame assistant coach Jim Gruden.

The Colonials, who play at Michigan City Elston Thursday night, will also be without linebacker Dave Beebe who is out for the season after suffering a spinal injury in an automobile accident.

SPORTS South Bend Tribune.

Clay hits quickly, but Blazers coast

By FORREST MILLER
Tribune Sports Writer

ELKHART — It took two hours and 36 minutes, and more than four pages in my notebook when the normal high school football game usually won't last three.

At one point the clock stopped on 10 consecutive plays, but no one from Elkhart Central was complaining Thursday at Rice Field.

Combining an explosive offense trigged by Eddie Words and David Robinson, plus an outstanding defensive game from lineb Brian Buckley, Central's Blue ers shook off an early 10-0 and whipped South Bend Clay

Central maintained its lead with a 6-1 record, and is 6-2 o Northern Indiana Conference Coach Tom Kurth's Blazers for the league title by defeating waka and Washington in the two games. Clay dropped to the league and 3-5 overall.

"We usually play the way our defense plays," said Central coach Tom Kurth. "We felt our offensive line was stronger than their defensive line."

There were 63 passes thrown and 18 penalties called (13 of them against Clay) by the 5-man officiating crew. Colonial quarterback Jon Gruden, scrambling constantly, passed for 237 yards but a lot of it was neutralized by 130 penalty yards. Steve Radde caught eight for 143 yards.

Tom Kocsis' fifth field goal of the season, a 36-yard shot before Central saw the football on offense, put the Colonials on top with 9:06 to go in the first period. Later in the quarter, after Greg Horvath sacked Blazer quarterback Andy Parmater for a 15-yard loss, Tim Smedley recovered a fumble at the Central 29.

Clay punched it over in plays as tackle cleared the way, dived the final made it 10 period.

and when No. 23 lines up in the backfield, you can bet something fancy is coming. Last week he scored on a 79-yard reverse — the first time he carried the ball all season. Thursday he went 66 on the same play the second time he carried the ball all season — with 7:32 to go in the half. Craft made it 14-10.

Even though Chris Cason's interception enabled Clay to keep the ball for the next five minutes, yards each and Clay never came that close again.

Buckley's third period interception touched off the other TD drive, a 64-yard, 11-play march. A 24-yard Parmater-to-Warren Roberson catch helped before Robinson went the final yard with 2:54 left in the period.

Richard Delks got another interception for Central, and Clay linebacker Dave Beebe grabbed two from Parmater in the second half. Midway in the fourth period Gruden hit Radde for a 66-yard gain to the 10, but Delks caught up with Radde and Clay lost 34 yards on the next four plays.

Robinson, who gained 92 yards on only three carries in the first half, finished with an even 100 on seven. Clay's Rick Perkins had 100 on 18 attempts and Oxley 50 on 13 car

Central hosts M
Clay is hom
Central

32

THE BOY WONDER HAD
THE BOYS WONDERING

MIKE RULLI

Mike Rulli, 39, played on the same high school football team as Jon Gruden. Today Mike is a Senior Application Engineer for Electric Power Marketing, Caterpillar, Inc. Mike lives in West Lafayette, Indiana.

Photo from 1982

Jon was a very intense individual, but for the most part he was quiet. He was all businesslike in the huddle. I was an offensive lineman, and I was blocking for this guy…and they think he is intense on the sidelines. You haven't seen anything until you've seen him with high school kids. As a leader, he's pretty much all business. He's very much the "This is what we're gonna do. Shut your mouth. This is what we're gonna do" type. Just the way you see him today. I don't think he has changed much at all.

I remember him going back and forth with Coach Britton. Jon has a very good football mind. He probably learned a lot from his dad who was a football coach at Notre Dame. He understood the game a lot better than a lot of us did at the time. He would have exchanges back and forth with Elmer. Nothing real bad, just, "Hey, we ought to do this." Elmer was kind of a stubborn individual as I remember him, a very good football mind, but very stubborn. You could see the stubbornness on both sides, and, of course, I'm the same way. I would have exchanges back and forth with people in the huddle, saying you ought to do this instead of that. Overall, Jon was a very good leader, very positive, very businesslike when he was there. I don't remember him being a super great athlete, nor was I, but we always seemed to find a way to get it done.

He would say stuff like "What are we doing, guys? Why don't we pick this person up? Let's get it done. Quit screwing around." They call him Chucky, which I think is hilarious. His facial expressions were the same back then as they are now. He was a very intense, focused individual. He knew how to get his point across. He didn't say a lot. I don't ever remember him being that vocal in the huddle.

Jon was class President. He was very well respected within his class and around school. He was a very good athlete, but he wasn't a stellar athlete. I never had the perception of him as being cocky. As I sit back and look at it from this perspective, he was always focused on football. After games and a lot of other times, he would just go home and watch film. He was the high school player going home after a game and watching film, either with his dad or with Radde. We had some film sessions too on occasions that we got together outside of football and sat down and he would go through things. At that point, you could tell he wanted to be a coach.

He was intense to watch film with. He was watching and pointing out mistakes, for the most part, from the receivers and the backs. It wasn't necessarily from the lineman's perspective, other than if the lineman missed something, and Jon got sacked. Of course he got upset about that. That's human nature. Did he have better mechanics than some of the other people? Yes. Once again, he didn't have great athletic ability, but he had different mechanics, especially when throwing the football. You could see it, and I think that was coming from his dad—the proper position of the body, and things of that nature.

We were in the locker room before a game one time…I forget who we were playing. Jon was lying on his back, and he was throwing the football up in the air. The ceiling in the locker room was probably a good fifteen, eighteen feet high. I was watching him do this and he had a perfect spiral on the football as he was throwing it. He was lying on his back throwing the ball towards the ceiling. That was pretty neat.

IF HE KNEW THE GRUDENS BETTER, MAYBE HE'D LIKE THEM MORE

MIKE SHINER

Mike Shiner was a 6' 8", 262-pound offensive tackle from Sunnyvale, California, who was recruited to Notre Dame by Jim Gruden in 1980.

Photo from 1982

Jim Gruden recruited me through high school. He didn't have to do much convincing for me to go to Notre Dame because I wanted to go there from the time I was a kid, but I grew an attachment to him and his family, and it was wonderful. It was a great experience all the way through. Jim gave me the opportunity to go to Notre Dame. I couldn't ask more of a man in my life. Kathy just happened to be there on the sideline and seemed to be just the sweet person that she is.

Jon was a junior in high school when I was a freshman at Notre Dame. I used to go over to watch him play because I wasn't on the traveling team then. He played for Clay High School.

My parents were awesome. I couldn't have asked for anything more from parents as far as I go, but when I was back in South Bend, the Grudens were my second family, easily. Coach Gruden, Kathy Gruden, Jon, Jim and Jay—I knew them all, like they were brothers. They're just great people. I don't know what else to say about them. They're people that you would *love* to have as family members. I consider them extremely close friends. They're just great people. I could give you examples left and right about what they meant to me while I was back at Notre Dame, but the basic line is that they were just absolutely fantastic people to know. If you were growing up in a neighborhood, and they were your next-door neighbors, you would be happy as heck to have them as friends because they're the most outstanding people in the world. You couldn't ask any more from anybody than that, as far as a friend goes.

I only knew Jon as a kid. The kid had more football intelligence than the college coaches had at that time. He knew more about **offense** and playmaking and whether to make an audible call. I'd go over and see him, just to see him, or go over to say hi to Kathy or whatever, and he knew what the heck was going on in a college football game as a junior in high school. Kathy taught grade school in South Bend. Blair Kiel and I used to go over to her school when we'd have a free period, or in the off-season. It was so much fun. She was so tickled to have players that actually cared to go over and say, "Hi, how are you doing?" We'd talk to the kids about football or answer questions about the team or whatever and give them autographs and it was a family atmosphere at the time.

Even when Jon was back in high school, he had football knowledge that amazed me. He sat and watched films with his dad. He knew about everything that was going on at Notre Dame. He knew the type of offense we were running. He knew everything that we were doing. He was sharp. He would bring up things to me. Even when he was a junior in high school, he had insight that was that of a college coach, at that time. Nothing that Jon has done has been a surprise to me.

Jon wasn't that great an athlete, but he tried harder than everybody else on the field. He ended up going to Dayton and was the quarterback there, but he had the smarts that nobody else had. He saw what happened. He could figure things out. The guy was just sharp. Unfortunately for him, he didn't have the size, but the guy knew football inside and out. He knew the pros and the cons. He knew everything about the game. The guy was smart. He's earned everything he's got. He's probably one of the sharpest head coaches in the league.

Jon was an absolute, complete football fanatic. He loved everything his dad did. He loved Notre Dame like there was no tomorrow. My personal feeling is that he still feels the same way about the place.

In the 1970s, a St. Louis Football Cardinals fan brought an ad in the *St. Louis Post-Dispatch* offering to sell the "Official Cardinals' Playbook" with "all five plays illustrated, including the squib punt."

Players and coaches get so close in the recruiting process that you attach yourself to an assistant coach. We would occasionally go over to the Grudens' house and see how things were going. I played catch with Jon in the front yard. It was just something to occupy our time off the field.

Plain and simple, I love them all. From Jim and Kathy, to Jay, Jon and Jim. I love them all to death. They are just absolutely fantastic people. They probably never will know in my life what they meant to me. I hope they do, but I don't think they will. They meant so much to me when I was back there at school. They came and saw me, they saw what was happening, Jim kicked my butt as offensive line coach. I know it's because he recruited me that he did that, but I love them all to death, and I wish them the best. I'm very happy for the success they've all had—especially Jon in the NFL, but Jim, too, recruiting for the 49ers and being a scout. And for Kathy, just for being who she is, because she is absolutely the rock where that whole family is embedded. You can talk about the boys and everybody else, but Kathy is the rock of that whole family.

I consider myself one of the luckiest guys who ever walked the face of the Earth because I've known the Grudens. I mean that sincerely.

Jon was a very easygoing guy, kind of quiet. Things didn't ruffle his feathers very much. He was an all around nice guy. I liked him. He was really cute. I guess there were a lot of girls who thought he was really cute. Our lockers were right next door to each other. We'd kid around a lot. He was just your typical guy. He wasn't a funny type person. He didn't have a real big sense of humor.

He was "King of the Prom", and he was probably one of the favorites out of all of the guys. But he wasn't a big show off at all. Some guys are real cocky and he wasn't like that at all. He didn't really shun anybody or anything like that. The girls liked him because of his blond hair and his blue eyes. He was a popular guy in our class—quarterback of the football team.

——KARIN WIRICK, 39, High school classmate of Gruden's

THEY SAY YOUR CAR IS A REFLECTION OF YOUR PERSONALITY. JON DIDN'T HAVE A CAR.

Photo from 1982

BLAIR KIEL

Blair Kiel was arguably the most recruited quarterback in Indiana High School annals. Jim Gruden landed him for Notre Dame, where Kiel forged a close personal relationship with the Gruden family. Kiel enjoyed a six-year career in the NFL with the Bucs, Colts and Green Bay Packers. While a rookie at Tampa Bay, he was diagnosed with Crohn's disease, a chronic inflammatory disease that causes scarring and thickening of the intestinal walls. Jon Gruden's coaching idol, the late Bobb McKittrick of the San Francisco 49ers also suffered from Crohn's. Kiel is an executive with Caskey Achievement Strategies in Indianapolis.

Jon's dad recruited me at Notre Dame. Kathy Gruden was like my mom away from home, both at Notre Dame and at Tampa Bay when I was drafted as a rookie. Jon was like a little brother to me. I couldn't have my car on campus 'cause I was a freshman so I kept it at the Gruden's house some and told Jon I didn't care if he drove it. So Jon borrowed my car, a white Firebird, on a few occasions. He and my brother would drive around the town and have a high old time. My parents had told me that if I got a full-ride scholarship, they would get a car for me. I was fortunate to get a scholarship, and they bought a car for me and gave it to me after graduation. Then for a Christmas present, they got me a license plate that said, "ND5" which actually turned out to be more of a pain in the neck. At different points in time, people bent the plate beyond recognition trying to steal it.

When I was at Notre Dame, Jon would come by and watch football practice. He was very close to Dan Devine as well. I went to some of Jon's high school games. He was a good player, very competitive. He was a natural leader, and you could see that.

Jon was always a tremendous fan of mine and a big supporter, both when I was at Notre Dame and at Tampa. Our paths didn't cross again until Mike Holmgren came in at Green Bay, and Jon was an understudy.

Jon was doing a lot of grunt work for Mike Holmgren, which you have to do in the NFL to get where you want to go. He was breaking down a lot of film and just taking in whatever he could from Holmgren. I remember talking to Jon, and he told me to just keep doing the best I could. He was always very encouraging and very supportive no matter what. That is obviously a trait that has stayed with him throughout his very successful career.

It was a little shocking to see Jon in Green Bay, but not surprising. It was great to see him. He had obviously matured quite a bit from when I knew him. It had been about nine years since I was at Notre Dame when he was there. It would have been about seven years since I'd seen him, and I knew he had coached at some other places.

Jon doesn't need *things* to be happy. He is, and always has been, very passionate about sports. He was constantly watching ESPN. He knew stats on teams and people and things more than anybody I've ever known. He was just extremely intense. It was funny because he's gotten nicknames in the past, but even when he smiles, he still has this growl about him, which is just hilarious.

I called him the year before last, and he called me back. I was just so tickled for him that he had done as well as he had with them, and I just wanted to let him know how proud I was of him. Here's a kid who was younger than me, who had idolized me at one time, and wanted to be what I was. Now look where he is, and look at how many people idolize him. His heart is probably as big as anybody I've ever met.

When I talk about Jon having borrowed my car, my friends mostly know the background of my being from Indiana and at Notre Dame and Jon being there then. People who I work with are a little shocked that I knew him as well as I did. Then they start asking questions. My whole family, including my brothers, used to run with Jon and do a lot of things with him. They all now have boys who just idolize Jon and want to be just like him. They have the pictures and all the other stuff. Obviously, the kids hear a lot of that from my brothers.

Jon's dad, Jim, was like my dad away from home—he was extremely hard on me, just like your own dad would be. My kids say that, when it comes to them, I'm harder on them than I am on most. He was the same way.

For somebody to be in the position he's in, and to have the success he's had, he's the most unassuming, give-credit-elsewhere-but-not-take-it-himself person that I could ever imagine. That's what is so neat about this whole story. Scrape bottom to get to the top! That is a true success story. Talk about the American dream—he's a guy who took nothing, rode his bike, carrying a TV as an NFL assistant, and then ended up winning the Super Bowl. There's no one more deserving of all the accolades than Jon Gruden.

One of the other amazing things about Jon was just the person he is. I think coaches have their favorites, and they admit that. I fortunately believe that I was a favorite of the Grudens at Notre Dame. I know my friend, Mike Shiner, was because Jim got very involved with his recruitment. It was the same with Vagas Ferguson—he coached Vagas and loved Vagas, who ended up being in Tampa with me as well when Jim was there. I think we were just fortunate enough that we hit it off and were the type of people that the Grudens wanted to be part of their family. I stayed there at their house sometimes once or twice a week at night, spent the night there. Jim had to be careful because that's a sensitive situation for him, but he would ask me to do it. He'd say, "I don't care. Just stay here. Just don't say anything about it." It might not bode very well for the rest of the team, so I respected that. I got up just like I was at home. Kathy would fix breakfast, and we'd hang out, and it was awesome.

I was very excited when I thought Jon might become coach at Notre Dame. There couldn't have been a better fit because Jon absolutely loved, and still loves, Notre Dame. I thought it would be an absolutely perfect fit. Now I am definitely a Willingham fan as well. I think he's a class act all the way. When it was rumored that Jon was going to be the coach, I thought, "Unbelievable! They're not going to know what hit them."

Chapter 2

The Old College Try

High Flyin' in Dayton
Joinin' the Fraternity in Knoxville
Showin' 'Em in Missouri

DAYTON—THAT TODDLIN' TOWN

DOUG HAUSCHILD

Doug Hauschild, 46, is Sports Information Director at the University of Dayton.

Jon Gruden was a three-year letterman at quarterback at the University of Dayton, graduating in 1986 with a degree in Communications. He was in school just after I was, and I was Sports Information Director when he played football.

My most outstanding memory of Jon would be his comment, going into his senior year, that his career ambition was to be the head coach at the University of **Michigan**. That jumped out at me. It's a pretty unusual statement for someone his age. Most guys say they want to be a coach. But to specifically say that he wants to be at one of the top programs in the country, and a program he had no ties to made the statement remarkable. His dad had coached here and then went to Notre Dame so any sort of tie he would have to a university would be to Dayton or perhaps Notre Dame. There certainly was no Michigan connection at that point in his life. He definitely had high aspirations and although he was not living up to his aspirations as a football player, he still had his sights set on being a high performer as a coach.

Jon was typical of our players. We're a non-scholarship program so you must be dedicated and really want to play football because you have to pay your own way or keep your grades high enough so that you can get some academic aid.

Jon Gruden is the second University of Dayton graduate to coach a winning Super Bowl team. Former UD co-captain and 1993 Pro Football Hall of Fame inductee, Chuck Noll, won four Super Bowls (IX, X, XII and XIV) as coach of the Pittsburgh Steelers.

He was really intense on football. I'm sure deep down he feels he should have played a lot more than he did. It's not unusual for someone to come through the program and be a starter for only one year. We really are a senior-oriented program and kids earn their dues and work their way on. We don't lose a lot of kids transferring or anything like that. The guy before him was pretty decent. Then, in Gruden's senior year, when he really looked like he had a shot, he was a little dinged up in camp, and Todd Morris, who won the job, was successful enough that he held on to the job. As it turns out, this guy was a junior, and he went on to have a real good year the next year, too, so it wasn't like we had to "settle" for him when Jon was there. Jon missed some rep days in camp, as the stories go, and that put him behind Todd. And, "if it ain't broke, don't fix it," so Jon did not play a whole lot, certainly not as much as he would have hoped.

In his senior year, Jon won what is regarded as the highest honor in our program, the Lt. Andy Zulli Memorial trophy. The award goes to the Flyer senior who best exemplifies the qualities of Zulli, a former UD football player who was killed in a military vehicle accident while serving in the Army in Germany in the 1950s. Although Zulli was not a starter on the football team, he was someone who everyone looked up to. That award is given at our last home game, and it really is a Who's Who of the best people who come through our program.

The Lt. Andy Zulli Memorial trophy award is given out at halftime of our last home game. The winner picks up the award from the founder. At the time that would have been Victor Cassano, a local businessman. There's no time for speeches or anything like that. It's *the* yardstick to measure someone who comes through our program. The football coaches make the recommendation and they and other people connected with athletics vote on the recipient. It's a strong recommendation from our football coaches.

Although I knew him when he was in school I haven't talked to him in a long time. When his dad took the job in Tampa, they moved there. I know he keeps in contact with Coach Mike Kelly, and that Jon sent Mike a box of cigars when he won his two hundredth game this year. Going into the Super Bowl week, Mike said in an interview, "I'm not a cigar smoker, but if the Bucs win the Super Bowl, I might just have to light one of these up."

THE POISE THAT REFRESHES

DAVE WHILDING

Dave Whilding, 53, was the offensive coordinator for the University of Dayton when Gruden played there. Whilding remains the Flyers' offensive coach and lives in Jamestown, Ohio.

W e recruited Jon out of high school. Then, he decided to go to Muskingum, which is in eastern **Ohio**. He went there—it was a Division III school and was a little smaller than Dayton. My feeling was he probably thought he could play a little faster. Then he decided that wasn't for him and he transferred in here.

I was the offensive coordinator when he was here. We're an I-formation team. So it was sprint draw. We'd run what we'd call freeze options. Speed options. Then just "I" formation with power off the tackle. We ran the isolation. He was a good quarterback and it was a good program. The kid had good blood lines and good background. He was a great kid when he came in to visit. He's a coach's son. He did everything you wanted. He'd pay attention to detail. He was very much detail oriented. He was going to do it just he way you told him to do it. He had been around it all of his life so he understood the game. That was the big thing. Everything was positive and he was a real good student and we have to pay attention to that kind of stuff.

It's a real pleasure to coach that kind of athlete. You never heard Jon complain about anything. He was always going to give you a great effort and that's what I always appreciated. There were some times that he wasn't playing and things could have gotten bad, but there was never anything like that. He just wanted to get better. He knew

Former Colorado Rockies manager, Jim Leyland, was once a second-string catcher for Perrysburg, Ohio High School. The starting catcher was Jerry Glanville.

coming in that we had a kid who was playing who was pretty good. He played ahead of Jon for two years. The guy was a good quarterback for us. So then you go into Jon's senior year and its his turn. Then he gets dinged up—he had hurt his ankle—and it just held him back so he didn't get off to a good start. I think it happened before the first game even. So he was gimping around for a while and he never did get one hundred percent and he never got it back.

He really paid attention to detail on everything and he was a good athlete. Everything he did he was athletic in the fakes and everything was carried out to the letter. He did everything well. I wouldn't say, obviously, it wasn't anything he was doing great or he would have beaten the other kid out. But the other kid was pretty good too. And we were winning. So it wasn't like he was coming into a down program that needed a savior. He knew it was a tough spot and he knew it would be competitive and a challenge and that's what he wanted.

Everybody asks if I've been surprised by his success. I'm not. He works hard and he deserves everything he's getting. That's the thing. In this business, it takes a measure of things falling into place for you, too. I mean, there are a lot of guys who work their butts off out there and don't win a Super Bowl. I mean, is it luck? There is some luck but the guy works his tail off. Everybody knows that.

He's loyal to those that he's been around. I know he thought a lot of those guys who were connected to the 49ers when he was out there at one time. Then you've got guys like Ray Rhodes who he has been around and I know he respects those guys. He appreciates the fact that they gave him a chance. Well, that's the way he was brought up. I can tell you that right now. That comes from his mom and dad. He was always taught to show people respect. Some of his elders, you know those guys who are older than him, gave him some shots, some opportunities coming through and he understands that. He respects that. He appreciates the fact that those guys gave him a chance to come through.

THEY BOTH FINISHED IN THE TOP 90% OF THEIR CLASS

AMY LOPEZ

Amy Lopez, 38, works as director of Kennedy Union and Conference Services at the University of Dayton. Amy was a classmate of Jon Gruden at the University of Dayton.

My first impression of Jon was that he was just a nice guy. He seemed quiet and reserved. He often walked around with headphones on. He sat right in front of me in speech writing class in my senior year. It was a senior course for communications majors. He looked just like he does now...he hasn't changed much at all. I don't remember any of the speeches he gave. Hard to believe these days.

There were probably about twenty-five students in that class. We were in the front row closest to the door, and he and I had talked all semester in class. I'd come and take my seat behind him and we'd just talk for a few minutes before class started.

One day, when we came into class I sat down behind him as usual. We talked a little bit as class started. He was sitting in front of me and I had my left ankle crossed over my right knee and had some gym shoes on. He reached around behind his chair and untied my shoe. Instead of pulling my foot away as I would normally do, I just kind of smiled and watched to see what he was going to do. He tied my shoe to his desk chair. He was just fooling around. You know, you're just twenty years old. When I looked at that and looked at him, we both started laughing...we had not been talking at that time.

The teacher's name was Mrs. Rang and she was kind of proper. She wouldn't even let us drink a soda in class. She was strict about behavior. So Jon did this, we both started laughing and she got irritated...rightly so. It was childish and it was rude in class. Another student was giving his speech so she asked us both to apologize to that student, which we did of course. We felt bad about that because we were interrupting things. When we came into class the next day the teacher was actually sitting in Jon's chair and made him sit in the middle of the classroom. So she separated us. She probably kept that up for a couple of weeks and wouldn't let us sit by each other.

Jon just seemed like a normal guy. You know, just "hi, how are you doing?" He was always nice. Nice pleasantries exchanged. He wasn't stuck on himself. He wasn't rude. He didn't think he was some big shot. Just a very nice guy. I don't think he would remember this story at all. Clearly, he has had much more exciting and serious things since that. But it's just one of those funny things that always stuck out in my mind. Then, when he became this head NFL coach I was like, "Oh my gosh, that's the guy who tied my shoe to his desk."

It's been funny to see all the attention he's gotten. When he was in *People* magazine's "Most Beautiful People" issue, another friend of mine from college called me up and was like, "Oh my gosh, did you see that?" I had to run out and get it just to read it. It's just neat when you know somebody from sixteen or seventeen years ago and have a little story to tell about it.

His success has been big news at Dayton. I am more of a college basketball fan. I don't watch pro football much at all, but you'd better believe I was watching the Super Bowl and telling everybody. I think a lot of people around here were really pulling for him, especially Mike Kelly, his former coach. That's a huge thing, because he's still here and he's a big name in Dayton.

WHEN GRUDEN CALLS, YA GOTTA ACCEPT THE CHARGES

TONY CARUSO

Tony Caruso, 45, has been the Equipment Manager for the University of Dayton since 1982 and remembers Gruden from his playing days there. Tony lives in Dayton, OH.

Jon Gruden wasn't very big when he and Larry Raville, from Gettysburg College, came in and had lockers next to each other. Jon lived in Florida, and I remember when he came back after the summer he looked nice and tan and golden-haired. He had the opportunity to be the quarterback his senior year but turned an ankle a couple of weeks into camp. After that he didn't get a chance to get back in very much.

Jon was a smart guy and you could tell he had been around football and sports. He would be in the locker room early every day. Usually, the team members would be in around 2:15/2:30, but he'd always be the first one in. He was prepared. He'd be dressed and ready to go out to the field when the specialist went out, and he'd work on his snap holds and the kicking game. Jon was the number one snap-holder on field goals and extra points, even after he hurt his ankle. He could always be found in the film-room watching film with Dave Whilding, who was the offensive coordinator. He just keep hitting the rerun button and watching films.

Jon was the kind of kid who never was a problem, and you always appreciate kids like that. It was always "Yes. Thank you very much. Yes sir. No sir." Since his dad had coached here several years before Coach McVay, Jon was familiar with the area and locker room facilities. He just had that presence and knew how to act in the training room and the equipment room. He knew how to get in there, get his stuff done and get out onto the field. He was always prepared, and he did his homework. Jon was the kind of guy who would have all his socks in order in his locker, everything hanging right and when his laundry would come in, he'd get it right out of the bag and put it in his locker the right way. He was pretty meticulous.

Back then I don't think we saw that crazy Chucky look everybody talks about now. It's funny because I have one of those balls for hell here hanging right above our telephone in the laundry room. I had it way before Jon was ever called Chucky. It's hilarious when people talk about that. We never saw that side of him. You could always tell he was intense because he was prepared. He knew where to be and when to be there. He was never one to be late for a bus, or for a meeting or for practice. He would have done just about anything to be a top-notch football player, but physically he just wasn't there—mentally he was. In his senior year here, the media guide shows he had stated as his ambition to be the Head Coach at Michigan. That was what he had written on his goals' sheet.

Jon came back a couple of years ago and spoke at the Dayton Agonis Club. I had not planned to go to the roast-type dinner, as I was working a high school tournament game. Jon called and said, "Hey, fat ass, come out and see me." I told him I was working, but he said, "I don't care. I only get into town once every fifteen years." I had a change of clothes there, so I got somebody to man my post, and I went to the dinner. Afterward, he asked me to give him a ride back to the hotel. He and I and a few of the guys who had played with him went to one of the local pubs. We had a beer and told old stories, and I got him back to his hotel about midnight.

I remember an article in the Dayton newspaper before the Super Bowl where he said he had talked to a couple of doctors here in town way back when about having trouble sleeping in the evening. I don't really know anything more on that. I think most college kids don't go to sleep until two in the morning anyway.

MISSOURI: THE SHOW-ME STATE. GRUDEN SHOWED THEM

BILL MASKILL

In March 1987, Bill Maskill hired the 24-year-old Jon Gruden as quarterbacks coach—his first full-time job as an assistant coach— for the Indians of Southeast Missouri State University. Bill is currently Head Coach at Midwestern State University in Wichita Falls, TX.

In 1987, when I arrived at Southeast Missouri State, I knew that we needed a good, young, enthusiastic, energetic guy who could coach the quarterbacks. I did a lot of research in trying to find the right guy and I talked with a number of people and interviewed three or four guys before I actually interviewed Jon.

I spoke with Gary Horton, a good friend of mine who has become a good friend of Jon's. Gary and I coached together at Arizona State in '78 and '79, and his career had taken him to the University of Tennessee where he was working with Walt Harris, who was then the offensive coordinator for Johnny Majors. I called Gary, who was on the road all the time, and asked if he knew any good young quarterback coaches? He said he did, and had the perfect guy for me. He told me about Jon and his work ethic. Jon was a graduate assistant at Tennessee at the time. So then I called Walt who said that while Jon was young, he was a lot more knowledgeable than his age might indicate. Then I called his coach at Dayton. The theme was always the same; that he was an over-achiever, he was a hard worker, he was dedicated, and was thirsting for knowledge. So I called Jon up and asked him if he had an interest and he said that he did.

I know that from Knoxville, Tennessee to Cape Girardeau, Missouri is probably about a six hour drive or longer and Jon got up at two or three in the morning and drove over and was at the office by 8 or 9 a.m. I liked what I saw during the interview but I didn't offer the job to him at that point. I probably wanted to do some more research, so I made a couple of more calls and talked to a couple of other people about Jon. Then I went back to Gary and asked if there was anybody else out there that he could compare Jon to. Gary said, "Let me just tell you this. If you don't hire him, he's a guy who in two years you'll wish that you had hired him." That's what convinced me to hire him.

His age wasn't a concern for me because his knowledge was well beyond his years. You could tell that after talking to him. If you want to measure his knowledge in coaching years, you would say he was probably 30 or 40 years old at age 24. His knowledge was well beyond what you might expect of a normal 24-year-old.

Jon is a coach's son and I'm a coach's son too. If you're a coach's son it means you're a gym rat and that you're always around the gym or an athletic field. And when you're always around you're going to pick up an instinctive understanding of how things work...an understanding that other coaches aren't going to have. Bill Belichek is a perfect example. I don't know if he ever played, but he hung out with his dad all those years at Navy and he picked up all of those innate coaching skills that made him so great.

I liked Jon's competitiveness. I liked his enthusiasm and energy. He was an exciting guy. So, I offered him the job and said just one thing and that was that I couldn't pay him until July 1. He said it was no problem and he'd be there. That was in March. He came in the middle of spring practice. I got there late March and I think that I hired Jon first because it was a newly created position for $15,000. Then Jon took that job and we put him up in a motel and fed him at the cafeteria and then he went on about his merry way.

That summer he went back to Knoxville and went back to Tampa and talked to a bunch of people and he came back in the fall. He did a great job of putting the play book together because he was computer literate and he typed. Computers weren't all that big back then, but Jon was always on the typewriter. He got the forms and put all the stuff together and he was very thorough. You asked him to do a job today and it would be done by tomorrow.

One thing Jon shared with me when he got to Southeast Missouri State was that he took notes in every meeting that Johnny Majors had at Tennessee and then typed up all of his notes. At that time, Johnny Majors was one of the premier coaches in the country and Walt Harris was his mentor as well. All of that was positive for Jon. He was just thirsty for knowledge and sat there and listened to those great coaches. I think Jon would be one of those guys who would just sit down and talk to one of them until two or three in the morning and it wouldn't bother him a bit.

Jon was very thorough in his teaching. He was tough…probably tougher than I wanted him to be on a quarterback and we had several discussions about that. He felt, though, that if it was tough on them during practice then it would be easier for them during the game. He was really aggressive with them during practice and I thought he did a great job of drilling them and schooling them. When he started with quarterbacks, he graded every play of every day in all phases of practice. Then he wrote that down and he went back and typed it up the next morning and handed it out to the quarterbacks the next day at practice.

Jim Eustice, who was the Indian's starting quarterback in 1988, called me right after Super Bowl and told me that when Jon first met him he said, "My name is Jon Gruden. I'm going to be a head coach in the NFL someday." I guess that's how he introduced himself.

I've been known to keep pretty late hours myself. Well, Jon was always at the job before I was. You know, a couple times I can remember he was waiting outside when I got to the office. I'd ask him what he was doing there. He'd say he was going to lift weights but he didn't have a key yet. I'd let him go in and lift weights and I'd go in and watch tape or whatever. After he got a key, there were many times that he beat me to the office. I don't think I could do what he does and go to work at three in the morning and go home at midnight.

Jon is kind of a health nut, you know. He lifted weights because he wanted his body to look good—and he really wasn't going to let it go at 24 years old…that's the prime of your life. He didn't waste time in the bars drinking a lot of beer. We always kidded him that he was a health nut and he ate all the right foods, or tried to. I remember that bowl of cereal he's famous for. Of course, at that time, he didn't have a big salary—he was trying to save some money too.

We didn't always agree. Of course, I don't feel like I have all the answers. Jon and I used to battle back and forth on his opinion and my opinion. But I valued his opinion and I think he valued mine. He's very competitive and very fiery and had done a lot of research to back up his feelings. He'd make his point and I'd make my point and then we'd go about our business.

He was not a "yes man" at all. I didn't want a "yes man." I'm not going to tell you that Jon and I are close buddies and that he and I talk all the time, because we don't. But we respected each other and we are a lot alike in a lot of senses. As a matter of fact, when we disagreed in staff meetings, I'd say, "Jon, you remind me of myself twenty years ago." Sometimes when you're young, as I was once, you only see things as they pertain to right now in the small quarters.

Jon wasn't the offensive coordinator then, but I gave him a lot of leeway to institute many of the things that Tennessee was doing. At that time, Tennessee was playing three wide receivers. We did quite a bit of that and were an "I" formation team and did a lot of play action and put in a lot of the stuff that Jon was working with at Tennessee. It really made us a better team.

He was well prepared when he came to us and still had years of growth to achieve. He sure had a nice feel for calling the game. He had a sense. Not to take away from the other coaches because they did a great job as well, but you could hear through the headphones that Jon was telling them exactly what they were doing and how they were doing it, and that doesn't surprise you any because his background was knowledge.

I can remember sitting down with Jon after the season—I don't know if it was late December or early January. He told me he was going with Walt Harris to coach wide receivers at the University of the Pacific. I tried to talk him out of it to stay and be the offensive coordinator and he just didn't want to do that at that time. He was getting

$15,000 and he went to Walt Harris and was getting $38,000. That got him exposed to the West Coast stuff.

Then Jon went to the 49ers. I don't know exactly what Jon did there. But my guess is that he got all of his work done so he could sit in the meetings with the coaches and gain from that knowledge and experience. I don't know if most guys could have had the energy to do their job, which is twelve to fourteen hours and then go sit six hours with coaches and be in on those meetings. When he was coaching wide receivers at Pittsburgh, I'm sure he learned from Paul Hackett because Paul is a very great X's and O's coach. I'm sure Jon just hung out in the office and listened to him.

Jon is no dummy. He's a bright guy and he formulates his own opinions, but I think he took bits and pieces of this and that to develop his offense and a lot of it is homegrown. I've been asked if I think, as Jon gets older, he'll be able to make the transition to being less of a hands on guy. I don't. Jon's going to run that offense. When you turn something over it's not going to be quite your trademark. And Jon knows the offense. He knows what he wants to do. My guess is that he didn't do anything with defense. My guess is that he hired Monte Kiffin and the coaches he's got and told them this is the way I'm going to run the offense. You're going to be the offensive line coach and I want you to protect these guys. You're the running back coach, you're the receiver coach. I don't even know if he coaches a position but Jon is going to call the plays. I assume that's what he's doing and I'm sure he's going to listen to input from everybody else. But at that level, it's not like you have to get out and recruit or you have to make phone calls to this guy or that guy. He can put that time in and he has the energy to put that time in. Obviously, you have to give a lot of credit to what Tampa Bay did, but its Jon's program.

Somebody asked me around Super Bowl time if I knew back then that he was going to be an NFL head coach. I said, "No, I couldn't tell you that at that time. But I could tell you he was motivated and goal oriented and he was working to gain more knowledge." He just has a tremendous amount of passion for the game.

THE DOs AND DON'Ts OF DEALIN' WITH JON GRUDEN: DO

MARVIN ROSENGARTEN

Marvin Rosengarten, 71, was the athletic director at Southeast Missouri State University when Gruden was an assistant. He is retired and lives in St. Louis.

Bill Maskill hired Jon Gruden here at Southeast Missouri as a quarterbacks' coach back in the spring of 1988. Jon was a good kid. Every time I saw him he was very nice and courteous. He was a gentleman. He was a hard worker. We had nothing but good things to say about him. I had to laugh because there was an article in *USA Today* about him making only a few hundred dollars a month working for us. I think they got that confused when he was a graduate assistant at Tennessee. He was making regular salary when he was at Southeast.

Jon was very polished. I want to say he was only about twenty-four, twenty-five at the most, and he was a gentleman. He was very polished, he stood out, and he was the kind of guy who everyone got along with. The kids really liked him. You could tell right away he had something special. Bill Maskill had a couple of guys like that at that time. Bill had a great eye for talent. I don't know how he found those guys. I think Jon was a graduate assistant at Tennessee before he came to us. He had a big family background in football so it wasn't like getting a typical twenty-four year old.

Back then Jon was the quarterback coach and he was like an offensive coordinator even though I don't think he had that title. I've read that he's famous for working late hours and the whole bit. Well, I have to tell you, if he worked for Bill Maskill here, he worked late hours. That's why Bill had trouble with the other coaches that were before he hired Jon. They all left and criticized him because he was one of those kinds of guys who was very demanding. After Jon left,

Bill hired Marty Mornhinweg who went on to become head coach for the Detroit Lions. Everyone who worked for him was the same way and Jon was of the same mold.

It's unusual to see a young man that focused. I thought it was because of the family background. I knew a little bit about his father and his family and I really felt that he was focused because of two things. First, he was working for a guy who was the most focused guy I had ever seen and, second, I think he was mature and he knew what he wanted to do from day one.

Jon was a good looking guy. He'd say "Yes sir. No sir." He had good manners. He was a gentleman. The football coach could hire whoever he wanted, but I had to give the final say and there was no problem there. They'd come to me and I'd sign a contract with them. Jon came and we talked for about an hour and I thought he was very polite. He was a gentleman. That's very unusual. Most guys like to think that they're hot stuff and you can't tell them anything. He's not that type of guy. He was definitely a listener. He wanted to hear my stories. He was very respectful. And you could see right off the bat that he was focused.

I give a lot of credit to Bill Maskill for hiring someone like him and I give Jon a lot of credit for being focused. Yeah, I'm proud that I know him. I sometimes feel like I'd like to call him and wish him well. I watched all of his games when he was with Oakland too. He's a gentleman, that's the way I'd like to say it.

> When Joe Girardi played for the Cubs, he caught a ceremonial first pitch from Mike Ditka. Girardi had a football curled behind his back. After catching Ditka's pitch, Girardi fired the football at Ditka which Iron Mike caught easily.

THE FIRST THING WE DID WAS CALL THE CLINIC...THEY SAID JON WAS OVER HIS SHYNESS.

JIM EUSTICE

Jim Eustice was the starting quarterback for the Southeast Missouri State Indians when he had his first meeting with a confident and determined 24 year-old Jon Gruden. Today, Jim is a vice president in banking as a business development officer. He lives in Ottawa, Illinois.

I remember the day I met Jon like it was yesterday. He had gotten there early in March 1988 even though his contract didn't start until summer. It was his first full-time job as an assistant after he got done being a graduate assistant at Tennessee under Walt Harris. Coach Bill Maskill called me down and introduced me to him. "Jon Gruden, this is Jim Eustice, quarterback." I stuck my hand out and he shook my hand and he said, "Jim, I'm Jon Gruden. I'm glad to meet ya. I'm gonna be an NFL head coach some day." Obviously, he just made quite an impression.

On that first day, I thought, "Wow, great!! This guy's got a goal." I never once thought that was a bold statement or anything. I really didn't think too much of it, but then, in talking with him over the course of the next days, I could see his passion. It didn't take long to figure out I needed to listen to this guy as much as possible. After seeing him for the first week or so, I just knew he was set on his goal.

He worked all through the spring. He knew what he was talking about. He really taught me the defense. He had boxes of 16 mm film and they were all spliced together from Tennessee practice game film. Each roll would have one play on it...one pass pattern. The first 30 times if he didn't get it done, so the next 30 were in the 2D zone, and the next 30 were 2D man under, the next 30 a man free. When he was done with that he would grab another 16 mm reel of film with another pass, broken down like that for just about every play. That is pretty amazing for somebody who was only 24 and who was just a graduate assistant up to that point.

I know he was the first one on the job and the last one to leave every day. I can't imagine that it wasn't the same thing when he was at Tennessee as graduate assistant. He must have just lived there to get all that film work done. I remember just watching it and watching it with him. Sometimes I would watch by myself. After watching so much film, I was more of a cerebral quarterback. After all of the preparation, it got to the point where games were pre-established and I could pretty much tell exactly what was going to happen. I knew where to go with the ball before it was snapped. Then, when the ball was snapped, I just had to look in one or two areas and see those guys one way or the other and it made it easy for me.

Jon believed that by the time you get to the line you should have a good idea—and by the time you are in your second step you should know—what you are going to do. As far as reading a defense, basically there are a couple areas you can look at in a defense to at least get an idea of what it is. These are called the triangles. If it is a true triangle, then the zone is based on which way the triangle is pointing. The wide outs actually would read all of that coming up. We had a real good group of receivers who studied just as hard. They would run the routes according to what they were supposed to do and give that coverage. Beyond that, there might have been one or two things I needed to see after we got the snap. That made it very easy to do it. His motto that year was an acronym HPD—which stood for hyper-sensitive positioning defense. In fact, he got the quarterbacks and the receivers and backs T-shirts with HPD on them. That was his motto from the time he got here.

One game mid-to-late in the year, we threw for 270 yards and had two or three touchdowns. That was just a really, really big deal. That was the one game from that year where it all came together. We were absolutely prepared. The game plan that Jon had put in for that week and then all of the rest of the offensive systems, as well as the preparation for the other positions, were just unreal. Everybody executed to a tee that day. It was just one of those when the hole in the mask looks like it's 50-feet wide.

I considered Jon not only a coach, but a mentor and I felt that if I had any problems I could talk to him. I was a fourth year junior, so I was 21 or 22 and he was 24. There really wasn't ever a problem with him being so close to my age. He could talk to you. He wasn't condescending and—just having been removed from college a few years himself—he seemed to understand what college life is like. His being so young was certainly not a problem at all.

He was a regular guy. In hindsight now, you might think that someone who is that focused on one thing is lacking in a lot of other areas, but he wasn't at all. He could talk to you about anything that might be going on in your life. He was a college quarterback himself and he was a regular guy. He didn't have to talk football 24/7. We could talk about something else. He was very personable and very funny. I loved being around him.

The way that he coached was fun. As serious as he was about what he was doing, he didn't take himself so seriously that you were uncomfortable around him. When you were around him, you just became captivated by his enthusiasm for the game and everything he did. I just loved to watch him, loved to hear him, and loved to listen to him talk. He would have jokes here and there. Just little things. There's not one specific incident that I can think of as far as jokes he told…I just remember just having a great time every time I was around him and for the whole year I was with him.

He left and went to the University of the Pacific. He said, "I'll never forget you, you'll always be my first quarterback no matter what happens, I'll always be around and call me any time you need anything, whatever." I learned a lot from him and I've always kept his drive and his focus in my business career. I remember my dad telling Jon, "I just want you to know that as a father I am very happy that you are in my son's life, that you are a person that he is looking up to down here and I feel very good knowing that he is under your wing."

IT WAS EITHER THE FLUTIE FLAKES OR WARNER'S CRUNCHTIME CEREAL

RON HINES

Ron Hines was the sports information director for Southeast Missouri State University when Jon Gruden was there as an assistant coach. Today, at age 60, he continues at the same job; Hines lives in Carterville, Illinois.

Although Jon Gruden was here for only one year, I remember him as being young and personable. He was not that far removed from college and he was very enthusiastic. He worked long hours and he didn't make much money here and he didn't apparently have much money. So the thing I remember most about him is that he kept a big cereal box and a bowl on his desk and he ate cereal three meals a day.

I don't remember what kind of cereal it was but it was a big box. That was his menu I think. I understand that one of the sports writers said he used to have a few beers with him so maybe Jon was spending his money on that and not on food. But he wasn't spending any money on food other than his box of cereal.

Gruden was the lowest assistant coach on the totem pole at that time. In the first couple of games I don't really know what he did. But by the second or third game he was calling all of the plays. That showed me he was making a rapid rise.

That's pretty unusual because he wasn't the offensive coordinator—he was the quarterback coach. Bill Meyer, the offensive coordinator, had been the head coach of a small college in Iowa and a former offensive coordinator at Iowa State. But Gruden started calling the plays. I'm not sure when the transition took place but it was early.

Southeast Missouri hasn't had a great deal of success in football here, although that year they had a winning year. Bill Maskill came in as head coach and he brought in a lot of assistants who have gone on to be very successful. He did an excellent job of bringing in people; many of them are head coaches or assistant coaches of bigger schools now. The guy who replaced Gruden when he left here was Marty Mornhinweg, who later became the head coach of the Detroit Lions.

So Maskill had a pretty good eye for talented people and I know he was excited they had Gruden here. They ran a wide-open offense—you know I hesitate to say it was a West Coast offense but it probably was at the time before that was popular.

Early on you could tell that Jon was a hard worker and he was really driven. He was enthusiastic. Sometime you see enthusiasm in young coaches but you don't see the "drive" I saw in him. I had no idea he'd be as successful as he has become, but you could tell that good things were going to come to him.

I remember that Jon didn't have much money, as most young assistants don't. I think he was well connected due to the fact that his father was in the NFL and his brother Jay was the quarterback at the University of Louisville. That probably helped open the doors for him and then he made the most of it when he got in because of his ability. I thought he would be in the NFL sometime because of his father but I had no idea he would have such a rapid rise.

He worked long hours. I do remember that. He'd be up there late at night. When I would stop in there from time to time for various reasons he was usually there behind the projector or eating that cereal. He had a good grasp of offense and he was in the press box at the football games. That's where he'd call the games from.

At practice, he was very animated like how I see him on TV sometimes. He was very animated on the practice field and that is sort of unusual for a young coach to do. Most of them are scared to say anything. They're afraid the head coach might hear them. But he got right into it right away.

For a school the size of Southeast Missouri it's quite an accomplishment in itself to have two former assistants who became head coaches in the NFL...Gruden and Marty Mornhinweg.

CAPE GIRARDEAU: WHERE THE FUN NEVER STOPS...TILL NINE P.M.

MARTY MISHOW

Marty Mishow, 43, is a sports writer for the Southeast Missourian *who covered Gruden when he was an assistant at Southeast Missouri State. He lives in Cape Girardeau, Missouri.*

In 1988, Jon Gruden was here at Southeast Missouri State in Cape Girardeau, Missouri for just one year. At least for a while, and maybe for the whole time, he just lived in a motel. At the time, he'd have been 24 years old, and I'm only a few years older than him. He was such a low assistant that I didn't really have a chance to get to know him a whole lot from a coaching standpoint. He was a pretty interesting guy, though.

A lot of times, I'd cover the practices, and after practices, or sometimes after games, we'd all go and have a few beers at a watering hole, The Playdium, right across from the stadium. It was a typical sports bar—pool, darts, jukebox, that kind of thing. I actually got to know him pretty well then. As we were having a few beers at The Playdium, we'd just shoot the breeze and talk about things. It strikes me as funny that, after all these years, when I read stuff about him he talks about the same things. He told me back then that he loved football and he can attack it so well because he needs hardly any sleep. He says if he gets two or three hours sleep a night, he's fine. It's funny because after reading stuff about him now, they say he gets to work like at four a.m. For whatever reason, he said his body just functioned great on two or three hours of sleep. That was one of the things that struck me as kind of unique about the guy.

Jon was a young, in-shape guy, and he still looks like he's in good shape. I couldn't say for sure if he was married or not when he was in

Cape Girardeau, but he didn't strike me as being single at the time. He might have already met his future wife. At the time, I hadn't been in Cape Girardeau very long. I didn't get to know him well enough as an assistant coach because we're such a small operation here. I don't have the luxury of dissecting the team every day and doing a story like a big-city paper would. I had to do so much other stuff. From his coaching standpoint, it really struck me when he was talking about the limited sleep he needs. I know most coaches don't sleep a lot, but when he mentioned two or three hours, I thought, "man, I don't see how this guy keeps going."

I knew at that time that his dad had a real extensive NFL background. I recall him mentioning that he really wanted to get in the NFL. That kind of struck me—a guy here starting out as a young assistant. I don't even know if he was a full-pay kind of guy back then. That struck me as pretty ambitious. Back then I didn't really know a whole lot about the guy. He never struck me as being cocky or arrogant. I thought he was a real good guy, but he did have that confident air about him which is very clear now. It makes sense how driven he is. You wouldn't normally expect someone so young to be that confident about his abilities. That really did strike me, too.

My lasting impression is just how amazing it is for a guy Jon's age to have accomplished what he's accomplished. I have admiration for him. I've written columns about him before, and I'm sure his dad being an NFL guy helped him get a little bit of a foot in the door, but not helped him get up there to be coordinators, head coaches, that kind of thing. It's amazing how the guy not only was able to get in the NFL, but at such a young age to be considered one of the great coaches already. That's an amazing story.

SHORT STORIES FROM LONG MEMORIES

My first choice for Notre Dame coach would have been Jon. I think it would have been an unbelievable choice for him to be there. I can tell you the alumni that would have just flowed in. But, that being said, Ty Willingham, has grasped the Notre Dame family big-time, not just because of what he did last year, but because of the type of person he is. He's a no-nonsense, no-BS type person. I think he brings a lot of respect to the Notre Dame program. I think he brings a lot of respect from outside sources. I think he's just a phenomenal coach, and I thought this four or five years ago. When they were looking for a new Notre Dame coach to replace Davie, I was willing to go with the Athletic Director's choice. I also knew that Gruden didn't have the choice at that time, unfortunately. He was tied up with the Raiders and there were other things going on at the time, but I knew that he probably wouldn't get that, even though he was my first choice. But I tell you what, Ty Willingham has made me a believer.

——MIKE SHINER, 41, *Former Notre Dame Player*

Jon's hobbies were sports, sports, sports, and more sports. He'd watch ESPN. He was very active in his high school sports. That's all he did. His older brother, Jim, is a physician now, and his younger brother, Jay, has had success in Arena Football. While Jim was a straight-A student at Notre Dame, and Jim, Sr. is very proud of that, Jon would tease him about being a bookworm. He would make fun of him a little bit even though he was very proud of him. Jon was the opposite. He would constantly be sports-minded whatever it was. When his dad was at Notre Dame, Jon ate, drank and slept Notre Dame. He absolutely loved Notre Dame. He came down to Notre Dame practice whenever he could.

——BLAIR KIEL, Former Notre Dame quarterback

Chapter 3

California Dreamin'

THE ODDS WERE A KILLION-TO-ONE SHE WOULD GET THE INTERVIEW

ANN KILLION

Ann Killion, a sports columnist for the San Jose Mercury News, *first met Gruden when he was with the San Francisco 49ers and then covered him when he coached the Oakland Raiders.*

My earliest memory of Jon Gruden is of this little kid walking out to the 49ers facility when I was the 49ers beat writer. He was walking out onto the field, and I had no idea who he was, so I didn't pay him another thought. Good beat writer that I was, I should have gotten to know him. I just remember this really young looking kid around the 49ers in 1990, which was my first year on the beat. It was quite a team and quite an atmosphere. I didn't realize that kid was soaking up everything he saw like a sponge and laying the foundation for his own success in the National Football League. I was pretty young myself, although I'm older than Jon, so I just thought, "Who's that guy?" I thought he was some glorified water-boy or something. Little did I know?

I still didn't know him when he left. There was a lot of upheaval on the 49ers staff, and the unpaid assistant was the last guy we were thinking about. I didn't know him at all until he was hired by the Raiders. When he was first hired by the Raiders, there was a certain amount of eye-rolling. Here's this really young guy coming in to be a stooge for Al Davis.

As soon as I sat down with him after he got hired, I had a pretty clear idea that he wasn't going to be Al's stooge. Jon had a mind of his own and had an idea about how he was going to do things. One of the main things that impressed me first was just how comfortable he was with the media. I don't know if you've spent any time around the Raiders, but people come in there scared. They do what the Raiders say and one of the things they say is don't talk to the media. Right from the start, Jon was extremely comfortable with the media, pretty honest, just clearly his own man. As a reporter, that obviously made an impression on me.

I met him before the draft, but the first time I remember sitting and having a long talk with him was probably early in that first season. I wasn't at the first press conference. I wasn't there the day he got hired. I was at Pebble Beach covering golf. The Raiders always do these things, like hire, when something else is going on.

He was just so young, and he had that bad hair cut. He'd had the Ricky Watters incident, and no one really knew what he was all about—maybe the guys at Philly thought he was an offensive genius. They were coming off the **Joe Bugel** thing, and so anything fresh and new was a good idea. They hadn't ever had a coach who really had a mind of his own except for Mike Shanahan who was a complete failure. Just given the nature of the Raiders' makeup and Al Davis, there was no reason to believe that he was going to be particularly different.

I have a very good rapport with Jon Gruden. When I was in Tampa before the 49ers were playing them, all the Tampa media people were like, "You're the only person who has gotten him to talk about the Raiders at all, or has been to his house since he moved here." Jon was honest with me. He had a few reporters he would go off the record with and talk to. I got to know his wife pretty well. She's pretty funny telling about the craziness of their lives.

Meeting him at his office in Oakland at four o'clock in the morning was pretty strange. Obviously, I had to arrange my whole schedule to get up at that time of the morning and drive forty-five minutes over there. He was there, and he came downstairs and said, "You tired?" I said, "Yeah, a little bit." He goes, "Ahhh yes," like he was wide awake and ready to go. He works in this room that's all dark with just one

> Until he was in his nineties, Joe Bugel's father would send his son, Joe, a birthday card every year with a ten dollar bill enclosed.

little light over the desk. He wasn't too thrilled about being disturbed. He was certainly focused on his work.

The phone kept ringing. First it was his mom, "Hey, I love you." "Okay, I love you, too." Then someone else called him, and then someone else called him. Everyone on the East Coast knew that was the time to reach him. Now that he's on the East Coast, I don't know when it's time to call him because no one on the West Coast is waking up that early unless they stayed up really late to talk to him.

Our early-morning meeting was more to observe him than to interview him. It was in 2001, right before the AFC championship game when they played **New England**. He knew I was doing a story, and part of that story was Cindy—what the other half of Jon's manic work life was like. He agreed to it. He wasn't that thrilled about it. I stayed about an hour. It was clear he had a lot of stuff he had to do. By the time I left around five or so, there were quite a few people there. He had a staff that worked that hard right along with him, and I'm sure they are probably doing that at Tampa, too.

That's the real deal with him. He was like that before. He told really funny stories when he worked for the 49ers that year. He never went home. He wasn't making any money, and he had a lousy little apartment so he just stayed there. He'd sleep in different offices. He never slept in Eddie DeBartolo's office. He wasn't allowed to sleep in Eddie's office, but he would sleep on a couch or all around, and he would stay up half the night with Ray Rhodes designing game plans. He was like that then. He didn't sleep. Bobb McKittrick, the great

> The New England Patriots once played a regular-season home game in Birmingham, Alabama, in September 1968.

> As a result of a public contest in 1960, the team nickname of Patriots was chosen. Many years later when considering a name change, they decided on the Bay State Patriots, but changed that because they're worried about Bay State being abbreviated in headlines.

offensive line coach for the 49ers, who died of cancer a couple of years ago, used to tell great stories about Jon.

Jon used to sit outside Bobb's little meeting room. Each coach had their own little meeting room. He would sit on the floor right outside Bobb's meeting room, and he had a little notebook and would write down everything Bobb said. He never came in to the offensive linemen's meeting. He would just sit there like a little sponge and just absorb everything. Jon says he still has all those notebooks. Bobb is the one guy who had been with the 49ers through every thing. He was kind of the original—he had the Bill Walsh system down better than anyone. He'd been there forever through all the different manifestations of it. McKittrick said to me that, aside from Mike Shanahan, Jon was the smartest coach that had ever come through that organization, which is a pretty high compliment.

A lot of people have accused Jon of having this media personality—like that whole "outworking everybody" thing is kinda for show, but it's clearly not. It's clearly when he does his work. All his kids have apparently inherited his freakish sleeping habits. Cindy says their house is like Grand Central Station at night. People are in and out of beds and moving around. She doesn't get any sleep at all. She's just exhausted all the time. She told me that in their new big house in Tampa, which is beautiful, she said, "Oh yeah, I just sleep on the floor," because there's too much traffic going in and out of her bed.

McKittrick is the guy that is the all-time idol of Jon Gruden. He's the kind of football coach, real super honest, didn't try to spin things. He was just all about football. Gruden really idolized him.

McKittrick once told Jon that he needed to be with his family. Jon isn't living by his advice. He tries. I think he knows, and I think when he's home, he's really home. That's the sense I get and that's what Cindy says. That he works like crazy, but when he's there, he is down on the floor wrestling with the boys. He's not in his office taking phone calls or looking at film. He's fully committed, but he's just a workaholic. The thing I worry about is that he'll burn himself like so many coaches do. But I don't know—so far he seems to be doing okay.

THAT'S BOBB WITH TWO "B'S," NOT TWO "O'S"

TECKLA McKITTRICK

The late Robert McKittrick was an NFL legend. His profile in Sports Illustrated *three years ago became one of the most discussed articles in the almost-fifty-year history of the publication. It detailed his amazing battle against dying, while continuing to coach the 49ers' offense. He was regarded as the consummate professional and became Jon Gruden's idol. Here, his widow talks about her husband's admiration for Jon Gruden.*

O ur younger son, Ladd, was a quarterback at Oregon State. Ladd grew up around football all his life. When we were at the Chargers, he was the ball boy for the quarterback. He went to Oregon State, and he worked at training camp for the 49ers. The 49ers asked Ladd to come down to be the practice-team quarterback so he worked there, and after the camp was over, **Mike Holmgren**, the quarterback coach, kept Ladd on as assistant to the offense since Ladd knew all the offensive plays. So he stayed on working with the coaches and was kind of the go-fer person. That was the first time they'd ever hired someone in that capacity, but now it's traditional—everybody has a defensive assistant-assistant and an offensive assistant-assistant.

Then the next year, it started out to be like a training job, an interim job for young people to come in. Ladd left, and they hired Jon Gruden to be the assistant. We knew Jim Gruden very well but didn't know Jon. Jon came and he was this firecracker and very industrious. Bobb was the offensive line coach and he came home and said, "This

> Mike Holmgren was an eighth round pick by the Saint Louis Football Cardinals in 1970. He was a back-up quarterback at USC.

is a very, very bright young man, very, very dedicated." Of course, we thought our son was very bright and very industrious, but he thought Jon was really good. Bobb was telling me that as the season went on—originally it was supposed to be only a training position during summer camp—but like they had kept Ladd on the year before, they kept Jon on. Bobb said he would be in his meetings with players showing film and the room would be dark. He said he didn't know it then, but that Jon would come in and sit on the floor inside Bobb's meeting room. He had his legal pad and would take notes while Bobb was talking and coaching and going over game plans and different things with the players. Then Jon would sneak out before the lights came back on. One time, Bobb turned on the light sooner than expected, and he saw Jon sitting there on the floor. He said, "Jon, what are you doing?" Jon said, "Well, if it's all right, coach, I'm just taking notes." Bobb said, "Fine, but you don't have to sit on the floor. You can sit up in a chair and join the group." So that's what Jon did. My husband and Jon became very, very close. Bobb commented that this was a young man who was going to go far in coaching.

Bobb had kind of pushed our son out of coaching. Our son wanted to go on in coaching, and Bobb said, "Get a life. You like to play golf. You're not gonna have time to do that if you're a coach." He kind of pushed our son into banking.

When Jon Gruden came along, Bobb said there was no changing him—he was going to be a coach, and my husband always knew Jon was going to be very successful. Bobb was so pleased when he got that first head job over here at Oakland. They always kept in touch. Bobb's big regret was that he never got to work for Jon. He had always hoped someday to coach under Jon. He knew right from the first that Jon was going to be an outstanding coach.

I got the sweetest letter from Kathy Gruden. It was so nice. When Jon's team won the playoff game, I called Jim and congratulated them, "I know you're very proud. Tell Jon that we're thinking of him and very happy for them." I just left that on their answering machine. I know how hectic and busy—just a whirlwind—it is when you're in the Super Bowl. The pressure on your time is just unbelievable so I didn't expect to hear anything. Then I got a very sweet letter from

Kathy thanking me for leaving the message and telling me how much it meant to Jon. She also said that they were thinking of Bobb. I know Bobb was up there looking down on him and saying, "I knew you could do it, Jon."

The thing Bobb worried about with Jon, and he often told Jon, "Jon, you've got to learn to balance your life. That's the hardest thing. Don't let your life go by so that you don't have time for your children or for your wife. It's a difficult profession. It takes a lot of your time." I know Bobb made it a priority that our sons were given what free time he had. I think Jon has this same devotion to excellence. He works till he gets the work done. They don't have much time for socialization. Jon was more dedicated than anybody I know. When we first knew him he was single and this was his life—football—and he was out to learn as much as he could. He was very fortunate to be at an organization like the 49ers. There's no doubt in my mind, and I know Bobb thought so, that Bill Walsh was one of the great teachers of football and put together one of the great organizations—the way everything ran very smoothly. He was very particular about who he hired, and it was important that everybody get along. Since there were no distractions from problems, you could devote your time to your work and could accomplish a lot. I think Jon learned that, right from the grass roots, and he was fortunate to be with an organization that had been built to be a very strong model, really, for a lot of teams now. Bill and all the coaches there were very good at what they did.

There are people who can do a lot of things and be under a lot of pressure and still keep their composure and keep their wits about them. Not many people can do that. My husband thought Jon Gruden was magnificent at doing that. I really believe that Bobb, even though he said he was ready to retire, if Jon had asked him to come coach for him, would certainly have gone.

We happened to be going up to San Francisco to have lunch with a friend, Lee Rogers, who is a talk-show host on KSFO. When we got there, Lee and Susie Rogers came running up and made this big fuss, and we couldn't figure out what it was about. Lee said, "Bobb, Bobb, I have to shake your hand." Bobb said, "Why?" He said, "'Cause you're about the greatest coach in the NFL. Jon Gruden just said it."

SOME PEOPLE FELT AL DAVIS WAS THE BACKBONE OF THE RAIDERS. MANY WOULDN'T PUT HIM THAT HIGH

SAM FARMER

Sam Farmer is the NFL reporter for The Los Angeles Times. *He was with* The San Jose Mercury News *from 1995 through 2000 and covered Gruden with the Oakland Raiders.*

When Jon Gruden came to Oakland, I didn't know too much about him. I had some friends who covered the Eagles when he was there. He looked so nervous in his first press conference. He was flanked by Al Davis and Bruce Allen. He just looked wide-eyed and rosy-cheeked and he wasn't as forceful as he can be. I didn't know what to make of him after that initial press conference. He really seemed like more of a peer when he was coaching the Raiders than he really did with the players and did with reporters too. I felt like I could say anything. I could give him a hard time about anything.

I was surprised by his voice. I mean when I first saw him, it didn't look like that voice would come out of that face. For a 30-year-old guy, it sounded like his voice was dubbed in by a hard-bitten coach. It sounded like a voice track. I know he's being steeped in coaching throughout his life. His dad being a coach and being surrounded by coaches, he sounds like a coach…like right from central casting.

I really didn't really feel like I started to know who this guy was until I talked to his mom and dad and his brothers. Then I started to feel like, "Okay, I've sort of drawn a bead on who this guy is." He was always extremely accessible. That's changed in Tampa. In fact, I went down there to training camp last year and I said, "I want to talk to Jon." He came out and I got him for probably about twenty-five minutes or half an hour or something like that. But a few writers came over to me and asked me, "What did he say?" I said, "What do you mean?" They said, "Well, we haven't gotten any one-on-ones with him yet. Even our columnists haven't." I said, "You've got to be kidding. He's been here for like four months." He's really more protected in Tampa. He's more of a rock star there. With us, it was this young coach that nobody knew anything about.

I wrote a story about him **punching** out a customer in the parking lot when he was working as a waiter at Bennigan's years ago. I guess some guy had insulted a waitress there and Gruden went over. He was a young kid and he said, "Hey, don't talk to the waitresses that way." The guy called him "blondie" and sort of brushed him away. Gruden followed him into the parking lot and smacked him. They called him "the Bennigan's Brawler." He was a hero to most girls there after that.

When his dad was working on Dan Devine's staff at Notre Dame, there was a drunken fan. Jon was about fifteen or sixteen. The fan was on the field and the guy was yelling things from the field level so Jon walked over and smacked him. Then the guy smacked Jon and gave him a fat lip. Jon was just a kid.

Do you remember the **Cotton Bowl** on New Year's Day 1979? Joe Montana began building his legend with the remarkable victory he directed over Houston when he brought the Irish back from a 22-point fourth-quarter deficit. The game was played in the worst ice storm Dallas had seen in 30 years. It was so cold and there was a danger of hypothermia. His dad was on the Notre Dame staff at the time, and Jon watched the first half on the sidelines, and then went

> In 1979 Ali beat Lyle Alzado in eight rounds. Rich Kotite, former head coach of the Eagles and the Jets, was once Muhammad Ali's sparring partner in Miami.

> The Cotton Bowl is nicknamed "The House that Doak Built," which is a takeoff of Yankee Stadium being known as "The House that Ruth Built." Babe Ruth's old school, St. Mary's Industrial School for Boys—now called Cardinal Gibbons High School—in Baltimore called itself "The House that Built Ruth."

and stayed warm in the team bus. When he saw his dad afterward he said, "Gosh dad. That was a great game." His dad said, "What are you talking about. I heard you went to the bus." He gave him a hard time. "You went to stay warm in the bus." Jon pretended like he was there the whole time watching it, braving the cold.

Then he had a game that he made up with his brothers and it was like a Strat-O-Matic game with football stats. It was the precursor to their version of fantasy football when nobody was doing that and he was just obsessed with the game. It was a dice game and they sort of made up the rules as they went along.

He was very well liked by the media. He'd say the same things, "I'll answer any questions." He still says that. He's a corker. I can't do an impersonation of him but we'd give him crap about anything. He got seriously razzed about the *People* magazine article but that was towards the end of his tenure there. In fact, I might even have been in LA at that time and joked about it with him later.

He certainly had a sense of humor about himself. He knows he's a certain way. In a group, he would always be different than when you got him aside. If you got him aside, one-on-one, he would joke. In a group, he was a little more straight-laced. In a group, he probably figures TV cameras are on. He is a guy who was very aware of the cameras. He knows how to work a crowd. He will always say, "I don't want to get too deep or philosophical." You've probably heard that before. That's his little ruse. Another thing, his dad would say, "If dog rabbit." That's what his family would say which was his dad's way of shooting down any excuse…"If the dog wasn't screwing around, he would've caught the rabbit." As soon as Jon started giving excuses for something, his dad would dismiss it lightly by saying say, "If dog rabbit." Jon still adheres to that, at least publicly. Privately, he'll pull you aside and remind you about the situation. He's like any coach.

I remember doing a story about Jon. It was a long, comprehensive story that went back to his childhood. I talked a lot with his brothers. His mom sent a bunch of photos from his childhood which we ran with the story. It was a nice story. It was just a story about who this guy was growing up. Then, my wife had a baby and one day we got a package with baby outfits from Jon's mom. Most of the time you don't even get a thank you note for a story. I thought this was a pretty classy thing. Jon is very close to his mom. He was very good salt of the earth. It really impressed me that she remembered to get three baby outfits. Whenever I talk to her she asks about my son and my daughter. I was very impressed.

This story is a bit of a departure. Rich Gannon was not an Al Davis type quarterback. In 1998, when **Jeff George** was quarterback, he and Jon didn't get along well at all. When Jeff George played a full season under Joe Bugel, he had a career year. Tim Brown, Rickey Dudley, and James Jett all had their career best years. The team went 4 and 12. So, Jeff was putting up incredible numbers but they were losing. They had a horrible defense. That was part of it. But how long could Jeff George stretch the offense? Gruden really pushed for Gannon. I remember calling Napoleon Kaufman the night they got Gannon. I asked him, "What do you think of your new quarterback?", and Napoleon said, "What are you talking about?" I told him "They're going to let Jeff go." Napoleon was surprised. "They're going to let Jeff go? Oh no! Oh man! Who did we get?" I said, "Rich Gannon." And he said, "Rich Gannon?" I said, "Yeah." He said, "We signed Rich Gannon?" I said, "Yeah." And Napoleon said, "Who's Rich Gannon?" I got a kick out of that. He had no idea who Rich Gannon was.

Gruden loved Gannon because he was so driven and he can be such a hard ass. One morning, about 6:00 a.m., Gruden was working in his office which was a second story office and he heard a rock at the window and then another one. He looked down and saw Gannon with what looked like a hand full of pebbles. He couldn't get into the building and was —— off. Gruden went to the balcony. Gannon said, "I can't get into the building. I want to come in and study film." So Gruden had a key made for him. Gruden loved that story. The Raiders are trying to make it like Al wanted Gannon all along. But it was actually Gruden who was the influence behind it all along.

Looking back on it, we knew they were going to go some different direction because Jon and Jeff George had different philosophies

Since the 1970 NFL-AFL merger, the starting quarterback with the worst winning percentage is Jeff George.

throughout the year. Jeff was hurt in the Arizona game. Nobody hit him but he was running to his right and he tore a groin muscle. He couldn't play. Donald Hollas and Wade Wilson filled in for him, but then, in the opening drive of the game against Baltimore—his first game back—Jeff reinjured his groin. He came back maybe one other time late in the year and then he went on Jim Rome's show and announced that he was pretty much done for the season. But he hadn't told Gruden that, so it —— off Gruden to no end. We knew that was the end of Jeff George at Oakland—going on a national radio show and saying his season was over. Gruden learned about it by listening to the radio.

Gruden is closer in age to the players than most coaches. Most coaches, especially guys who have played, have those bowed knees. They're sort of knobby and they limp along. Gruden does not have that beat-up body. He spends a lot of his time in his little office at the Tampa Marriott. He would put in like an hour and a half a day on the StairMaster. He used to cuss these guys out like crazy. He would get right up in their faces. It was very entertaining to just watch him coach. Some of the stuff you'd hear was just shouting at the guys.

Gruden definitely is a master motivator. The first year that he was coach, I remember Tim Brown telling me that, "This guy is not going to last. This guy is going to burn himself out real fast. He's so intense. He's so 100 miles per hour that he is going to burn himself out." Obviously, that hasn't happened. That's the way he is. I saw him the other day and he was pretty funny. He had a great line for someone who asked, "Have you thought about retirement after twenty years." He said, "Yeah. I thought about it."

The intensity stuff is a little bit overblown. You hear this stuff about him waking up at 3:17 every morning…there are lots of guys like that. He's actually a pretty normal guy. But he perpetuates this myth of a guy who is just off the cuff. You know he's trying his hardest. Probably some of the Gruden stuff is true. I'm sure he slept in his office. But look at Dick Vermeil. The guy was a nut. He had a couch in his office. He didn't even go home.

One thing we tease Jon about, and certainly other players will tease him about, is that he thought he was a good quarterback in college. Remember when he played being Gannon in practice on the Thursday before the Super Bowl and completed three passes. I think John Lynch said something like, "We were all just doubled over laughing until we let him complete the passes." It was funny.

Gruden had a real hard time with Jerry Porter. Jerry Porter drove him crazy. He was a second round pick out of West Virginia. He was a bit of a reach. He played a lot of defensive back in college and maybe even some quarterback. So, as a receiver he was a reach for a second round pick. Here is a guy who hadn't really played much as a receiver. But he was still athletic. Jerry came in and he was sort of like passive-aggressive. He was real laid back and countered Gruden. It nearly drove Gruden crazy that he wasn't high-wired all the time. Gruden would say, "How're you doing Jerry?" You know, get right up in his face. Jerry would say, "I'm chillin." It —— Gruden off. Gruden started calling him "Chillin'" It wasn't exactly a term of endearment.

Gruden got the bad apples out of the Raiders' locker room. That was a big deal. Chester McGlockton was a bad apple. He'd show up late at meetings. He tried to lead a little mutiny. One time, he came to practice and went through drills in a full length coat and wouldn't take it off. It was one of those coats like you'd wear to stand on the sidelines in bad weather. He went through drills like that and wouldn't take it off. This was before Gruden got there. Gruden didn't have to deal with Chester.

Jon's agent, Bob LaMonte, took a hard line on the Raiders. They were not one year away from the Super Bowl. They were four games away from zero wins. The Raiders always portrayed themselves as great news. Al Davis had two long interviews with Jon and really liked him. I think Al and Jon were the same guy. As a young guy, Al Davis always had ideas, always worked long hours, and was always thinking football. That's all he had in his life. He was a coach at a young age, an offensive guy. What Al Davis was in 1963 is what Jon Gruden was in 1995. Maybe he saw himself there. I wasn't around every day when people said they never talked. I think their relationship sort of withered over time as Gruden got stronger. There might have been an element of jealousy. A lot of people think that that was one of the reasons Al had the falling out with Marcus Allen is because he became symbolic of the Raiders. There was a word association game. If somebody said Raiders you'd say Marcus instead of Al Davis. That clichéd shot that they used to always show on **Monday Night Football** of Al Davis grimacing in the owner's box was replaced by Gruden grimacing on the side lines. Gruden became the rock star. That might have bothered Al.

I don't think Gruden ever got too too close with anybody in the media. There was a professional distance there even though you'd like to feel like you knew him, like he was one of your buddies because he was around your age and you joked about it and you laughed about it. You might even have had a beer with him. But it was a good, professional, journalistic relationship. He wasn't going to let you in on any trade secrets. You weren't going to let him off the hook because you felt beholden to him for being a nice guy. But he understands when you had to hold his feet to the fire in a story. I think he steeled himself to that. I can't remember him being extra sensitive. Bugel was very sensitive.

I've been the beat guy for Mike White, Joe Bugel and Jon Gruden when they were with the Raiders. Jon had so much control over the players that he commanded the respect of the players so much more than the other two. That was evident early on. For the longest time, some people might have thought that Gruden was playing favorites and that he loved Gannon. He and Gannon used to get into it on the sidelines like nobody's business. They would be screaming at each other on the sidelines. Even with guys he liked, particularly with players he liked, he would tear into them. He didn't want to be their friend, even though he was close to a lot of them.

> John Lennon's death was first reported to the nation by Howard Cosell on Monday Night Football...In 1999, Monday Night Football became the longest-running prime-time entertainment series ever, breaking a tie with Walt Disney at 29 years...Even when *Monday Night Football* ratings hit an all-time low, it still ranks in the top five during prime time for the entire year.

There's a funny story about Gruden when he was with Green Bay. There were a lot of funny things in Green Bay. Ty Detmer was squeamish about worms. When the practice field was watered, it would turn up all these worms. So Gruden would stick worms all over his helmet. Detmer hated that. In fact, for a while, Detmer didn't know that Gruden was the guy putting the worms in his helmet. Finally, he figured it out. One year when the 49ers were playing Green Bay, Detmer found out where Gruden lived and went and covered his car with worms.

They used to call Gruden "Miss Daisy" in Green Bay because he drove Mike Holmgren everywhere.

Gruden was a young receivers coach and Holmgren said, "Hey. Go tell Sterling Sharpe he's running his curls two yards too shallow and we want him to go a few yards deeper." Well, Gruden was scared of Sharpe. He wasn't going to tear into him in any game. Gruden walks over. He notices Holmgren is watching him. So Gruden affects this like really angry face and then starts screaming but it was during the game so nobody could hear him. Nothing is coming out of his mouth. He was pretending that he was yelling. Sharpe was just looking at him like, "What the hell are you doing?" Gruden didn't say anything. He didn't even make a sound. Then he walked back over to Holmgren and said, "Yeah. I told him." But he really never said a word.

Gruden was too afraid to say anything. You know, being a little guy, a young guy and Sterling Sharpe didn't like to be bothered during games and stuff. He didn't want to be coached up during games.

It remains to be seen how success is going to affect Gruden. He's already less accessible and more on the Presidential schedule than he was at the Raiders. I imagine he was even more accessible when he was a Philadelphia assistant than the offensive coordinator. I'm sure there will be a lot of time for people. Beyond that, I don't know. It remains to be seen. He could become aloof or he could be the same but I can't really predict how it will affect him. I've always known he was ambitious. He's the most ambitious guy I've ever been around. He's always looking ahead to the next thing.

OOOH, RICKY, GRUDEN JUST PUT THE RAIDERS IN THE VITAMEATAVEGIMATIC

RICKY RICARDO

Ricky Ricardo, 57, is the owner of Ricky's Sports Theater and Grill in San Leandro, California. Gruden and other Gruden family members occasionally frequented Ricky's. Ricardo lives in Castro Valley, California.

The Raiders fans loved Gruden. He is the best. You meet him, and if you don't get excited about football, you must be dead. You gotta be dead. There was that story that Gruden could make a dead man get up and watch football. This guy has so much energy and so much enthusiasm, and he just is a good person. He wanted to see Jay, his brother, in an Arena Football League game. He just came in one day and brought his mom with him and they watched a game. He was so enthusiastic. I have never met a nicer guy and a nicer family. His mother is terrific. He said he joined the Raiders and looked up and he saw Jerry Rice and Rich Gannon and Tim Brown. He said he just couldn't believe it. You could feel the excitement when he talked to us about that stuff.

When he was here watching a game, he asked, "Have you been up to training camp?" I told him no. "Well, I want you to be my guest at training camp." I've been a Raider fan for a long time. We are known as Raider Land. He is the first head coach, while he was a coach, to be in the place. We took all of our employees to training camp. The Raiders aren't big on opening up the training camp, and I think they have locked it up since that time, but it was the experience of a lifetime.

We rented a big ole' stretch limo, a fourteen-seater, a truck-type one. We piled in at seven in the morning, and we drove up there and got to training camp and watched them. The training camp is in Napa, about an hour-and-a-half drive. Sixteen of us could go at that time. I couldn't have thrown a better party for my employees. Jon was great when we got there. He was busy, of course, but he always had time at the afternoon session, and he would stop and talk to people. He was right there. You could see him doing his job. He was just real cordial, real nice and the same way he is all the time. When Jon was around, you could see them working and doing their stuff. We had the greatest time. He was great. He talked to everybody and was real nice. He is a once-in-a-lifetime kind of guy, as far as I've seen coaches go. I think that is pretty evident with what he did in Tampa Bay.

When they were playing **Oakland** in the Super Bowl, fans had big expectations, but it was pretty dismal in my place. Jon just had the game plan down. He knew what was going on. He knew what Gannon was going to do before maybe Gannon even knew what he was doing. For the Raiders, it couldn't have been a worse match-up. If they had played the Eagles, they would have probably won the game, but Gruden knew exactly what was going on. He knew what the Raiders were going to do. It was a big party, but it didn't turn out the way the Raider fans wanted it to turn out.

It was an exciting time when Gruden was here. He brought spark and enthusiasm. I'm an older guy, so he reminded me of the Kennedys in the White House. You gotta look like "a bright future ahead of ya," is exactly what I saw when you see Jon Gruden. He just gets you excited. The atmosphere was so great. Besides being a great guy, he was a great marketing tool for the team, and everybody loved him. I heard a story that he went out to visit some kids at a school in Pleasanton where his kids go to school, and he was in a class there and they almost had the whole school shut down.

> The Oakland A's colors are green and gold because their late owner, Charles O. Finley, grew up in LaPorte, IN and loved Notre Dame...when he bought the Kansas City A's, he changed their uniforms to those colors.

OOOH, RICKY, I WANNA BE IN THE BOOK TOO

TINA RICARDO

Tina Ricardo, 45, is married to Ricky Ricardo, the owner of Ricky's Sports Theater and Grill located in San Leandro, California. Tina lives in Castro Valley, California.

Jon Gruden with Tina Ricardo, 2003

When Jon was coaching for the Raiders we got to know him a little bit, and his mom and wife used to come in to Ricky's. They are probably the nicest people you ever want to meet, really, in your life. They are just great people, and they always had time for everybody. Jon would sign autographs, and when they left Mrs. Gruden wrote us and thanked us for being nice to her. We actually got to know them more when they left than when they were here. I went down to a game in Tampa, and they invited me to go with them in their box for a playoff game against the 49ers. I went to their house and talked to Jon afterwards. Look at what he's done. He's amazing. He brought the Raiders back—they were eight and eight for how many years? Until he came along. He gave everybody something to believe in. They loved everything about him.

The first time he came into our place, he walked in the liquor store and was bent down where you really could not see who it was. He was buying a bunch of Chucky shirts, and he started talking about the first time when they had just got Jerry Rice. Jon was talking about being in the huddle with Jerry Rice and Tim Brown and how awesome that was. He was like a little kid talking about heroes.

He is a great guy. Anywhere he goes he is going to inspire a lot of people. The day he first came in, he told me he was going to a **golf** tournament. He said "Don't tell anybody I'm buying these." I go, "I'm telling everybody I know." He used to come in and watch his brother play with the Orlando Predators and sat there and watched the game, right up front, and would talk to anybody that came and talked to him, not like a lot of the players who are too important to sign anything. There was another couple who came that he had talked to before. They had been to an autograph signing and Jon had talked to them as he was signing a book. Six months later, they were at some other autograph signing, and Jon saw them in line, and he goes, "Hey, I was thinking about you guys. You had an earthquake up there." It was the little things that he remembered the most. He loved the fans. I don't know if the Raider fans remember that, but he loved them—whatever the story may be.

He liked Coors Light. All the waitresses kept his empty bottle, and his chair, and his menu, pretty much anything else that was there. He was wonderful to everybody. Another couple came in one time and they were up at the training camp. They didn't have tickets, and they were just standing there watching all of the players, and he goes, "Well, aren't you going in?" They said they didn't have tickets and he goes, "Well, then be my guest." I mean, how many people do that? He is the best. The best. I was a Raider fan for forty years but when all that transpired with the Raiders, that was it. I'm a Buccaneer fan.

His mom—how many people would pick you up, take you back to their house, take you to the game? I had one ticket to go to the 49ers game. Ricky was sending me. I sent her a note and said, "If you have a chance, call me. If not, go Bucs." She called me, she picked me up, she took me to the game, she took me down to see Jon. I mean it was amazing. I went to Tampa for that. It was fantastic.

> The average score of the average golfer is 91.6 strokes. Better get your ball retriever regripped.

> Chris Evert and Martina Navratilova once went on a double date with Desi Arnaz, Jr and Dean Martin, Jr...to a drive-in movie.

Chapter 4

Super Bucs,
Super Bowl,
Super Man

The West Coast Offense
Meets the East Coast Defense

WE KNEW THAT ELVIS WAS THE KING BECAUSE HE DIED ON THE THRONE.

WHITNEY JOHNSON

Whitney Johnson, 42, is sports director for WDAE- AM 620 in Tampa. He has been doing sports talk radio for 15 years and lives in St. Petersburg, Florida.

Like many of us, my earliest memory of Jon Gruden comes from watching him on TV and seeing this intense guy every time they showed him on the sidelines. The first time I met him was at the press conference when the Buccaneers announced he was coming to Tampa Bay. It was kind of neat at the press conference where everybody was asking questions, and he showed he was pretty intense.

Reggie Roberts, the Bucs PR guy at the time, was there. When I walked up, he said to Jon, "Oh, coach, stay away from this guy. Stay away from this guy." Gruden kind of looked at me as if to ask "What's this guy all about?'

Then I asked him what his three favorite albums are. I wanted to find out what the guy was all about, rock 'n' roll wise, because that's always a fun angle to talk about. He answered that his three favorite albums were anything by Stevie Ray Vaughn, Van Halen's first **album** *Van Halen*, and John Fogarty's, *Centerfield*. I don't know if we clicked, but his eyebrow didn't shoot up when I asked him that. I

> The band, Pearl Jam, was originally named Mookie Blaylock, after the NBA player, and they recorded their first album, *Ten* under that name. In 1992, the band Mookie Blaylock changed their name to Pearl Jam after a hallucinogenic concoction made by lead singer Eddie Vedder's great-grandmother, Pearl.

heard his answers, and I said, "Boy, those are the same three albums that Coach Dungy liked," and he started laughing. That is my first meeting with him. He has been very cool ever since.

My niche is to be the rock 'n' roll guy, and I always like to find out what other people are listening to. That goes for anybody—the average Joe on the street, the head coaches of teams, whoever. Over the years I have asked everyone I've met what they like and what they listen to, and it's become a habit. Now, when someone is coming to town or in an interview, people always ask me to make sure I find out what their three albums are. Some people are real receptive to the question. Over the years I've heard some of the coaches say, "Ask a football question." When Dave Shula was coach of the **Cincinnati Bengals** I asked him about his three favorite albums in a conference call one time. He said, "I'm here to talk football." Over the years, other guys like Mike Holmgren, Dennis Green and Tony Dungy would talk a lot of music, so it's kind of fun to see which direction these guys go in when you ask them that question.

My favorite story is about Jimi Hendrix's birthday. It was the day before Thanksgiving, and Roy Cummings of the *Tampa Tribune* and I were over there at One Buccaneer Place talking to Gruden. I said, "Coach, you know tomorrow is a national holiday, being Thanksgiving, but today would have been Jimi Hendrix's sixtieth birthday. Don't you think today should be a national holiday?" He just looked over and started laughing. He said, "You know, if we had a holiday for all of our fallen rock stars, every day would be a holiday, kind of like it is in your world." He was pretty funny. "Every day would be a party," he said, "Kind of like it is in your world." I asked, "You listened to Hendrix lately?" and he said "Man, not lately, but man, I do love the guy."

> The Bengals, owned by the Paul Brown family, were named after the Massillon (Ohio) High School Tigers, the team Brown coached before he became head coach of Miami (OH), Ohio State and the Cleveland Browns.

> Do you confuse Miami (Ohio) with Miami (Florida)? Miami of Ohio was a school before Florida was a state.

I asked him when he listens to music, "Coach, you know with your schedule, you get up at 3:17 in the morning and you're here till midnight. When do you get a chance to listen to music?" He said, "Oh, driving in to work, you know, the CD, I got it blastin', I have them blastin' in the morning." At training camp last summer in Celebration we were out there talking, and I asked him if Elvis or Chuck Berry was the real king of rock 'n' roll. He looked over at me and said "Well, you know you gotta go with Chuck Berry." Then he stopped and thought and said "No, you know, Elvis is the King, man, Elvis is the King, but Chuck Berry is not bad either." So he was kind of laughing about that. I don't know if he listens to music when he watches tape. I'm not that close to him. I heard somebody say that he cranks up the music and watches tape.

We were out there at training camp and after he got done talking to everybody, we were walking off. He was just standing there, and he looked over.

Gruden: "How ya doin' man?"
Johnson: "I'm all right. Coach. By the way, I got some Stevie Ray Vaughn bootleg CDs a buddy of mine gave me. I know that you liked him. I remember you telling me that."
Gruden: "How did you know I liked him?"
Johnson: "Remember the first press conference you had over at the hotel. I asked you what your three favorite **albums** were and you said Stevie Ray Vaughn, Van Halen and John Fogarty."
Gruden: "Oh, yeah, yeah."
Johnson: "Well I got a couple bootlegs."
Gruden: "Man, I would like to get a copy of those."
Johnson: "As soon as I get a copy, you get one."

Of course, my buddy's CD burner went on a fritz that week. Later, Jon came by and asked if I had any word on those tapes, and I said, "Hey, as soon as I get them Coach, you get them." Sure enough, I finally got them and gave them to him. He just looked at me and then

> Phil Rizzuto is the only baseball person to earn a Gold Record...his game calling was in the background of Meat Loaf's *Paradise by the Dashboard* Lights.

gave me the "I love you, man" treatment. It was funny because you see him on the Super Bowl stuff and he's telling that to everybody. Then I asked him what else he listened to? He says, "Oh, you know, Southern Rock; so I had a Lynyrd Skynyrd bootleg made up for the playoffs and gave it to him. I go, "Here is a special little boost for the playoffs, Coach," and he goes "Oh, man!"

I asked him what kind of music he listens to during the playoffs and if he changed his music styles. He said, "Yeah, I go back to the old school, you know, AC/DC, Zeppelin, even *Hair of the Dog* by Naza-reth." I said, "Well you know, two out of three ain't bad. I had a Led Zeppelin bootleg CD taped that somebody had made for me so I gave that to him and again I got "Oh, I love you man," handshake and everything.

He has a little bit of a rock 'n' roll streak in him. He seems to really know what's happening, and he knows his music. Anyone who likes Stevie Ray Vaughn is okay in my book.

Jon has been aces with the media and cooperation. He comes in, "Hi, I'm Jon Gruden." You see him on TV with the Chucky face and think that he is going to be a hard ass, but, in my book, it has been directly the opposite. He has been very accommodating. He would stay at training camp and over at the Stadium and talk to you. He doesn't blow you off or do those "next question" type of things. He has been great—aces!

I was at the Super Bowl when they had the last press conference, where they bring him in and you stand up and say who you are and you ask the question. The final press conference he had, I did stand up and asked him "Coach, you know, you told me that you change your listening habits for the playoffs, that you went to old school, and Zeppelin and AC/DC. Will you change your habits for the Super Bowl, if you get a chance to listen to music at all?" He just looked over and for the first time during that press conference he laughed. He said, "As you know, I have quite a CD selection. I'm going to have to think about that one."

ENJOY A SHOT OF THE TRUTH. MAKE IT A BOTTLE, I'LL BUY.

MARTIN FENNELLY

Martin Fennelly, 44, is a sports columnist for the Tampa Tribune *and covered Gruden's first year as head coach for the Buccaneers. Fennelly lives in Lutz, Florida.*

I was covering the Winter Olympics during the hiring process. I kept hearing these rumors "Gruden might get hired." Writers from the West Coast kept coming up and saying, "You guys are in for the ride of your life. You've never seen anything like this guy. You've never heard anything like this guy. He's gonna be a trip." I was very curious.

Gruden basically went into the bunker—the media couldn't get at him for a large amount of time. He was cramming on the Bucs. He was studying all the stats and everything like that, studying tendencies, watching films. That's what I kept hearing every time I tried to get in touch with him.

The first time I met him was at mini-camp. Some guys in the military have this thousand-yard stare—I immediately noticed he had a thousand and two-yard stare. He just looks over the horizon and tries to see if there's a nickel back there. He looks at you but he's not really looking at you. You pick up on that immediately with him. He's focused, but he's somewhere else at the same time. It was definitely intriguing. Also, he talked like us. I'm in my forties and he made references to *The Brady Bunch* and stuff like that, so I realized immediately that this guy's my age. He's got the same frame of reference as me. I immediately thought, "This is going to be pretty cool."

I was determined to get to him. We went through training camps, and the Bucs kept putting me off. At training camp, he once again dove for cover. He could only give me fifteen-twenty minutes, and I really needed some time with him. I'd always heard about this ballyhoo that he gets up at 3:17 a.m., and I talked to some of the security guys and one buck said, "Yeah. He rolls on in here." And he would bring doughnuts for them and knew their names. So it really is legitimate. He usually is in the office by 4:00 a.m.

Five days before the season, I went to his office at four-thirty in the morning, and I spent about three and a half hours there while he worked. He was drawing up play cards for that day. He draws them all himself. On a lot of teams, you have the assistants, the interns, or the go-fers do it. You can't completely describe Gruden's office; you have to really stand in it. There is really no light in it. One of the requests he had when he came to the Bucs was that they cover up the window, dry-wall it over, so he has no windows in his office. It is a cave. I got there at four-fifteen, and I forget the name of the security guard, but there was a call like, "Jon. This is Charlie. That guy's here." It was dark out. You could hear the bullfrogs croaking in the little ditch across the street. It's totally dark out. The streets were empty.

Charlie took me back to this labyrinth of rooms and knocked on the door. I heard a voice go, "What do you want?" The guard replied, "This is Charlie. I got that guy." "All right." I went in, and Gruden sat there for about three and a half hours. He was in sweats, and the only glow in the room was from his computer screen. He had a TV in the corner that had the **New Orleans Saints** goal-line defense on it. That was my introduction to him.

We sat there and talked about a little bit of everything that day—life theories, how he got his start in coaching, what he was proud of, what he wasn't proud of—a lot of off-the-record stuff—what he really thought of this team. Basically, the gist you get from Gruden is that when he came here—typical Gruden—he looked at the board, and said, "What the hell have these guys got? They've got nothing." But

At halftime of a New Orleans Saints game in 1968, Charleston Heston drove a chariot and rode an ostrich while filming the movie *Number One*.

that's just the way he is. He prefers to be the most miserable man on earth. It's the way he functions in life.

Rich McKay said during the season that he was told before Jon came here, "If this guy's two and ten, he's gonna be the most miserable two and ten guy in the world. If he's ten and two, he's going to be the most miserable ten and two guy in the world." That's just the way he is. That's the way he works. The sky is falling. It's creative tension for him. His best mode is to be miserable. That's also what Sherry Gruden, his sister-in-law, told me, "Jon isn't happy unless he's miserable."

He takes you in and off-the-record with incredible ease. Actually, I was a little surprised at how early he did it. But the whole cue with him, I think, is that he likes the attention. We've seen it after the Super Bowl. He digs the attention. He doesn't mind being portrayed as 'Chucky.' He doesn't mind being portrayed as this hot-shot, sexy young football coach. He really digs it. Because, when you cut through it, you discover he's a worshiper of coaches himself.

There are certain coaches and certain work ethics he worships. During his entire coaching life he has been trying to put himself around the **smartest** people he can. He's a sponge, and he's been one since his first job. He takes in all that information so he's probably a real mish-mash of all the people he's worked for. He's intimidating like Mike Holmgren, who has about eight inches on him. He's funny like some of the other coaches he's worked for. George Seifert was kind of an existentialist, and Gruden cannot be existential. Gruden's proudest statement is, "I'm a real shallow guy." Early on someone taught him that being a real shallow guy implies that you only think about football. So that's really a line he's adopted. He told me in that meeting "I'm a real shallow guy." I said, "Why do you draw these

> The NFL since 1968 has given every player the Wonderlic test (a human resources test measuring the ability to acquire and use job knowledge). In a recent year, 118,549 non-NFL people took the test and only four had a perfect score of 50. In 30-plus years, the only NFL player with a perfect score was Pat McInally of Harvard in 1968. McInally starred with the Cincinnati Bengals as tight end and punter.

cards?" He said, "Well, I could have someone doing it, but I want to have it done right." I guess my real problem is that he showed me this card that already had the circles and boxes drawn on it representing the linemen. He goes, "This is a real —— to me. I used to practice drawing circles. I wanted to be the best damn circle drawer there was when I did these cards. When I was growing up, I said I was going to draw circles better than anybody could draw circles. You've got to really care about what you do, bro, you really do." That was an early tip-off. This guy wants things just right. He wants things to go just right. That was a fascinating meeting and was one of the best interviews I've ever had.

There really wasn't an interview. Basically, I'd ask a question and about fourteen minutes later, Gruden would stop talking. It's not that he's so talkative. But on some subjects, his mind was just wandering while he was working. But he never stopped working. That was the amazing thing. He talked for three hours without stopping. He continued working, looking at film, talking, drawing, talking, drawing up plays, talking, personal stuff, talking. Then, finally, he got up and walked out into the hall and looked outside, and the sun was up. He goes, "Damn, another night." Just walked down the hall right into a meeting.

He's a likeable guy. I guess he's likeable because maybe in the jockocracy of it all you think that if you're a guy who likes to watch sports and like to drink a beer, this is your guy. This is the guy. He likes to drink beer and he uses salty language—probably the way you would talk if you were watching a football game on Sunday. That's this guy. He's legendary. And this guy gets into Arena Football— what more do you need to say? His brother, Jay plays for the Orlando Predators, and Jon sits in the stands. Sometimes he has to sit in the upper deck because he wants to be where he can just focus in on Arena Football. Right off the bat, that makes him extraordinary because he's probably the only human on Earth to focus in on Arena Football.

I guess the security people have moved him from time to time because he was causing such a racket, making so much noise, not all of it pleasant, that they wanted to move him away from children. He's a nut. Sometimes we call him 'Nut-boy.' But we love that about him too. We love the energy. This guy's got the juice, and he kinda plays along with us. There's this whole Keyshawn Johnson stuff. He'll say, "I really wish we could have gotten the ball to Key more," and then kinda giggle. He's very likeable. He tries to act like one of the guys, and to a large extent, he is. But he isn't—he's the head coach.

There weren't really any rifts with the media, even when we were writing stuff about Keyshawn. It wasn't really bad, and we'd rip him. He did get a little tired. His usual thing when you knew he was —— was, "Hell's bells." And it turned out to be quite prophetic because he kept saying, "You people, you guys, all I know is that we're eight and two, and you guys are talking about 'This isn't working, and that isn't working.' Let me tell you something—a lot of people would trade their right arm to be eight and two in this league right now. Yeah, we've got some problems on offense, but we're getting better."

Of course he would scold us for that, but privately he was climbing up the wall. He was under a lot of pressure when he came here. He won't admit how much he was under, but I've talked to other people who'll tell you. When the trade-off draft picks were made on draft day, he had to sit there day while draft expert after draft expert crowed, "Oh, the Raiders really cleaned out the Bucs. I don't know what the Bucs got in Gruden." Then he came in, and he only knew one person here—Monte Kiffin, the defensive coordinator. He didn't know any of the other coaches. He didn't know any of the players. He'd never worked with them before, so he knew no one. All he had was that office and that glowing screen. He had a couple of acknowledgments from the owner. They paid him all that money, but it was a crushing weight on him early in the season. His natural reaction was to want to blow everything up. But I give him a lot of credit for what he did. He realized what he could do, and what he couldn't do. He realized who he couldn't go and get and who he could go and get, and he worked with it.

He's always dealt well with the media. He has scolded us. On one hand, he loves to be 'prophet of doom.' But it got to him a little bit when we were criticizing him a little much: "How is this different from Tony Dungy?" When in fact it was, and he deep-down knew that. We knew it in the last three games of the season.

Giving the players a kick in the pants was Gruden's theory from very early on. I remember that day in the office, he said, "Deep down, I really believe players want discipline. They want direction. They want to be led." And, he followed through on that. He came at the perfect time. He came at a time when the defense had had an off year and everyone was wondering, "Is the defense being down?" He came in and said, "You're not down. You guys are going to be great."

The players didn't quite know what to make of his energy. In the first mini-camp they had, at the end of practice, the whistle blew and all the players had to huddle up around Gruden. He said, "I didn't like the way you guys huddled up. Everybody go back to where you were standing." So, they looked at each other. "I mean, go back to exactly where you were standing." Then he blew the whistle again, and they had to run. He said, "Run. I don't care if you don't have enthusiasm. If you have to, fake it, and sooner or later, it'll be there."

I think John Lynch's first conversation with him was by phone, and the last thing Gruden said was, 'Oh, by the way, we're gonna kick your —— a time or two." Right there, Gruden challenged him.

A lot of guys on this team get revved up—Sapp is the perfect example. What the players related to was that Gruden is kinda like a player. Through them, he's vicariously living the life he never had. They joked around all season about how Gruden was never good enough to play. He told me he threw a touchdown at Dayton. Of course, he didn't. He threw like four balls. They would joke about it—Brad Johnson would say, "Yeah, he's trying to live the life—I'd say he was trying to recreate his college days, but he never had any."

Although he'd won the World Championship and was King of the Football World, one of the things about Super Bowl Week that Gruden is proudest of is that he played quarterback on the scout team during practice to give the defense the look on Rich Gannon. He was so proud of how he threw the ball. In fact he told me about throwing the ball the morning after they won the Super Bowl. "Oh man, I zipped a couple of balls in there." That's Gruden.

The players are impressed by how he relates to the media. I'll never forget one day late in the season, there was an important game coming up, like the Eagles' game. I see a radio guy come up and he gives him a disk with no labeling on it. I go up to him, and here it is the week of this big game, and he holds up this little disk, and he goes, "Zeppelin, *Bootleg*." This man coaches a team. Can you see Lombardi doing that? "Beatles, *White Album*." Like, the week of the game, holding up a vinyl.

There was juice all the time. Gruden is known for giving incredible speeches, too. He's gleaned those off of all kinds of people. He didn't say much before the Super Bowl. He said a lot before the game in Philadelphia for the NFC title. He turned his back on the defense, looked at the offense, and said, "I know these guys on the defense. I don't need to talk to them. They're going to do their job. What the—— do you have today? What do you—— have? Are you gonna show?" That's the way he is. He really challenges them. Eventually that message will wear thin. It's natural in any sport, but it was just what they needed this year. It put them over the top. It made them do things. I still can't believe they won the Super Bowl.

Gruden did find a way to light a fire under Sapp. Tony Dungy had come right in and said, "You're the guy. Nobody zips around you and Brooks." That's all Sapp needed to hear. When Gruden came in, there had been rumors of Sapp getting traded. But Gruden shook Sapp's hand and what he said was a variation of the same theme. You've got to get somebody to go on the record, but that's what he said. Now there's something right there that Sapp can relate to—a little different from what Dungy would say. You can probably paraphrase that—that's like the first thing he said to him. I think Sapp thought, "Well, we're going to go to town here."

What Sapp wanted—and all that the defense ever wanted—was for the offense to be held accountable. If there is one thing in Gruden's world, it's accountability. Not everybody dug it. Keyshawn Johnson didn't always dig it. Their relationship got better, but it's amazing how a relationship gets better as the wins pile up. His credit was very good with them as the season went on. In fact, when they lost in Philadelphia the first time during the season they got their butts kicked. I was in the locker room afterwards and the buses were loading up and guys were getting on. Sapp and Simeon Rice were both sitting there naked. Gruden came over and knelt in front of them. "You——— guys. You ——— stay with me here. You stay the ——— with me." They were nodding their heads and Sapp said, "We ain't going anywhere." Rice said, "Cool, man, cool." That's Gruden, kneeling down between them, "You stay with me on this." That's Gruden. I think Sapp was reminded of that all through the season, "Stay with me." And they did stay with him, and to a certain extent, we all did.

Gruden is a very unique individual. He's a truly weird cat. He's fully capable of doing it. He'll be very good at adapting to players. He's always gonna be able to change, because his whole life has been about learning from other people. He learns from Monte Kiffin right now. He's learning something from the defensive line coach, Rod Marinelli. He's capable. I don't think he'll ever morph into a Bear Bryant or anything. But the guys he admires—for instance, Steve Spurrier. Spurrier is still considered a players' coach, and he's in his late fifties, because, in his own way, he's got that energy, that "Let's go get 'em. Let's show them something" —attitude. As opposed to a Bobby Bowden, who's more the grandfatherly type. Spurrier still has juice. Players can feel it. "Let's go get them." I think Gruden is turning into something like that. Maybe someone who doesn't show up at 4:00 a.m., but still has that. To me, Spurrier still seems youthful—and he's fifty-eight. I think Gruden's always going to be that. Gruden's always going to be the 'sandy haired boy.' I don't think he'll burn out. I don't see that.

Gruden really did handle the situation with Keyshawn perfectly. Early on I think it bothered him sometimes, but never to the point where he started venting in the press box like Bill Parcells would have done. He just didn't do that. He realized very early on that Keyshawn's noise wasn't as divisive a force as people made it out to be. And it isn't. I know Keyshawn. I enjoy Keyshawn—even when he's saying something I don't agree with. Maybe Jon doesn't. Very early on, their divide was over how Keyshawn didn't show up for some voluntary workout in the spring after Gruden was hired. Gruden had a problem with that. Deep down, there's something about Gruden that thinks, "Ah, Keyshawn, West Coast guy. A hundred deals-going-at-once guy. A restaurant guy." I think Gruden had a hard time in his own mind, "Nice guy. Soft guy," which I don't necessarily think is true. If you tried to raise Jon Gruden in the neighborhood that Keyshawn Johnson was raised in, he wouldn't make it out alive. All you need to do is go to the street he grew up on in south-central LA and look at the depth chart on who lived and who died. That's something you have to deal with.

Keyshawn could say anything he wants because a lot of it is noise. It took Gruden a while to realize that when Keyshawn's talking, Keyshawn's *just* talking. That's what Keyshawn does. We breathe. Keyshawn talks. He wasn't getting the ball as much, but the bottom line is he had better yards-per-catch average this year than last year. He caught more touchdowns than last year. He caught what turned out to be the winning points in the NFC championship game. He had some big catches for Gruden. Gruden just believes in spreading it around.

Gruden wants everything. He wants Terrell Allen. He wants Marshall Faulk. That's just the way he is. It's the classic kid in the candy store syndrome. "I want this. I want that. I want something better than Keyshawn." And yet, the fact of the matter is, for everything he wanted that was better this year, no one could be better. He got as much out of those guys as he could. No doubt about it.

Gruden's wife Cindy is a beautiful person. I did an article on her. I had been fascinated by her all year. "Who is this woman who puts up with this nut cake, this guy who comes down from the second floor of the house because the kids forks are tinkling against the bowl of the cereal or spoons. "Could you please get them to stop that?" Some of the things she said were extraordinary—how little she sees him during the season.

There's a great story about them on one of their early dates, and this is a true story. He was some punk, graduate assistant at Tennessee. She was a cheerleader, and she kinda liked him. They go out for a date. He's twenty-four, and he sits there in the diner, and he says, "I'm gonna be this. And one day I'm gonna be an NFL head coach. I'm gonna be one of the best." She's fascinated by his dreams. "I'm gonna do this, and I'm gonna do that." The check comes, and he goes, "I'm penniless. Do you have any money?" He can't even pick up the check in the diner. "I'm gonna be the next Lombardi." She was just fascinated by him, by his dreams. Basically, she's a willing accomplice. I went and visited her during Super Bowl week. She was staying in a suite they had set up for her. I don't even know if Jon was staying with her. She'd been there three days, and she'd seen him about twenty minutes. I walked in that room with the three little boys—and it looked like a Toys 'R Us had exploded in that room.. She's just a great person. She told a great story.

This is another true story. They have fun with each other. When Gruden was named one of *People* magazine's "Fifty Most Beautiful People" she said he just came home and had a copy of the magazine, threw it on the kitchen counter, looked at her and said, "You want me?" She said, "Of course I want you. I want you to pick up your socks." He doesn't hang up his clothes. He doesn't hang his pants up 'cause he doesn't know how to fold them right. Stuff like that. I think when I had talked with him he had misplaced his driver's license four times in the previous year. He doesn't know how to write a check. She writes all the checks. She keeps track of things. When I talked to him, he had just lost all of his identification at an Orlando Predators' game. She had to send away for all that stuff. She takes care of him. When he's home, he gets on his knees in front of the couch, and the boys try to play goal line with him and score touchdowns.

Their son, Deuce, is actually Jon II. Cindy told me Jon calls him Deuce after Sterling Sharpe, who's nickname is Deuce. She said originally he wanted to name his first son Jon James so he could call him Johnny Jam. She drew the line at that. She said, "No. You're not calling our son Johnny Jam." He wanted to call him a football name. But they play goal-line defense and I guess he had stuffed Deuce on fourth down so Deuce came up and just gave him an elbow in the face, gave his father a bloody nose. Things are tough in the Gruden household. They go hard there.

Cindy is Joan of Arc. She is Jackie Kennedy. She is Betty Ford. She is Eleanor Roosevelt. All rolled into one. It's funny, because when I wrote that article, I got a lot of negative feedback from women. "How dare you cast her in this light?" Well, she wants to be cast in that light. That's what she does. She's crazy about her man. She still sees him in that diner with all those dreams, even though he's achieved many of them. It's the same thing with the kids. She wants to be called Mrs. Gruden, not Ms. Gruden. That's her deal. I'll never forget. We were trying to take a picture of all three of the kids. The youngest one was hiding behind a chair so there's Cindy trying to lure him out from behind the chair with a Reese's Peanut Butter Cup. It was tremendous.

Jon goes to the beach two weeks a year, and it's pretty serious. They collect shells. Sherry Gruden, Jon's sister-in-law who is married to his younger brother, Jay, told me this story. One year they went to Redington Beach, and Jon bought this crappy little **fishing** net, and he's standing out there barefoot in his bathing suit and keeps casting it in the surf in the gulf. He keeps casting and pulling it back in, casting and pulling back in. Sherry walks down there after two hours and there's two fish you wouldn't even keep—some little fish flapping on the sand. She says, "Jon, what are you doing?" He looks at her, and his eyes narrow, and he goes, "I'm —— fishing. What are you doing?" He won't even rest. "What are you doing?" That's Jon. Here he is on vacation, and he buys a crappy little net and he keeps casting it out. He's the "Young Man and the Sea." He doesn't reel anything in, but he's doing something. He can't sit around. He can't talk on the phone with you. After two minutes on the phone with him, it's "What do you need?"

My first meeting, I'll never forget, he was showing me the phone numbers he had written down on his grease board. He'd been at Tampa five months at that point, and he was showing me the numbers. The sixth one down there didn't have a name next to it. He goes, "Aw. That's my home number." He didn't even know his home number. He had to look at the damn grease board to get his home number. You've got to be kidding me. "It's like when my wife leaves me a message, 'Hi. This is Cindy. I love you, Babe. Call me.' And she'll leave me her cell number or the home number. I'm a real genius. A friggin' moron, my wife has to leave the number every time she calls from the house."

Jon Gruden is a piece of work. He made my year.

There are more fishermen than golfers and tennis players combined.

TO SEE THE BUCS UNDRESS THE EAGLES

JOE LETTELLIER

A native of Lafayette, IN, Joe Lettellier is a long-time, towering figure in Tampa business circles. He has been a Buc season ticket holder from three years before Day 1.

Having been a season ticket holder since 1976, when the Buccaneers started, and actually three years before that, when we had pre-season games in town—I was a season ticket holder for those three years for three pre-season games a year. The stadium was built, and it had been worked out with the NFL that three pre-season games were played there. The **Dolphins** would come up and play another team. We really had our appetite whetted before Hugh Culverhouse bought the team in '76. Our town was starved for football so the crowds were pretty good there in the "Big Sombrero." Back in 1977, I was actually one of the few Tampa people in New Orleans for our first win after twenty-six losses. There weren't very many of us, but I was there. The city was ours.

At the half-time of that game we were leading there in the Super Dome. Hank Stram was coaching the Saints. As he came back onto the field after half time, they showed him on their huge Jumbotron, and he was carrying his rolled-up little game plan. Someone had typed in a message: "Oh, God, don't let it be me!" Nobody wanted to be the first to lose to the Bucs after twenty-six losses.

> The undefeated 1972 Dolphins (17-0) beat only two teams with records over .500. They were actually three-point underdogs to the Redskins in Super Bowl VII.… Miami Dolphins defensive end Jason Taylor is the first home-schooled student athlete to play in the NFL.

We went to a lot of out-of-town games over the years, and when we had a chance to go up to Philadelphia for the second game of the playoffs, I took my young son, Matthew. There weren't many Buccaneer fans going. I felt that it couldn't be that bad, but I had been warned. I'd been to Philadelphia before for a game, and it wasn't exactly pleasant, but it wasn't that bad. We could at least stand up and cheer. At this game, there were very few Bucs fans, and we went to the local bars there before the game, and my eighteen-year-old son was wearing a Bucs hat. Upon advice, I was wearing neutral colors. We were in this one bar, and there were at least four hundred people there. They pointed at his hat and just unanimously all chanted, "____, ____." This was in a bar right next to the stadium. They were joking, but not really joking—*they were serious!* He had been warned not to wear his hat in the stadium. My son's reaction was, "Oh they're just kidding, just good-natured ribbing." I told him those folks were serious.

We got to our 700 section, and I went to buy beer. At the vendor area, they had a sign up—NO BEER SOLD TO BUCS FANS. If you didn't have on Eagles paraphernalia, you could not get a beer. I did not get a beer the whole game.

As we entered the stadium we stopped beside a cop. The cop said, "Move on. Get away from me." He said, "Why?" The cop said, "I don't want to get hit with anything." "You're here to protect me." He said, "Not as a Bucs fan," and he moved away from my son. By this time, easily two thousand people, the whole end-zone section, started pointing up there and chanting the same thing. It was just not comfortable.

When I had bought the tickets, I'd had to buy four, so as soon as we got there, I sold two of them. This big guy standing next to us turned to my son and said, "Look, I drove five hours to see this game. I didn't drive that far to lose. But since I got the tickets through you, I'm going to protect you." I never once felt like I could cheer for the Bucs because I genuinely felt that somebody up there would have hit us. I'm not necessarily afraid of things, but I felt that if we had jumped up and cheered, somebody would have thrown something or hit us. It took me about half an hour before I had enough confidence to ask this lady behind us to take a picture of us with my camera. I can honestly tell you that most of the people in those stands would have taken my camera and thrown it. These people booed the warm-up high school band during half time. They booed the rapper. Then, they had an award for a fireman who had saved somebody's life, and they booed him. I'm not talking about a few boos. I'm talked about the whole stadium. It was the darndest thing I've ever seen. It was awful.

Early in the fourth quarter, the big guy next to Matthew says, "Look. This isn't looking good. I strongly urge you not to be in this 700 section if we lose. You don't need to be up here." We went down to the lower level, and when Barber intercepted that pass and went down, I've never experienced anything as eerie as the quiet that came over that otherwise boisterous stadium. They had been making a comeback there for a while. We were in the standing-room area there, and we could not yell for our team, for a legitimate fear of our safety. At the end of the game, we went over by the Bucs bench, and I'll bet you there were only three hundred Bucs fans in that whole area, and they were still being harassed and jeered at by Eagles' fans.

After the insults we got, it just made it all the sweeter to kick their butt. After leaving the bar, we got back to the hotel and gave the car to the valet. But, somebody jumped in our car and started driving away. The valet rushed to open the door and the thief kicked him away. He fell into the street, which is only about ten yards from the police station. About half an hour later, the police called me down from my room to answer questions. The lady cop asked me where I was from and I said, "St. Petersburg." She said, "You're a Bucs fan." I said, "Yes ma'am." She said, "Why am I doing this for you?" I said, "Well, it's your job." She said, "Not for a Bucs fan." This was a cop.

Gruden just doesn't want to lose. He's prepared. He knows the talent level of his players, and he gets the most out of them. He just loves football. His intensity is what I like best.

> Fuzzy Zoeller is from New Albany, Indiana.
> Fuzzy got his nickname because of his initials:
> Frank Urban Zoeller.

IF YOU PLAY THAT FILM BACKWARDS, IT LOOKS LIKE SAPP IS HELPING THAT PACKER OFF THE GROUND AND SHOWIN' HIM ON HIS WAY

STEVE SABOL

NFL Films was established in 1964, when Ed Sabol, Steve's father convinced then-NFL commissioner Pete Rozelle that the league needed a motion picture company to record its history. NFL Films has mushroomed well beyond the role of mere historian. The entity has won 82 Emmy awards for outstanding cinematography and sound, and it represents the quintessential standard for sports filmmaking. From theme programs, such as NFL Films Presents, to team highlights to emotional behind the scenes detailing the nuts and bolts of HBO's **Inside the NFL**, *NFL Films, as an independently operated arm of the league, captures the essence of football like no other visual entity.*

Jon Gruden is an interesting dichotomy as far as his personality because number one, he is one of the new breed of coaches who is aware that the game is entertaining. That it's entertainment. He is also a guy who is contemporary. This is someone who can talk about Eminem and Doctor Dre. To me, a lot of coaches, in the past, have been fatherly. In a way, Gruden is like an older brother. Just in the way he coaches and relates to his players. The thing is that, even though he's young and contemporary and relates to the players, he's more old school in the way he runs his practice. This is a guy who was a real disciplinarian. When I've been at practices with him, he reminds me of a lion tamer. His tongue is his whip. One quick snap of the tongue and the big cats jump back on the stools.

> *Inside The NFL* on HBO is the longest running series of any kind of cable television.

He's got the respect of the players because of two things. Number one, he's got a clear view of the big picture but, simultaneously he's always aware of the smallest details. When we've had him miked in practice, he'll come up to a player and want to look at his spikes, you know, how long his spikes are.

Another great example of that was with the gloves. He made Brad Johnson wear gloves before the Eagles game…something Johnson had never done before. Gruden experimented with them. He took the gloves and submerged them in ice water in a test to see if that would affect the grip. That's an example of a guy being aware of the big picture and still have an understanding of the little details.

On the practice field, Gruden has a very high energy level and is a very active participant in the strategy and the fundamentals. A lot of head coaches today have, as they say, "Given up the chalk." Meaning that they let the offensive and defensive coaches devise the strategy and tactics. Gruden is still the guy in control of the chalk. He is still is the strategist, as well as an overall general coach.

Today, it's a bigger challenge than ever before for a head coach to be close to the players and be an effective leader at the same time. It's a difficult thing to do. **Don Shula** was that way when he started. He was in his mid-thirties. I mean here was Don Shula, he was coaching **John Unitas** who was older than him and was already acclaimed as one of the greatest quarterbacks that had ever played. Shula had to earn his respect even though he was in essence a contemporary. I think Gruden has been able to do that.

He's been able to do it because of the respect the players have for him, because he's smart and also because of his work ethic. He's got that mysterious work ethic where he shows up at 4 a.m. The other thing with Jon is that he's very sure of himself. He's an instinctive leader. When he

> When Don Shula retired, he had more victories than over half the NFL teams.

> Two of the greatest quarterbacks of all time, Johnny Unitas and Dan Marino, have the same middle name, Constantine, and both are from Pittsburgh.

tells you something, it's with a lot of authority. You have to consider his background too. When you come from a background where your father is a coach, you learn about the time and the commitment that it is going to take to be successful. Jon has learned that from his father.

Another thing is when you look at great leaders—and I'm not just talking about coaches—they have distinctive voices. Look at Lombardi…he had a very distinctive voice. Martin Luther King had a very distinctive voice. Kennedy has a very distinctive voice, FDR. Gruden has a very distinctive delivery and a very distinctive voice. I think that probably goes back to polemics class in college. I've talked to him about that, about the way to deliver the message emphatically and with clarity. That's all part of the components of being a head coach.

I first became aware of Jon when he was with the Eagles. I remember him there but I never spoke to him. Coaching staffs now are fifteen, sixteen people and Jon was so young when he was with the Eagles, you wondered if he wasn't a ball boy or a training assistant or something. When I got to know him better I discovered that he was sure of himself. Confident. He had an air of leadership that you just can't be taught. It's something that's there and I became aware of that when he was up in Green Bay. Then, when he took over the Raiders, it was obvious to me the first time I watched them practice.

Jon has a certain charisma about him that we thought would appeal to our audience. One time we had him miked for practice. Then we did a piece on him when he was with the Raiders. It was about his work ethic. Jon has that mysterious work ethic—that thing where he couldn't sleep and he would get up at 3:17 a.m.—and has a general command of the practice field. And he is so young and young looking and contemporary in a profession where that isn't always the case. A lot of the coaches might be up to date on what's happening within the white lines, but when it comes to relating to the players as far as lifestyle outside the field—music, entertainment, etc., here was a guy who was their age and was commanding their respect on the field but off the field they could look at him and say, "Hey. This guy knows what's going on."

With Jon, we had to work the beeper quite a bit. But profanity is not unusual with head coaches. You're in the heat of combat and sometimes profanity is the most direct and best way to make yourself understood but I wouldn't say that Jon uses any more or less profanity than other coaches. I mean there are some coaches who just do not curse at all. Then there are others like Marv Levy who has a master's degree in English History from Harvard and yet he could blister you with profanity.

Part of being a contemporary coach is understanding the media and being cooperative with the media. Jon is a successor of Hank Stram, who was the first coach who ever understood that professional football is not only a sport—it's entertainment. He understands the role the media plays in sports entertainment and knows what's expected of him.

At NFL Films, we only have three cameras at a game. We really can't just put a camera to capture a coach's facial expressions. There were times when we would mike Jon. We would have a camera on him for the whole game. But that was really more about his field generalship and his ability to get the most out of his players. Coaches today are mood shifters. They're manipulators. They're called on to be so many things and Jon gets an "A" in all of those categories. He gets an "A" as a media personality. He gets an "A" as a football coach. And he's won a world championship. He's the kind of guy I could see being around in the league for the next thirty years. He'll probably coach at least one other NFL team before he retires.

On the Friday before the Super Bowl, I went in to set up a meeting with him to see if he would wear a microphone in the game. That's something I do as sort of a secret every year and we don't release it to the media and nobody knows about it until the game is over. I spoke to his assistant, Mark Arteaga, and Mark set up a meeting at 6 a.m. Friday morning. I was led through this maze of curtains and security people and I finally got into Jon's suite. He was sitting in the living room suite and he had a big table in front of him in the shape of an "L" and on both sides of the table were two giant plasma TVs. There must have been at least a hundred game tapes on the table. He had game tapes on both screens and he had remotes in either hand. This was the Friday before the game. I walked in to say hello to him and he was just so engrossed in what he was doing that it took me about five minutes to really get his focus and talk to him about what we wanted to do. And he said he didn't know if he wanted to do it because there's a perception that he's kind of a media whore. I said "NFL Films is the media whore history." He said, "You know, you're right. I'll do it."

Part of that tape is in the DVD of the Bucs World Championship video. It was terrific. We're probably going to have a whole ESPN special just on him and his strategy and how it evolved into the Super Bowl. It's probably going to be released on the new NFL Channel in September.

We taped a show called *Holmgren's Heroes* at the coaches meetings, the March meetings in Orlando where we brought Mike together with six of his former assistants at Green Bay who currently were head coaches in the National Football League—Steve Mariucci, Andy Reid, Jon Gruden, Dick Jauron, Marty Mornhinweg and Mike Sherman. Our talent coordinator Maryann Wenger is unbelievable at getting coaches and making arrangements and she coordinated it and it doesn't hurt that she's a beautiful redhead. She got all the coaches together and she made the arrangements. When the idea was presented, I thought it was great but we'd never get the coaches together. But she set it up and all the coaches showed up at the golf club at 7 a.m. We had drivers pick them all up and deliver them to the golf club where we did the interview.

I think it was a great thing for Mike Holmgren and really it was about him and yet all the assistants agreed to show up and we had him for forty-five minutes and we sat down and just started talking. Jon was very respectful of Mike and the opportunities that Mike had given him and he was also respectful of all the other coaches. I think that goes back to the fact that his father was a coach and he understands the profession and he has a respect for the profession and all of the other men that are in it.

Jon's the youngest coach to ever win the Super Bowl. That puts you in—you've already made a mark in history just with that. The fact that he's got, in my opinion, another three decades to go, you're talking about someone that has the potential to be one of the greatest coaches of all time.

When you look at the greatest of all time you look at Tom Landry, Bill Walsh, Joe Gibbs, and Don Shula. They're the greatest because of their contributions to the game, their winning records or their longevity as NFL coaches. You know, to me, Joe Gibbs is in that league, not because of longevity but because he took the team to the Super Bowl with three different quarterbacks. When you look at all the other ones—Bill Walsh, there was Joe Montana; Tom Landry had Roger Staubach; Don Shula had John Unitas on one hand…but Shula went to the Super Bowl with the late David Woodley, too. With Shula it's longevity. The other coach that I neglected and you have to put in there is Paul Brown. Paul Brown is the Thomas Jefferson of the game. He gave the modern game its shape and structure. He took his team to a championship game ten straight years. I've got to put him maybe at the top as the greatest coach of all-time. It's hard when you're at that level with Walsh, Landry, Gibbs, Shula and Paul Brown. They're like saints.

When you look at the guys who achieve longevity as head coaches in the NFL you're really looking at their ability to adjust. That's almost a given—to be successful you have to be flexible. I think Jon will be able to adjust. Paul Brown used to say that a football season is always a work in progress and a career in the NFL is a work in progress. Look at Don Shula. I mean Shula won with defense. He won with David Woodley. He won when he had Don Strock. He won with Dan Marino. Look at Joe Gibbs. He had three different quarterbacks— Doug Williams, **Joe Theismann** and Mark Rypien. None of them will ever be in the Hall of Fame. Maybe the only one who wasn't that flexible was Landry who had a system so effective and so complex that he didn't need to change. He had such a great draft that they knew the exact kind of players who would fit into their system. Shula just changed his system to fit his players. Landry had a system so good that he would draft the players to fit that system and continued to win for twenty years.

Running NFL films is like the supreme job. Every day is like winning the Super Bowl. Well, maybe not, but I sure am lucky…and Jon Gruden's performance made our job easier.

Joe Theismann holds the NFL record for the shortest punt that wasn't blocked—one yard.

SHORT STORIES FROM LONG MEMORIES

South Bend Clay High School is one of six high schools in the South Bend community. We're about two miles north of Notre Dame University. In fact our school song is patterned after the Notre Dame Victory March. The week of the Super Bowl, some of our teachers who were on staff twenty years ago when Jon was here got together and developed a good luck telegram that we faxed to the hotel where the team was staying. We assume he got it although we've not received anything in terms or a thank you or anything back in return. Obviously he's been a very busy person.

Everybody watched him on David Letterman a few weeks after the Super Bowl. It's a kick to have such a celebrity be from here.

It's been interesting having all of the reporters come around. It really started a year ago when Jon's name was surfaced in connection with the Notre Dame job. We had people from *Sports Illustrated* calling and inquiring about him. We e-mailed them some pictures of the yearbook and stuff like that. He's in the '82 yearbook and he's got about four or five shots in there.

Having Jon be the winning Super Bowl coach…you know, that's a real feather in your hat. He's obviously one of our more famous alumni.

———GREG HUMNICKY, Athletic Director, South Bend Clay High School

When Jon first started working with the San Francisco 49ers, he wasn't making much money. He had this old Delta 88 like John Candy drove in the movie *Uncle Buck*, and the players called him Uncle Buck. He said he would always try to park his big old beater right in between the expensive cars Jerry Rice and Joe Montana drove. He said these guys would get out and say, "Hey, Uncle Buck watch out man, move your car. Why do you gotta park next to my car?" He'd reply, "I just want to let you guys know how good you got it." So, when he wasn't making much money, he was still goofing around and having fun.

———BRIAN TRANT, 39, High school friend

Chapter 5

Sweet Home Tampa Bay

I LOVE YA, DOUG
I LOVE YA, MAN
CAN I HAVE YOUR BUD LIGHT?

DOUG WILLIAMS

Doug Williams stunned the NFL twice. In 1979 as just a second-year quarterback he led the three-year-old Tampa Bay Buccaneers to the NFC Championship Game. Then, after appearing in only five regular-season games with the Washington Redskins in 1987, he led a second-period explosion by passing for a Super Bowl record-tying four touchdowns, including 80- and 50-yard passes to wide receiver Ricky Sanders, a 27-yard toss to wide receiver Gary Clark, and an 8-yard pass to tight end Clint Didier. It was the greatest quarter in Super Bowl history. In December 1997, Williams returned to Grambling, his alma mater, to take over for retired legend Eddie Robinson as the first new head coach there for more than 50 years.

I have always kept up with the Grudens over the years. I always liked his dad, even before Jon got to Tampa. Any time Jim saw me, he used to always say that when he was in Tampa I gave him the opportunity to put a screen porch on the house, because we went to the play-offs. He figured that extra money put a screen porch on his house. To this day, Jon Gruden always says the porch was the thanks of Doug Williams. He always said, "Man, I love ya, man, I love ya, you know." He is just a realist.

I remember Jon Gruden like it was yesterday! On game day, he and Rich McKay were there to warm me up. Jon used to stand side by side with Rich. I would either be throwing to Jon, and he would throw it back to Rich, or I would throw to Rich and Rich would throw it back to Jon. That's my earliest memory of Jon.

His dad was assistant coach there and was on the sidelines. Jon Gruden was exactly the way he is now. He wanted to be around it, he loved it, he wanted to be near it, he wanted to see what was going on. That's the reason why he is where he is—that was his life.

He went to Dayton and after going to college, he realized that his calling might not be as a player in the league, but that did not turn him off from the NFL. He realized back then that he wanted to get in there and learn as much as he could. Because his dad, Jim, was around it, that really gave an opportunity to stay in the loop. Jon is the same guy—he hasn't changed looks-wise except maybe he's a little taller.

When Jon called me he said, "Man, you know, we can't do this thing, if you ain't here, we cannot do it. You gotta come to camp and talk to these guys" I had something scheduled, but I thought it was worth my time and effort to change it to get down there for that weekend, and I did that. He gave me an opportunity to talk to the team, during the mini-camp. And we sat in the meetings and sat at the practice. Actually, what he has given me is an open invitation to be a part of the Bucs whenever I am down there, just like I belong. That is a great feeling. If the Buccaneers keep Jon there, he can do more for the guys that came before these young guys and make them feel part of the organization.

It was a great night! They blocked off half of Hooters. You got to see all of the older guys that had played with you, and some who played after you, and Jon Gruden was so laid back. The fact that he used to work at a Hooters made it a special night. Everybody was able to eat, drink and be merry and hobnob with everybody. It was just a great day. He singled me out to get a jersey, and I've got my jersey hanging up. It was a super night. and it was real big of Jon Gruden to do what he did. I think we all just wanted to feel like we belonged there. To be honest with you, my whole mentality has changed. No matter what has happened to me in the past, going to Washington, winning a Super Bowl, I still feel like it all started in Tampa. What Jon did put the icing on all that.

Sitting there watching the Super Bowl, I remembered the time the Bucs were so close, and to see them go to the Super Bowl and win—nobody gave them a chance. I mean, it's not a game of chance, but they figured going to Philadelphia, it wasn't going to happen. The win they had up in Chicago, the first in cold weather, that win was the one that gave them the confidence to realize that it doesn't matter where they play, they can win. It worked out that way.

Jon has overcome not having been a professional player, and Joe Gibbs was the same way. I don't think his success has anything to do with that. I think it is opportunity. If you look around, most of your best coaches weren't good players or didn't play, but they were around it most of the time. Jon Gruden grew up around it, and it gave him the opportunity to be the coach that he is. I think from a player's standpoint, players are usually able to communicate with other players in getting their respect because they did play it. I think that makes a difference.

When the Raiders came here to play the Saints in New Orleans a couple of years ago, he invited me onto the sidelines. I went down to the sidelines and was there after the game. They won the game, and he came and hugged me. I didn't throw any passes that day. A couple weeks later I got a game ball. That's Jon Gruden, "Love ya man." If a player doesn't like Jon Gruden, there's something wrong. He is all about business. He is going to make the decision that's best for the organization, but the players that are there like Jon Gruden. I put them in the same boat. I would have loved to play for Jon Gruden. I think he would have loved me to play for him.

He won the Super Bowl at 39, and a lot of guys have been coaching for years and haven't won at all. It's so tough to repeat and to continue to dominate. Does Tampa have a chance? Yeah. Keeping Coach Kiffin really gave him an opportunity, and they can keep most of their players together. They have a chance to repeat.

More NFL games have been played at Wrigley Field than at any other stadium in the country. Mile High Stadium in Denver was in second place until demolished in 2001

GRUDEN'S COACHIN' IS LIKE A HOOTERS T-SHIRT. YA ONLY GET OUT OF IT WHAT YOU PUT INTO IT

ED DROSTE

Ed Droste, 52, is one of the now famous "Hooters Six"—six businessmen with absolutely no previous restaurant experience who decided to open a place they couldn't get kicked out of—Hooters. Droste lives in Clearwater, Florida.

Jon Gruden and I were at a baseball game and were comparing notes of his days with Hooters and of a lot of our activities with the NFL. He was animated about how aggressively he was going into the free agency pool to try to fill in his team. I said, "Well if we can ever help with chicken wings or Hooters VIP cards, let me know." We give this stuff to a lot of the teams. About two weeks later, on April 18, 2002, both sports pages came out with the headlines that the Bucs signed Ken Dilger to a three-year pact. Then in the story it said "Hooters discount card seals deal for the tight end." It was funny. In his press conference, Dilger reported that a lot of teams had been chasing him and that Jon had bugged him the most and was the most aggressive. He said that he actually had some higher offers, but that finally on his fourth or fifth call, Jon threw in a Hooters VIP card and he couldn't turn down the deal. Jon actually had some of his meetings with free agents at a Hooters restaurant in Indianapolis during the NFL Combine. We only had two stores in our area there.

I knew Jon when his dad was a coach for the Bucs...so it was like, "Hey, there's the coach's kid." He was a good looking kid and aggressive and just cool. I never hung out with him—I was running too crazy back then.

It is just great having Jon back in the area. The best part about it is that he hasn't forgotten his roots. He is wholesome. What you see is what you get. He is full of passion. It is a dream come true to have gone to the Super Bowl, but everybody was just glad to have that kind of energy and passion associated with the team. We had a feeling that whether they made it there or not, things were going to get exciting.

He actually did something really smart when he came to Tampa when he recognized that there had been a lot of history with the Bucs. Even though the Bucs had a lot of losing seasons, there had been many good players and he wanted to bring them into the fold and bond the organizations—the old with the new. We had a little event in the back room—not publicized—where he invited a lot of the old players and honored Doug Williams with a jersey. He reached out and said, "Hey, this is going to be a whole age-long Buccaneer effort." He said he was going to need their support, and he got it. It was a wonderful way to kick off the new age very early in his tenure. He is going to continue that going forward.

Jon challenged us to get him on one of our billboards instead of Lynne Austin, our billboard girl for years. At that party, we rolled out a prototype of the billboard. But instead of Lynne's face, Jon's face was superimposed on her figure. It got quite a chuckle out of the crowd. We had a lot of fun with that.

> Superstitious Denver Bronco Terrell Davis, who recently retired, demanded that the name tag above his locker always read "Joe Abdullah," and Bronco center Tom Maler won't wash his practice gear during the year because he feels that he's giving the equipment "natural seasoning" to shield "evil spirits."

THIS IS WHERE GRUDEN GOT THAT "AW, SHUCKS" ATTITUDE

DAVE HILDENBRAND

Dave Hildenbrand, 40, is the General Manager of the Hooters restaurant in St Petersburg, FL. In 1985, when he was the kitchen manager, Dave hired Gruden to set up trays, shake wings and shuck oysters. Hildenbrand lives in Brandon, Florida.

When Jon Gruden first came aboard, he told me he was only going to work for us for three months. I've seen a lot of employees who know they're not going to stay here and the majority of them just go through the motions. Not Jon. He showed up on time and had a great work ethic. I'm sure he still does.

He always carried an athletic bag. I don't know if he played tennis or what he did, but he always had that bag with him. He looked like a beach boy—he was in pretty good shape, he had a red face from sunburn, blond hair—much like he has now.

He did both set up and oysters. The way the kitchen was set up, I would be cooking and would yell down "Hey, Jon, a dozen raw." He would go get a dozen raw oysters and shuck them right there at the end of the bar. He was very quick at shucking oysters and the quicker you can get the product prepped and out to the table the better—it's all about timing. Shucking oysters is a fine art. If you've ever shucked oysters before, you know that it's not just *done*. It can be a hazardous job at times. It's not easy to do and if you don't know how to do it, you can really cut yourself. You also need to concentrate on what you're doing. If someone calls your name and you look up while you are still shucking, the next thing you know the shucker is going through your hand.

It was a pleasure working with him.

WORTH EVERY PENNY

JIM McVAY

Jim McVay is the President/CEO of the Outback Bowl and a long time friend of the Gruden family.

I've known Jon a long time and consider him to be a dear personal friend. Jim Gruden, Jon's father, was an assistant coach for my father, John McVay, at the University of Dayton from 1969 to 1972. Jim Gruden coached me, and I remember his three little blond-haired boys, Jim, Jon and Jay, were always following him around everywhere. So I've known this family for thirty-something years.

His growing up in locker rooms and being around football before he knew anything else helped make Jon the coach he is today. His dad was a very successful high school football coach. He coached at Dayton and at Indiana where helped turn that program around back in the early 1970s. He coached at Notre Dame during **Joe Montana**'s playing days before coaching with the Buccaneers. Jon's seen it all. He grew up lifting weights with these guys. He didn't know any different. He's got the advantage of listening—his dad's got three Super Bowl rings. He's not gonna be overwhelmed by anything.

When Jon was assistant coach in the NFL, he'd come down here to Tampa and spend time with his parents, Jim and Kathy. We'd go out golfing and have a couple of beers and run around and have fun. It's tough to go places with him. He's so popular now, and he's such an engaging guy. People want to meet him. They want to talk to him. They want an autograph. It's just one of those things when we go places and do things. You've got to pick your spot.

> Joe Montana did not start until the fourth game of his junior year at Notre Dame...Montana was awestruck by Huey Lewis and once sang backup with his band.

He is as popular a sports figure as you will find in the country today. And you won't find a more engaging guy in terms of dealing with the fans. We were over at Orlando, and these guys are there for summer ball. Jon gets there a couple of days early and he's grinding away. He gets up in the middle of the night, stays up late. He's watching more film than any coach will ever imagine. The guy has got these guys wanting workouts, and they get after it. He's got a high tempo, aggressive practice tempo, that he likes. They're working hard. After practice, he walks straight over to the fans and will stand out on that field talking to the fans, after both sessions, for forty-five minutes or an hour signing autographs, posing for pictures, and meeting people. That's highly unusual. He really does have a very engaging way as well as patience and a desire to mix with the fans, which is kind of unusual. Sometimes these coaches, at that level, will sign a couple of autographs while they're walking on their way to lunch or getting ready for something else, but Jon really takes time for the fans. He's very good. He likes to interact with the fans.

Jon has reached a level of success that is just unimaginable for most people. When he's out on the sideline coaching, he's in the middle of a battle. He's in the heat of the moment and he's a fiery, demanding guy. He is successful because he's driven, he's aggressive, and he's ambitious. But he's not always coaching and he is a fun person to be around when he's not. When we're having a few refreshments or playing golf, he gets a little different temperament. He knows how to enjoy himself. This is a guy's guy. He is a football guy. He's a sports guy. We've been going over to Orlando to watch Jay, his younger brother, play Arena Football. He gets excited when he's watching his brother play. These guys are close. Jon is just as nutty a fan as any one of those Orlando Predators or Tampa Bay Buccaneers fans when they're watching Jon coach. He should be one of those guys with the crazy hat on and the makeup on and the shirt—that's how excited he is when he's rooting for his brother. He's no different than any other fan, and maybe a little bit more fanatical, but it's his brother.

Out on the golf course we're all competitive. The last time we played it was Jon and I against his dad Jim who is a great golfer, and John Brunner, a former player and coach who is now a scout with the

49ers. Jim is the one who is the real **golfer**—he's probably like a two handicap, maybe scratch. Jon and I always get strokes and do a little scramble—we want to beat these guys, and they want to beat us. There's definitely conversation going on during putts. He's got to make his shot. Occasionally we have some fun with it. But if we're playing for five bucks, or a pitcher of beer, believe me, we want to be able to say we won. Yeah, it is competitive. We're not as successful as we'd like to be since Jim is such a good golfer that he's tough to beat.

There are funny stories about Jon in San Francisco. He didn't have much money. He was just a young struggling kid, trying to get a foot-hold. He used to ride a bike to work sometimes. Somebody gave Jon a TV to put in his apartment. Jon tells the story of riding down the highway on his bicycle carrying a TV. He never had any furniture in his apartment because he was never there. He was always in the training complex. He had ridden that bike for a long time, but then he stepped up and got that old beat-up car and said he paid about five hundred bucks for it.

He used that beat-up car to go to the training complex. He tells a story about that car. The 49ers had a big Monday Night Football game once. Jon's car was not very dependable. The players used to make fun of him and pick on him, but he was a worker and they liked and respected him because he was always there—work, work, work. But he was just a young guy on the staff. So, they're getting ready for the game and **Charles Haley** tells Jon, "I want you to pick me up for the game in your car, in that old beat-up piece of —— you have. That's the mentality I've got to have for this game." Jon was a nervous wreck. He didn't know if the car was going to get to the stadium or not. He was worried that if he picked Haley up, and the car broke down the coaches would be mad at him for having that beat-up, old, undepend-able car bringing one of the most valuable players in the league to the

> While playing golf in 1567, Mary Queen of Scots was informed that her husband, Lord Darnley, had been murdered. She finished the round.

> Charles Haley was the first player—or coach—to earn five Super Bowl rings.

game. He picked Haley up, and they were driving down the street. He's got this big defensive end in there. Jon's heart was pounding. He was afraid the thing was going to break down. But he made it to the stadium and he was never so relieved in his life.

This is a football guy. This is one of the truly gifted guys in terms of football knowledge, in terms of work ethic, aggressiveness. He didn't just stumble into a Super Bowl. This guy willed this team to a Super Bowl victory. If you look up and down the roster, how many super, outstanding, Pro-Bowl playmakers are there on offense? Off the charts! Jon gets these guys playing unbelievably well. The guy's a truly, gifted, talented head coach. Right now you have to say this is the top coach in the National Football League, hands down.

This guy earned his stripes. This isn't just some guy who showed up and said, "Hey, I want to take a shot at this coaching thing." He worked his butt off, coaching as a graduate assistant at Tennessee, went to Pacific, coached at Pittsburgh, and was around the 49ers. He's the first one in the office and the last one to leave. He used to sit in the hallway in San Francisco and listen to coaches lecture their different units, taking notes. He'd be there late at night following coaches around saying, "Why did you do this? How did you do this?" This guy trained. You talk about having a doctorate? This guy's got one. He earned it. He knows every position. He knows everyone's responsibilities. He's not just some glamour guy who knows how to drop back and throw the ball. This is a guy who is as thorough as you will ever find, and that's why he landed the Super Bowl.

The Raiders could have been in the Super Bowl last year. They could have been in the Super Bowl the year before. They were 8 and 8 his first two years in Oakland. He took over a terrible football team. He got the head coaching job because of what he accomplished in Philadelphia as an offensive coordinator—as a young kid. When he stands up in front of the team, he's got the chalk in his hand, he's on the grease board, and he's got the marker. The players immediately know that he knows his stuff. You can't fool the players. They know immediately if the guy knows what he's doing, and if he has the mental toughness, the work ethic, the aggressiveness and the knowledge to be the right guy. You can't BS the players.

When you can get a guy like Jon, you do whatever you can to get him. Jon felt a certain amount of pressure because it took a lot of money and draft picks. He wanted very badly to succeed. Whether they had paid that much or not, Jon was going to give the same effort. He only knows one effort—and that's all out. He doesn't know how to temper things. Whatever the most you can give, you are going get out of him. He just goes full throttle. Go over to mini-camp. Watch him. Go and listen to him talk. Talk to the players about him. Talk to the coaches about him.

Did anybody think he'd win the Super Bowl the first year? I'd be very surprised if anybody was convinced that was going to happen. They just kept gaining momentum, and every week they got better. The players were into it, and they wanted to succeed. All of a sudden there was a whole new level of energy that came out of these guys—offensively and defensively.

Jon's wife, Cindy, is a star. This is one neat girl. She and my wife, Lori, are good friends. Cindy has a lot of responsibility. They've got three little boys, Jon II, Michael and Jayson. Here's the odd thing. Jim and Kathy have three boys: Jim, Jon and Jay. Jay has three boys. Jon has three boys. It's eerie. They've all got three boys. We go to Tampa Bay Storm games or sit up in the box and watch the Buc games. We had three boys in our family. It's very similar. Three little boys running around. And the poor mother's got one on the hip, chasing the other one, and the other one is running down the hallway with a balloon hat on. You put your soft drink down and you come back, and it's full of ketchup and mustard. That's what little boys do.

Cindy has a great demeanor. You can tell that she has been exposed to this stuff. She knows how to deal with it. She's smart. She's strong. Cindy's the best. It's vital to Jon because he knows that his three boys are in good hands. You see her do interviews. She's great with people. She's great with the camera. She's very supportive. Jon would not be able to function the way he does because he's a working maniac—in his time and his commitment. He couldn't do that without the support of a woman he knows is there running the house, running the show.

The Tampa market needed a guy like this. They never had a champion, and this market is a great sports market. Great football passion here. Bucs fans have been loyal for years with a bad owner. I mean a *bad* owner. He was a terrible owner for this team, but the fans stuck in there, hung in there. They kept coming back, coming back, following, hoping, begging. It wasn't going to happen with Hugh Culverhouse. It just wasn't going to happen. There's a deep long history of Buccaneer fans. Now you get a Glazer team in here. Jon's here. They win the Super Bowl—these fans have been rewarded. These fans have been there for twenty-seven years. He's given the community an identity. He's made every sports fan in the market feel proud to be able to say, "Tampa, Tampa Bay, St. Pete, the Bay area." We haven't had that. It's given us an identity. It's a young fresh enthusiastic state of the art cutting edge, hard working, glamour feel for this community. That goes right through the football team, right through the Super Bowl, right into this market and affects everybody's lives. Look around. Look at the cars—the flags and the banners and the Buc shirts. It's galvanized a community. It's united a community to be proud of something that we have in terms of sports.

Are sports teams the most important thing a community has? Absolutely not! But they certainly can be a symbol for a community. This is a window to our community for those outside the Bay area to get a chance to look at us now, and all of a sudden there's more stories coming out of Tampa, St. Petersburg, and Clearwater. Now there's more beach shots and palm trees. From a sports standpoint, this has become "the cool place." It hasn't always been that way.

We had the struggling Devil Rays, the struggling Lightning, the struggling Buccaneers. Well now we've got a Super Bowl champion, and you can never take that away.

FSU-Miami, 1991, "Wide Right I"—FSU kicker Gerry Thomas missed by inches; the year before the goal posts were 12" wider on each side. Thomas quit football and Bobby Bowden never saw him again after that day.

HEAR ME NOW, LISTEN TO ME LATER

SCOT BRANTLEY

Scot Brantley is a former NFL player who played with the Tampa Bay Buccaneers from 1980 to 1987. Scot is now a radio broadcaster for WQYK in Tampa.

I've known Jon for over twenty years since all the way back to 1982 when John McKay hired a running backs coach out of Notre Dame by the name of Jim Gruden. When Jim and his lovely wife Kathy came down to Tampa they had two young boys—Jon and Jay. Being sons of a football coach going through the college ranks—where you're used to hanging around the Notre Dame locker room—they used to hang around our locker room. They came in the off-season obviously and we'd go over there and work out daily and those kids would be around. They were young. I don't know, I think Jon was going to be a freshman at Dayton and Jay was still at Chamberlain High School. It was just unique. They were young guys. They were bright eyed. They were great guys.

I can remember chasing Jon out of our locker because he kind of followed us around the locker room. I dipped Copenhagen and I'd always have some in my locker that they'd send me. Jon would always go in there to steal my Copenhagen out of the locker. I remember chasing him out of the locker room and telling him he better stay his butt out of my locker. He kind of gave me that look like, "Hey, if I wore a size thirteen, I'd steal your shoes too." But that was just Jon. Then he went away to college and I ended up seeing Jay a lot more than Jon. But we created a friendship, especially with Jim and Kathy Gruden. And they loved Tampa so much even after Ray Perkins came in and let Jim and the other coaches go. They wanted to be in Tampa and stayed until Jim took a scouting job in San Francisco and have been there ever since. Wonderful guy. Wonderful family. Just a model American family. If you could model an up-and-coming family after anybody I think that Kathy and Jim Gruden ought to write the book on it.

Jon still has those down home values. Even winning the Super Bowl hasn't changed him at all in my opinion. I was with him for an hour and a half yesterday, and Monday I called and he answered the phone. I was like, "Hey, I know you're busy this week but Ronnie Lane—you may remember him as the Night Train—is out of town. Can you come in and do the show with me? What day do you want to come in?" "How about Wednesday?" he asked. I said, "Okay I'll see you Wednesday." That's just the kind of guy he is.

The one thing I love about Jon is his love and respect for the game of football, especially the National Football League. Although he played some in college, he never had an opportunity to play in the National Football League because of his size, but he has a distinct appreciation and love for this game and he understands the history of this game. He's not one of these new kids on the block trying to make a name for himself. He's a guy who actually loves the game, knows the game, appreciates the history of the game and he loves the alumni. That's the beautiful thing. Very early in the off-season, after he was hired in February, the first thing he did when he got to town was to call me and say "Hey Scot, how many guys can you muster up? We want to have a little alumni gathering with ex-Buccaneer players." Between Jon, Andre Trescastro, the head of security, Jeff Kamis, the Bucs communication manager, and myself we called some ex-Buc players. He expected like twenty guys to show up at Hooters, but the total count was somewhere around eighty. Eighty guys! He was just floored by that. It was a new day, a new beginning.

Without a doubt, this was the first time that anybody had offered an olive branch to the alumni of the Bucs. That kind of a thing had been pushed under a rug for forever...maybe justifiably so after some lean years. But it's still part of the foundation. It's still part of the workings of an NFL franchise that should start to create a little bit of a history when you've been around for twenty-six years. It's time to start doing a little bit more for your alumni. They're part of your building blocks and are as much a part of you today as they were then. I know that the logos change. The colors have changed. But still, they were once the Tampa Bay Buccaneers.

That night at Hooters was very special. I don't think there is any question about it. When he started this little deal Jon said, "Hey, I don't care how, we have got to get Doug Williams back." He understands that the quarterback is the field general. On any level, on any team, you look to your quarterback as your field general. This is coming from a linebacker's standpoint. Doug Williams was our general before from '78 to '82 and in '79 we went to the championship game. It wasn't about statistics, or about numbers. It was about leadership quality and there was no doubt that Williams was that guy. The Bucs ended up paying airfare, hotel and everything else so Doug could be a part of that night. It was great. It was a thing of beauty to see all the old guys. Most of them I see around town but a lot of them were flown in and that just added to the entire equation of why he wanted to get this done. That all came from Jon Gruden's decision.

Over the years, I had stayed in touch with Jon in a roundabout way through his father and when he'd come down to Tampa in the off-season. Shoot, I've been in radio since I got out of football. I'd find out from Jim and Kathy when he was going to be down staying with them or staying at the beach. I'd always get a number from them and contact him to be on the show or contact Jon to grab a beer or meal one night, just to keep that relationship together.

I had no idea in the world that he'd end up being the head coach of the Tampa Bay Buccaneers. I remember the day Tony Dungy was fired. I went on a little bit of a campaign saying "Hey, I know he's under contract for one more year, but find a way, somehow, someway, that Jon Gruden can come here to Tampa Bay." At the time there was so much going on with the speculation about Bill Parcells, Marvin Lewis, and go right down the list of some other guys and I said "Man, you've got to do the right thing. Gruden's the best guy for this job right now. It's night and day. You're going from Tony Dungy, "mister laid back," arms folded, great human being. But you need a guy to come in here and light the fire, stoke the fire, and get these people's attention because that's what this team needs more than anything in the world right now." And lo and behold, it all culminated in a great year, a work in progress, and a Super Bowl XXXVII Championship.

After he was hired, I went with his father to his first press conference down at the Tampa Marriott Waterside Hotel. He was glad to see me with his dad and I was able to chat with him and get him on the radio at the press conference. We exchanged numbers and he gave me his home number. Once the season started, though, it was on. He's always called me up on this radio show I host every Monday. I said, "Hey, come up here and sit with me, you know, and we'll discuss some things." We have a genuine friendship that I think is only going to grow and get better. Obviously being in the position I'm in, he knows that what he can tell me, he won't be able to tell anyone else because I understand what I can say and what I'm not going to say. What's between us is between us, and he understands that. It's a good thing to have.

The one thing about Jon is that he goes and goes and goes. I know it's all very well documented about his waking up early and going to the office at 4 a.m. and that's so true. Even on Monday, after a long trip or coming in and getting home late, he's still on that routine. The alarm clock in his head goes off and he goes to the office. I remember going there one Monday to do the show. Jeff Kamis, his director of communications, met me and said, "Hey, give him a little time, give him a little time." I asked what was happening. Jeff said, "Well he's been on the floor sleeping there for about the last forty-five minutes." This was totally unusual…it was almost like his battery had run out, and he had to charge his battery. Then, boom, he turns a light on and pops up to the chair. We did an hour show and he didn't miss a beat.

That's the kind of guy he is. Relentless. A lot of people say that can be damaging after a while but I think—for what the Glazers gave up to get him—he feels it's his responsibility to pay them back. And the only way I can figure for him to pay them back is to bust his butt every day. Go above and beyond the call of duty and mold this thing together and make it work. That's exactly what he's done this year. Most people thought this would be a three-year project. Maybe four. Put everything together the way he wants. But no, he did it in one year with a brand new offensive coaching staff who didn't know each other from Adam. That's the most amazing story, I think. How could you not be impressed? Andy Reid, give me a break. How is he "Coach of the Year" over Jon Gruden? That's a travesty. That's Jesse James. That's stealing, because Jon was definitely "Coach of the Year".

Yeah, Monte Kiffin was there and didn't have Tony overseeing him. Jon said, "Hey, Monte, that's your defense. You do whatever the hell you want to do with it. It's y'alls, baby." And look, with no handcuffs, no input, that's Monte Kiffin's defense. He turned them loose and that's why you got the product you got. It's all about delegating authority and nobody does it better than Jon.

I noticed how Gruden handled the different personalities on the team. One thing that comes to mind is how he handled Kenyatta Walker. He sat Kenyatta's rear end on the bench, and he said, "Hey, you're just not getting it done, and I don't care if you went to Florida. I don't care how much money you're making, or what round you were drafted in, sit your butt down until you work back into this position." To me, that was probably the best thing that ever happened to Kenyatta Walker to make him more of a productive player down the stretch. That's just one example that really sticks out in my mind. Although he wouldn't admit it then, I think Kenyatta would tell you now that it was the best thing that could have happened to him at that time.

Then there was the thing with **Warren Sapp**. The tight-end thing was probably to give him a little extra motivation and add a little bit for fun. Look at the productivity. He knew that if he put Warren into that situation, Warren would take pride in it. Other guys would just kind of rumble in there, and just go through the motions, and big deal, "Why do I have to do that?" But Warren wanted to do it. The minute Jon Gruden walked onto that practice field, Warren Sapp's whole perception of football really changed. It was more like he wanted it to be—not laid back, not just structured, but a "Hey, get after it and kick-butt" type attitude. And that's what Warren thrived upon. That's why he would volunteer to do goal line. I'll guarantee you one of these days he'll catch a touchdown pass in that position on

William (Refrigerator) Perry, "the Galloping Roast," had a grand total of three touchdowns in his career.

a tight-end delay, sneak out into the flat, and Warren catches a touchdown. I envisioned that to happen this year, and it didn't, so it'll happen next year.

The Gruden family is a great competitive family. Jay was always the bigger of the two, and still is. But Jon's the kind of guy who depended on his attitude and his fire and his toughness. Most little guys are the tough guys because they're the guys who have got to fight all the time. Did you ever see a big tough guy—and I think of **Shaquille O'Neal**... that sucker ain't never fought in his life, but he's always been the biggest, and the strongest, and the baddest. When has he ever had to fight for anything? You meet a little guy, any time, and I'll give you a guy that's going to grow up into a hard-working, strong-willed person. That's exactly what Jon is. I'm not saying Jay isn't, because he's got a lot of the same qualities as Jon has. Even before Jay stepped foot over there on the field with the Buccaneers as a quality control coach, or whatever you want to call it, I predicted that he will be an offensive coordinator in the National Football League within five years. I still stick to that. As a matter of fact, Herm Edwards wants to hire him as a coach right now. That bloodline flows—it started with Jim, and he developed it. Jay's already developed it up there in the Arena Football League as a world champion Arena Football League coach. So it's there. It's going to happen for Jay. I think one day, you'll see Jay and Jon go head-to-head in the National Football League as head coaches.

It's all about that family, having that comfort of family and friends and old friends and acquaintances to really build it. I think that comfort zone is there right now for Jon and Cindy Gruden more so than it's ever been because they've been everywhere back and forth across this land in the coaching profession. That's the nature of it, but I hope Jon has found a home here as the head coach for a long time.

With free agency, there probably never will be another twelve-year coach in one place because after four or five years, players get bored.

In March 1954, the Lakers and the Hawks played a regulation, regular season NBA game using baskets there were 12' high rather than the usual 10'...the next night they played each other in a doubleheader. True facts, believe it or not!

They're making too much money and they want some change. But I think Jon's the only coach, out of the thirty-two right now, who has a chance to be here for the long term, and I hope that's the case. Tony Dungy did his six years, and it was time to change because, and I hate to say it, his action was getting old. That same old stuff, something needed to change. Jon is ever-changing because he is young. He's vivacious. He has all the great qualities that keep it fresh, and that's the most important element that a lot of these coaches will never get. I think Jon will always understand that and keep it fresh for all players who want to come to Tampa Bay and play.

When you go with Jon to an Arena Football game to watch his brother play, you drink beer and you have a good time. It's not a time to get too analytical. It's fun. After he won the Super Bowl the Orlando Predators played a nationally-broadcast game. I didn't even care to go because I knew Jon would be put down in front and the cameras would be on him. He couldn't be himself. To be honest with you, he'd rather go to the top of the stands, have a cold beer, dip Copenhagen, and reminisce with a couple of coaches and friends. That's his idea of a fun. Now when you win the World Championship, a lot changes because of the attention you're going to draw. He came in here under the microscope, and he's under a huge microscope right now. Like he said yesterday, "Brans, I wish we could just go find a dive, just a little old hole in the wall, with nobody there but a bartender, and we would just go in and drink beer and listen to rock and roll music." That's Jon Gruden. That's all-American Jon Gruden. He's got three wonderful kids and the greatest wife in the world.

He is the most fun guy in the world. When you've got three kids under the age of ten, obviously that pretty well dictates what idle time you have, but he loves to include the kids. He calls me about fishing. We're getting ready to plan some fishing trips, and I've got a couple of tournaments coming up. We're going to involve the boys. That's the fun part of it—doing little things like that, and at the same time having fun and still doing your duty as a father—nurturing those young kids that are growing up. They want them to experience the other things that a lot of other kids might not have that chance to do.

Chapter 6

The Write Stuff

LaSalle's Briscoe tips Clay in overtime

By FORREST MILLER
Tribune Sports Writer

Donald Briscoe, scheduled to attend the funeral of his grandfather this weekend in St. Louis, trapped Clay for 178 yards in 22 carries and scored all three touchdowns in LaSalle's 21-14 overtime victory over the Colonials Friday night at Clay.

It was Briscoe's one-yard, second-effort, fourth-down smash into the end zone that broke a 14-14 deadlock and Clay, which had chosen to play defense first in the overtime, couldn't recover.

LaSalle's comeback season now stands at 4-2 with Elkhart Central coming up at School Field next Thursday. Clay is 2-4 and faces Adams at School Field next Friday.

Emotional Mike Sacchini emphasizes the word "love" when talking about or to his team, and Friday night there was a lot of love overflowing among the Lions.

"This was an outstanding high school game," said Sacchini. "We were going to run Briscoe on that trap until Clay stopped him."

The 5-9 senior cracked Clay for a 60-yard touchdown dash in the first period, carried the ball six consecutive times on LaSalle's first series of the second half and scored on a six-yard run, then nudged across on the dramatic game-winner in overtime.

Clay, unveiling a wishbone offense but lacking the outside speed to make it effective, scored first on an 11-yard run by Mike Barrix, and beat the halftime clock by 24 seconds on a 21-yard Jon Gruden-Steve Radde pass. Radde made an outstanding catch, just as he had a moment earlier on a 43-yard pass when he out-battled defender Tony Mabry. The latter had intercepted one in the first period.

Conversion kickers Bill Lewsiewicz of LaSalle and Tony Wise of Clay were both perfect. Lewsiewicz tried to win it for LaSalle with fourth-quarter field goals, barely missing short on a 37-yard kick with 7:30 to play, and missing wide on a 30-yard attempt with 1:31 to go.

The Lions were experts at turning mistakes into positive yardage all evening. Several times quarterback Richard Whitfield fumbled the snap, quickly recovered and ran for good gains — including a nine-yard run on the first play of the overtime.

Clay's defense, led by Dave Beebe, Kevin Grunawalt and Kevin Sinclair, stopped Whitfield on second down and Tyrone Ware on third down and Tyrone Ware on third

LaSalle 26 helped Clay's opening TD drive — a match that ended with Barrix' 11-yard run with 4:26 to in the quarter.

Only 65 seconds later Briscoe gehtly placed the ball in Clay's end zone after his 60-yard run. It was 7-7 until Radde's two fine catches, the second with 24 seconds to play, gave Clay a 14-7 halftime lead.

A partially blocked punt — a kick that netted only 11 yards — gave LaSalle the ball at Clay's 38 in the third period. After one pass, Briscoe carried six times in a row and ran 13 yards on a keeper to go in with the

Clay, unveiling a wishbone offense but lacking the outside speed to make it effective, scored first on an 11-yard run by Mike Barrix, and beat the halftime clock by 24 seconds on a 21-yard Jon Gruden-Steve Radde pass. Radde made an

	LaSalle	Clay
Yards rushing	253	112
Yards passing	28	75
Passes	5-7-0	3-8-1
Punts	4-24	7-27
Yards penalized	40	65
Return yardage	0	2

The Fourth Estate
Doesn't Take the Fifth

JUST WON, BABY

TOM McEWEN

Tom McEwen long-time sports columnist for the Tampa Tribune *has known Jon Gruden and the Gruden family for years.*

T he first thing I remember about Jon Gruden was when he had a press conference and walked into the Tampa Marriott Water-side Hotel. He was walking through the line and he stopped in front of me and said, "Are you still providing those breakfasts?" I said, "Yeah, sure am." Then after he had his first conference, he stopped on the way out and said, "Can I come to see you?" He did. He went over to my house.

When Jon came over here to a party at the house, it was kind of funny. He had already talked about the fact that he had worked at Hooters. He said he was shucking oysters. He also later said that wasn't his first job at Hooters—his first job was cleaning the smashed chewing gum up off the sidewalk. What kind of a job is that?

Later, he was over here at my house at a function. He walked in and he was early, and there was only one other couple here at the time. He walked right over and said, "Frank Campisi." Well, that just tickled the hell out of Campisi because he didn't think Jon knew who he was. "You're the tomato man here." Camp said, "How the hell do you know that?" He said, "I worked for you for two weeks, worked for you and Jimmy Fisher. I worked for you for two weeks trying to clean up and select some of those tomatoes for you, and it was too hard. I left. I quit that." Campisi is out of the business now, but he was big in tomatoes around here for years out at the Farmers' Market so it was clear that the kid was running around trying to get jobs anywhere he could.

He's got a lively personality. Here at Tampa, we went from zero to a hundred on the personality chart, we went from zero to a hundred on the enthusiasm chart, and we went from zero to two hundred on the profanity chart. You know that Dungy wouldn't say "———" if he had a mouthful. Jon will say it whether he means it or not. You've seen where some of those players said that the first word out his mouth when he introduced himself to the team was a profane word. And I'm sure I can tell you what it was. I'm sure that was a hit with them, and they said it was, and he immediately got to their level to get them going.

On that first visit here, I said, "I don't believe you can win with Brad Johnson at quarterback." He said, "Why?" I said, "Well, he hasn't demonstrated that he can win anywhere really. He's been kind of bumped around. He's a big guy, but he can't "move around." He asked about the others, and I said, "I don't know about the others." At mid-season I told him the same thing. I said, "I don't believe you can win with Brad Johnson." That how much I knew.

But the truth is Brad Johnson was terrific toward the end of the season when all that he was force-fed by Gruden just went right into his skull and right into the huddle and right into his arm and right into the plays that came out of it. It was perfection in those last three games, as you well know. My judgment is that this man got this team going because he force-fed his scheme of things, got them into believing in him, and he won just enough to get into the playoffs and get that "bye" week. That allowed him then to have the time to give them the polish they needed. Now, that's my opinion because he did say the key game was the Carolina game that they pulled out without Brad playing, so they could rest him and get him well.

He understands the media very well. He says to me all the time, "Love you, man." That's what you see him saying all the time when a player comes off the field. "Love you, man." It's clear that he's been on the sidelines to watch this through the years as an assistant coach in the pro ranks, and with an assorted bunch of head coaches and an assorted class of media.

His daddy said, "I honestly don't think any of us will realize for a long time what kind of a job this kid, my son, 'did.' I don't know of anyone, anywhere that's ever left a team—left all of his coaches, left all of his players, came to a place where he didn't know any player, where he didn't know anybody, where he didn't know the owners, where he couldn't bring any of his coaches but one assistant, Mark Arteaga, who was a personal assistant—Davis didn't want to let him go. He told him he would sue to get him. He was the only one he brought. He could walk in here and start from scratch like that without any knowledge at all and bring in his own scheme of things and get it done.

It had to be a powerful personality, and you can see it. He admitted he got a lot more confidence in his own personality because you can see how he became livelier on the sideline and how he was more outgoing and outspoken as the season wore on. He's showman enough to understand that the cameras are on that face of his so he could guess about when it was there—like Sapp, of course. Nobody can follow those cameras better than Warren Sapp. You can almost see in Jon's eyes, that he knows the camera is on him so he's not going to give you a wink, but he's gonna scrunch his face up a little bit. I think he's probably as appreciative of television and the media as anybody around.

It's all still unfathomable around here to all of us—even today the Bucs are still pinching themselves trying to believe what happened.

We were in the stands at the Super Bowl. It's the first time I've not been in the press box. I decided I wanted to work in the stands and sat there pretty close to the wives. No one in the stands could believe what was happening. No one. Not the Buc fans and certainly not the Raider fans. We had them around us, too, and they really quieted down. I tell you one of them actually turned around and shook our hands. They were not ugly at all afterwards…except for one drunk.

Gruden is that way, and he remains that way. His father said, "I don't believe any of us can appreciate what this young man did." He's got a tall quarterback, and he's got big, strong, tall receivers. No speed, but a lot of tall receivers, except Joe Jurevicius, who ran fast as he could in the Philadelphia game. I think tall-for-tall is so important, because Brad is going to throw it up a bit, and they go get it.

Steve Spurrier was very admiring of what he had done. He said, "The biggest thing in my mind was that Brad Johnson can throw that

> Steve Spurrier was the only quarterback to go 0-14 in one NFL season, with the '76 Buccaneers.

short slant as good as anybody, so if you've got a 6' 5" receiver who weighs two hundred and fifty pounds going across the middle, and he puts it in him, you're going to always make six-seven yards. There's not a defensive back in the world that can break that up without fouling." It's a good point. You saw how many times they threw that on first and second downs to get important yards. Jurevicius had a seventy-one yard run and it was a six-yard pass right over the middle. He had the option to make it a slant, and he did. That's very important—two big receivers and a big tough quarterback.

Regarding this Super Bowl, I think the best quote I heard was from safety, John Lynch who said at the half, "We haven't seen one play we didn't see in practice." That's amazing. He was anticipating what Rich Gannon, the quarterback, was going to do. Gruden even got in himself and played Gannon in one of the practices out there. He used even some of the terminology that Gannon used in practice. The Raiders didn't show them anything new that they hadn't seen. That late touchdown, that wasn't a touchdown—that was a terrible call.

I've seen so many losing Buccaneer games, I offered to write a course at the University of Florida on "The Art of Writing About Losing." I had used every adverb and every adjective and every preposition and every descriptive phrase and every simile and every anecdote about losing that I could think of.

I had to get used to this winning right here after all the losses. They'd say you could walk through our press box at Tampa Stadium and most people, when they had won, had not started writing because they didn't know how to do it. People were late because they had to write about winning, and they didn't know how to do it. They were so stuck on losing they couldn't get out of that mode.

The bottom, I think, was during the Leeman Bennett and Richard Williamson periods. There was just no way. There was nothing here, and the coach had no magic at all. Of course, they clearly did not have the know-how that they began to have later with their scouting department, with Ruscal and that crowd that grew with this thing. They had to learn, too. The bottom, to me, was in the 1980s after John McKay left. I guess if you had to say the worst, probably Ray

Perkins. The team was bad, and the coach didn't like to be the coach here, and didn't like the media. The media didn't like him. There was no pleasantry. There was nothing pleasant or fun either about coaching or writing about the Buccaneers during those years. He didn't just have a thin skin, he was a mean man who didn't like the media—I don't know of anybody he did like.

There are no jerks on this team. They've always had a few jerks on teams, but they're not on this team now. I don't know of any. Gruden has gotten them all thinking like he does, or he will go along with a player who's different from him to get the most out of him. I would imagine that so many coaches would not have been able to go with Keyshawn Johnson in the middle when it was clear that he was arguing with the coach on the sideline. The coach never got upset, and he never chastised him after that. He said, "Oh, he's a California boy." That was about it. He wasn't going to say anything to lose him. He kept him, and, my goodness, how valuable he was in the playoffs. Clearly, Gruden saw the value of that. I didn't, but he did. I thought Keyshawn Johnson might be divisive. He wasn't. Gruden wouldn't allow anybody to be divisive—if he could see it coming he would cave enough, just enough, so that they both stayed on the same track.

I've know his dad a long time, and everyone in that family is smart. Everyone is smart, the mother, she taught school, the father, all the kids. She had seventeen years of teaching here at Berkeley, and she is a quality lady that you would enjoy knowing. I know I enjoy the family. I like to be with them.

Gruden's shortcoming is that he does not return a lot of phone calls. Neither does his associate. They need to return more phone calls. When the San Francisco 49ers made that move on Monte Kiffin, the defensive coordinator, Gruden said, during that time, "Monte, you stay and you be the head coach, and I'll be your offensive coordinator." How nice is that. Does that make you want to stay? He has the ability to do that. He's a smart guy.

I think he does have an ego, but I think he knows how to harness it and steer it in the right direction. I guess a lot of that comes out from his yelling and screaming and dancing and jumping all over the place.

His communication skills are wonderful. His similes and anecdotes are good. His comparisons are good. The lines he'd take are good and unusual, and they're tacks that you don't expect him to take. I think he's a wonderful speaker on his feet. He has got just enough enthusiasm that he can say, "I love you, man," and "Pound the rock. Pound the rock." How corny is "Pound the rock?" How old is that? Didn't that start at **Clemson** with old Frank Howard? He could also take that simple corny stuff and make it sound very important. I guess people like **Knute Rockne** did the same thing.

This area hasn't had anything like him before. Phil Esposito has got a lot of personality, too. He yells and screams at players, and that sort of thing. They're the only two I know.

Gruden followed a taciturn man who was intelligent; he just didn't believe all that enthusiasm was required. Tony Dungy was such a man of faith that he thought that right would win out. He thought that if he did the right thing, good things were going to happen to him. He wasn't nearly as aggressive as this man was about changing and believing that such a thing could motivate his team.

Gruden is an old-fashioned coach. The upscale part of that is the use of his computers. His dad said, "You've never seen anything like this man with a computer. He lives by the computers." I've been in to see his office. His office is dark. He doesn't have lights. You go in during the daytime, and he's got those computer screens. He works them all the time, puts everything on there. He's always been that way.

Sapp loves him, and we all are happy that Sapp loves him. Gruden decided early on that Warren Sapp was one heck of a ball player, and

> When Clemson University plays in a bowl game most of their fans pay their bills with $2 bills to show their economic impact…and increasing their chances of a future invitation.

> When Knute Rockne was killed in a 1931 plane crash, where seven other people perished, it was the largest disaster in U. S. aviation history up until that time.

he was going to see to it that he had every advantage to use all his ability to a max, especially his leadership ability. He very quickly anointed Sapp as a leader. He anointed him as his trusted leader and friend. My goodness, he was. Whether it was *his* playing, or his being the center of attention on the defense, it allowed other people to do things, and that did happen because they never failed to double-team him. It didn't matter. Gruden allowed Sapp, and Sapp allowed himself to be part of the team. Remember how, when Anthony "Booger" McFarland got hurt, Gruden was able to fit in these people we hadn't heard of. Greg Spires, my gosh, he could hardly play at Florida State, and yet he was very important in the Super Bowl. Then Ellis Wyms—where did he come from? To my way of thinking, no one on that team was more invaluable to that team than the big end on the right-hand side, Simeon Rice, the philosopher. He's a beauty there, a thinker and a well-read guy. He uses all these quotes and takes on all these little forums and goes on little pathways that you'd never expect.

Prior to Gruden, I don't know that I've seen anybody here who could be your friend and still be a disciplinarian. This is the only real coaching success we've had besides McKay, and he didn't want to be close to his players unless they were from USC. Of course, McKay was older, too, and that is a factor. Age, and the fact that Gruden is "age with youth" allows him to run with them. Have you watched them practice? He runs all the time with the offense. He runs all over the place. Up and back, yelling and screaming, up and down, all the time. And Mark Arteaga—the kid he brought in that he calls his aide—is a leader in practice. He carries a clipboard, and he holds it up high, and they all read off that clipboard. He works every minute, and then he's also his personal assistant.

And that motor he's got—I don't know where that comes from. I don't know how long that's going to last. I don't know how you can drive yourself that much. I can't do that. Most coaches, when their motor begins to slow down, learn to adjust. They begin to delegate a little bit more when they can't do it all themselves. People like Ara Parseghian, the Notre Dame and Northwestern coach, who was involved in every phase of his games was the very same way. Steve Spurrier is the same way, and he's gotten a little older. There's very good respect between Spurrier and Gruden. They like and admire

JON GRUDEN: ALL IT TAKES IS ALL YA GOT

each other very much, and they're a lot alike—they both get in the quarterback's head the same way.

Spurrier called here once early in the season:

> **Spurrier:** "What you got down there? That Gruden? Got an offensive coordinator?"
> **McEwen:** "Not really."
> **Spurrier:** "Like me, huh?"
> **McEwen:** "Yeah."
> **Spurrier:** "He coaches quarterbacks?"
> **McEwen:** "Yeah."
> **Spurrier:** "Like me, huh? Calls the plays on the field himself?"
> **McEwen:** "Yeah?"
> **Spurrier:** "Like me, huh?"

It was clear then that they like each other and that they do a lot of things alike. I thought it was a definite possibility that Spurrier would have gone with the Bucs, and I think if timing had been different, it would have happened. But the Tuna—**Bill Parcells**—shot him out of the water. They fell in love with him, and things just fell in place for these people to get the guy that wanted to come here from the start.

I've seen Jon a couple of times since the Super Bowl. This is one thing I'm finding out about him right away that I like. He seems to have a real respect for people before him. He certainly doesn't take away from anybody, and he elevated Dungy. Dungy almost declined to accept it for a while, I don't know why. He gave the coaches before him credit. I haven't heard him put anybody down. Just from my being here all those years, he knew who we were, that sort of thing. Linda cooked him some grouper. It was just the three of us. He always talks about those breakfasts I used to have. They were nothing really, but he used to like that. Back here after the Super Bowl, he was just getting ready to tape something. I don't think I'd seen him since

In 1969, the famous "Joe Namath" Super Bowl, Army assistant football coach Bill Parcells watched the game at the house of Army's head basketball coach, Bobby Knight.

California. I said, "Holy, Lord, what a great thing you've done here." He said, "I ain't famous. You're the famous man. You've got a street named after you there on that stadium place. You've got a press box named after you. You've got everything there. You're a lot more famous than me, man. Love you, man." All that is not true, but that's a great tack, and I suppose he does mean it. He means that you're an achiever, and he likes that.

His dad just keeps saying what all his kid has been able to do. He can appreciate it because he's been a trudging assistant coach for years, and now is scouting. He probably surprises all—even surprised his family, and maybe even surprised himself. I've been around his family at games and at the Super Bowl. They're just a bunch of proud people who love it. They went down and hugged each other all during the game. They kept hugging everybody around. They're big huggers in that family. By the way, he had Phil Mickelson there in his little group. He loves to fish because he can take the kids with him. He doesn't get to see much of them. He loves those little freckle-faced kids, Deuce, Mike and little Jayson. She had all three of them there at the game.

Except for availability, he's pretty down to earth. He's got to get himself a line of communication that a real good secretary could help. He's okay. I could call over there. If I had a problem with him, I'd call his mother.

GREEN BAY: COME SMELL OUR DAIRY AIR

BOB MCGINN

Bob McGinn, 51, is the Green Bay Pack-ers beat writer for the Milwaukee Journal Sentinel. *He lives in Green Bay, Wisconsin.*

When I see Gruden competing on TV, or holding the Super Bowl trophy, I think about how he started out and that was one of his jobs was as the driver for Mike Holmgren. The Green Bay practice field is more than a quarter mile from Lambeau Field. The team doesn't go anywhere during training camp. They stay in the dorms at St. Norbert College, about six miles away, but all the practices are right at the Packer facility. The coaches would be maybe half a mile away in a headquarters area right smack on Lambeau Field. They would have to drive down or walk the half mile to this practice field. In his first year, Gruden's job was to ferry Mike Holmgren back and forth.

As the staff got bigger with the addition of Ray Rhodes and Sherman Lewis later on in Holmgren's years, they hired an administrative assis-tant to do these mundane things. But that was one of Gruden's deals. I would be talking to Holmgren after practice and there would be Gruden with the car warmed up in colder weather. They would be practicing outside in October. Just outside the gate, Gruden would be out there waiting—and that was his job! He would drive the guy back and forth.

Gruden was always talking to me about the Arena Football League. His brother Jay plays in the Arena League for the Orlando Predators, and Jon was always talking about that and about how he was scouting the league on his own, coming in early in the mornings and watching film. He knew everything about the Arena League. I assume he was probably scouting the CFL and every other damn league at this time too, and he was just so into it.

This was a young coach who was originally in quality control. I didn't really know that much about how hard he was working on his craft to know the system, how much he was bugging Lewis and Holmgren to teach him things. A real good friend of mine was Bobb McKittrick from San Francisco. I knew him really well for a lot of years. We always talked about Holmgren and Sherman Lewis and Dennis Green and different people like that, but I know Gruden has said he has learned so much from McKittrick.

The first year, Holmgren had Sherman Lewis coach wide receivers, in addition to his job as offensive coordinator. Then, the second year, he promoted Gruden from quality control to wide receiver coach. I believe it did get rid of his driving duties. In 1992, Gruden was offensive assistant quality control. Green Bay was in the throes of a twenty-five year downturn, and it was just horrendous. People thought they could never win here again. That's what Frank Deford basically wrote in *Sports Illustrated*. From that staff, who went on to became head coaches? Okay, we've got Ray Rhodes, Jon Gruden, Dick Jauron, Steve Mariucci, and Andy Reid—five head coaches out of that staff. Sherman Lewis moved on as offensive coordinator with Minnesota and was just named offensive coordinator in Detroit. Greg Blache became a defensive coordinator with the **Chicago Bears**. Gil Haskell became an offensive coordinator in Carolina and Seattle. Three guys became coordinators. That was quite a staff.

In 1993, Gruden was promoted to wide receivers coach by Mike Holmgren in the off-season. He had been offensive quality control coach his first year. Then he coached wide receivers for the next two years. Immediately, the question was: could this twenty-nine year-old guy handle Sterling Sharpe? Sterling Sharpe was brutal. He was really tough on coaches, writers, and teammates. He was kind of an

> The Chicago Bears wear blue and orange because those are the colors that team founder George Halas wore when he played for the University of Illinois.

overwhelming personality. Coaches would say if he didn't want to practice, the team wouldn't even practice. If his mood was down and if he was screwing around at practice some days, they just couldn't turn the thing around. This was probably Gruden's first major test in coaching. That was when Sharpe was not talking to me or almost anybody else in the **Wisconsin** media. I remember talking to Gruden and to other players about that. All indications were that Sharpe respected Gruden almost immediately and I didn't see any problems they had at all. I thought that probably kept him in good stead when he had to deal with Ricky Watters in Philly.

They were a crazy bunch—Ty Detmer's crazy sense of humor, Favre would have been in that, Gruden, Mariucci. They had a good time. In 1994, the Packer quarterbacks in camp were Kurt Warner, Mark Brunell, Ty Detmer, and Brett Favre.

Jon was with some really veteran coaches, guys who had a million Super Bowl rings in San Francisco and Green Bay. Jon was just so young. I do remember that he would ride his bicycle through the snow at Green Bay. That would be down that half mile slope from the locker room area down to the practice field.

After games, it always helps to have a position coach explain good plays and bad plays in the locker room. After Gruden became wide receivers coach, he was always willing to do that. He was a young coach, 30 or 31, and he did not shy away from that. I relied on both him and Mariucci. I tried to get one or both after games. Jon was more than willing to explain good and bad, to stand there after defeats, just the two of us. One day I said, "You know, this is probably going to help you when you become an offensive coordinator. That may not be too far from now." I never realized he was going to be a head coach sooner than later, either.

> Arnold Schwarzenegger graduated from the University of Wisconsin-Madison in 1979.

NO OFFENSE
NONE TAKEN

DAVID WHITLEY

David Whitley is a Sports Columnist for the Orlando Sentinel.

I think anybody who says they weren't surprised by the whole turn of events that brought Jon Gruden to the Buccaneers is lying. And speaking of lying, it started with the Glazers who got up and told the world that they had no contact with Bill Parcells. You could just see their noses grow longer and longer during that press conference. Their noses got so long, they needed to move that press conference outdoors. We all got out of there saying, "These guys definitely came out here saying the sky is green and the earth is flat." Everyone knew that Parcells was their guy.

Subsequently it came that sure, they talked to him. Then, a year later, they even said they had a contract with the guy. Everyone knew it was going to be Parcells and when he begged out then they got totally behind the eight ball. They were scrambling around and Marvin Lewis was all but hired...his assistant coaches were being lined up and the Bucs' assistants were being held up. Monte Kiffin and those guys, the defensive guys.

Then that didn't pan out so they went out west and Steve Mariucci had this long drawn out emotional thing, "Should I go or should I stay?" Then he told them, "No, I can't do it." Now they had nobody and they needed somebody. They had just fired Tony Dungy, the beloved Tony Dungy, even though they had every reason to get rid of the guy at that point. He had been there for six years and hadn't taken them as far as they could go. But, the way they handled it, it was like they just shot Jesus Christ. He was a martyr at that point and you don't replace Jesus Christ with—hello—Mickey Andrews or Ralph Friedgen, which is what they were down to. They needed a big name guy. They're sitting around and there was Chucky.

It was all done so quickly there was no way anyone could say that this was part of some grand plan on the part of the Glazers or anybody else. It was serendipity! He was there. He was available…although he came with a price, of course. Had he not been available, I don't know what they would have done or who they would have gotten and it would have been a disaster. But he was probably the only guy they had who they could get to make up for the big fiasco that it had become as far as hiring a head coach. **Jimmy Johnson**…he wasn't going to come. They needed to land a big fish at that point. They were lucky to get him. It gave us a whole year to speculate who got the better end of that deal—the Glazers getting Gruden or Al Davis getting the picks and $8 million. It certainly made it an easy angle for stories leading into the Super Bowl. I guess in the end, we all got our answer.

Gruden is a very compelling character. There aren't many NFL coaches who rise to the level of where my mother—who doesn't know anything about sports—recognizes that person. If you just happen to tune in to an NFL playoff game like the Snow Bowl game, you'd see him on the sidelines. He catches your eye because of his whole facial contortions. He is very telegenic and he puts on a good show although it's not an act, it's his thing. Whether he could coach or not he seemed like a very interesting guy and would be interesting to cover and work with. I've never really had a big sit-down with him myself. But when I've dealt with him, he is genuine. He is that character that you see.

He is very much just a football guy and focused on football. If you're into social criticism of him you could disparage him and other coaches for devoting so much time just to their jobs at the expense of

Coach Jimmy Johnson and Janis Joplin were high school classmates at Thomas Jefferson High School in Port Arthur, Texas. Jimmy Johnson didn't know she sang. They hated each other. She called him "Scarhead" and he called her "Beat Weeds."

their family life. He is that way but, the people who are really affected by that don't seem to have a problem with it. His wife knew what she was getting into. I mean she has said over and over that she met him when he was a graduate assistant at Tennessee. Graduate assistants usually work 110 hours a week and he was probably working 500 hours a week. So she knows this is his passion. This is what makes Jon Gruden love football. So that's the tradeoff she gets. She gets everything in the world. I suspect he's a very good father and husband. Ten months out of the year he's up at 3:17 a.m. and he's out the door and you don't see him until late that night.

Judging from his family, this is a pretty smart crew. His brother James is head of Cardiothoracic Medicine at Emory. Jon has sufficient brain power that he could have pretty much have done anything but he chose to focus all his energies on football. It turns him on. You have to be a pretty smart guy to be a successful NFL coach and very smart to be a successful as he is.

He can just play off that stereotypical dumb football coach image when you ask him anything world related like, "What do you think of the Iraq and the S2 missiles." Well, if he wanted to read up on it, he could give you a very good opinion but he's so much into football, he'd just say, "I'm not into 'philosophical' or any big picture stuff." In a way it's easy for him to deflect any deep questions he really doesn't want to answer.

Or, if you asked him, "How do you think your relationship with Al Davis would have turned out if you had been....?" "Well, I'm not really into 'philosophical' because I'm just a football coach." It helps him to come off as just a guy who is simple and there is a great advantage in being underestimated.

Anyone who underestimates Chucky at this point is just an idiot because he's proven there is so much more that goes into coaching than just Xs and Os. You need the whole package.

Gruden remained consistent through the whole season and that was instinct. There is so much emotion invested by fans and the media in every game. People overreact negatively and positively. I remember that first game. Their offense was awful and they lost. Fans were thinking, "Oh, my God. We could have won this with Dungy." I remember thinking, "Give the guy a chance. It's just one game and Rome wasn't built in a day." You don't rebuild the Bucs' offense in a day much less a year—although somehow he managed to do it.

He knew what the Bucs had. They had a great defense and an offense that sucked. If you could just get something out of that offense, squeeze it out of them with some luck on a good run, you had as good a shot as anyone.

Talent-wise, I don't think that the offense was that much better than what Dungy had done. He definitely upgraded the wide receiver. He gave them Keenan McCardell. The offensive line was mediocre. Brad Johnson is a good quarterback, but he needs help around him and he needs to be able to stand up for more than three seconds in the pocket. That didn't happen the first half of the season. The offensive line was terrible, yet they still managed to keep their heads above water. Eventually, he figured it out. Squeezing an offense out of that offensive line is just a great testimony to his coaching. I think he maximized every point he could out of that offense. I thought it would take him two or three years to get it going…and that's if you question whether the defense was still dominant. Over the last four or five years all they ever needed was just a few points because the defense was just grasping at any life preserver it could get in the way of touchdowns.

He gave Brad Johnson just enough time to find the receiver. His strength was his accuracy. He's never going to be a **Michael Vick** but, with that offense, he doesn't have to be. If I'm an opponent, that's almost scary. That's what he did in Oakland. That franchise must be the toughest place to coach in the NFL because you've got the Godfather overlooking everything. You're a coach but you're also a figurehead and you don't know if you have any authority. He was brought in and he got it going. You're never going to become bigger

Saints quarterback Aaron Brooks and Falcons quarterback Michael Vick are cousins. In 2001, Michael Vick said, "I've got two great things goin' for me: my arm, my speed, and my brain."

than Al Davis out there, yet that's what he was becoming. He came in there and, within three or four years, he made Oakland and turned them into the best offense in the league. He turned Rich Gannon into a Joe Montana. You can see what he had to do with that in the Super Bowl. He knew exactly what Oakland was going to do offensively. I think Bill Callahan, who replaced him, was a good coach but not that good. He did nothing whatsoever to throw Chucky off the scent. It was the same offense. He figured, well, we can execute. Nonsense, you couldn't do that.

Gruden went into Oakland under terrible circumstances and built them up. Then he went into Tampa with no assistants and he's turned them around right away in spite of the pressure on the guy, on top of everything else, to justify the price the Bucs paid to get him. I mean he was the highest priced coach in the NFL history. Nobody really cares about $8 million out of the Glazers pocket, that's pit money for those guys. In fact, I wish it has been $80 million.

You know those **draft** picks, that's a heavy price to pay. He knew it too. If anything was a sensitive topic with Chucky, it was the price that they paid for him even though it wasn't his fault that they got themselves in that position. He knew that the whole franchise had put out a lot and had a lot riding on him.

I thought he would get it going decently but that it would be a two or three year process before they seriously got an offense good enough to make a run like they did. But it just all fell into place. They got healthy and they were the best team. But it just takes a lot of luck to get hot at the right time in the NFL because there is such desperation to get by week to week. To get Brad healthy was huge. After that, if you look at it, they just laid waste to everybody. That Super Bowl, it could have been 65 – 10 if they had really kept it going.

They destroyed San Francisco. And Philadelphia—talk about a facial. That was the ultimate "in your face" for Philadelphia because, when

> During WWII, the NFL did not refer to the team's selections of college players as a draft. It was termed the "preferred negotiation list."

they went up there, they weren't just beating a team, they were beating a whole culture. Like, "Oh. We're rough. We're big and tough." The talent was there but Chucky knows how to get guys motivated. He had them so ready to play. He knows how to pull the right strings on all these guys.

As far as coaching goes, it's all about ego management. He did a real good job with that. Keyshawn Johnson is still an issue...they don't call him Meshawn for nothing. He's the kind of guy that, while he's happy with the ring, he'd be almost as happy if he had had 15 receptions for 300 yards or whatever and they had lost. Warren Sapp is definitely a self-promoter but, in the end, he is willing to subvert himself, if it means winning.

Sapp took some winning over because he was very skeptical at first because he didn't know Gruden and also, he was such a Dungy guy. Dungy was his neighbor. He really saw him as a father figure. So he came in with a chip on his shoulder. Gruden dealt with that and he won him over. Even Sapp had to realize that Dungy had taken the team as far as it could go and that at least Chucky had a clue how to score touchdowns...or that he would put people in charge who knew how to get a first down. So Sapp got behind Gruden.

That's part of being a coach. You have this mass of egos—some of the biggest in the NFL—right there and they don't get along. Johnson and Sapp come from two different worlds. Sapp is just a country guy from Apopka, Florida who's smart and has answers. Johnson is the Los Angeles, California pretty boy. So they just didn't see eye-to-eye. They just didn't hit it off. They've both had their turf that they wanted to protect. Gruden managed that very well. Keeping that from exploding and becoming a divisive issue was big...as was keeping them motivated. Keyshawn is the kind of guy who, if he's not happy, will just go through the motions. I think Chucky wants to get rid of him just because although he brings a lot, for the amount of money they pay him and the aggravation he brings, there are fifteen other receivers who are just as good.

From a football standpoint, it makes some sense that letting Sapp play some tight end had something to do with winning him over because he could play that position. Keeping Keyshawn relatively happy was a big thing. It's fortunate that a lot of the stalwarts like John Lynch and Brad Johnson don't have the egos that need massaging. These leaders just go out there and do their job.

You had more good lively quotes the first week of training camp from Chucky than you did in six years with Tony Dungy. That is not really knocking Tony. Your personality is what you are. Chucky knows the role of the media. Like Parcells is always good to plant stories…if he wants to motivate someone he'll say something and someone will read it. I don't know if Chucky really did that this year. He is smart enough to know that he needs to play a role in this whole thing and if you feed us and throw us peanuts and make us think at least we're your buddy that it helps you out. The only problem I heard is that sometimes he wasn't that accessible because he was just busy. It wasn't like he was forever with the hacks. He knows how the modern media works, how to give a good sound bite.

In training camp we found some kid who had done up his face as Chucky and Gruden was happy to stop and pose for five minutes through the whole thing. That's what some people don't like about him. They say he is a self-promoter with this Chucky thing. He is and he isn't. I think he is generally that way, and he doesn't try to grimace and play up the thing too much, but when people ask him about it he's happy to talk about it. Some people might get tired of it over and over again but I've never seen him go, "Oh God. Another Chucky question." He will happily talk about it.

He really has something. I read in one of the sports magazines about what a hot property he is. The trade people like him. He sells products. He's good-looking. The Chucky thing is good. I think of him more as a Dennis the Menace than as Chucky. You know the cowlick, the blond hair. People just like him and they can relate to him. He was acting that way before anybody ever knew him so it wasn't like he decided I've got to concoct this character. I think he's always been that way. It's just that the more exposure you get, the higher you climb, the more cameras are going to be on you, so people just started seeing the way he has always been. He is that guy.

ROOTIN', TOOTIN' GRUDEN

PAT YASINKAS

Pat Yasinkas writes on sports, specifically the NFL. He was formerly with the Tampa Tribune, *and now writes for the* Charlotte Observer.

I've been covering the NFL now for seven years or so but it really seems more like ten. I knew of Jon as an assistant in Philadelphia and that he was so well thought of especially as a young, incredibly young, offensive coordinator. Every football coach is intense but this guy just carries it on. I mean no other coach gets up at 3:17 in the morning every day and that's just a classic example of how intense this guy is.

John Fox, the guy I cover here in Carolina is very intense as well but Fox has a rule that he's done working by 11:00 every night. He doesn't think that anything can be accomplished after that. He doesn't take it to that extreme. That's more the norm. Gruden is obviously the exception. A big part of what made him so successful is his work ethic and just how far he carries things.

First of all, he took a good career path. He started in San Francisco and then went to Green Bay. At the time he was in Green Bay, it helped that Mike Holmgren was a hot commodity—the whole Bill Walsh family coaching tree was—everybody wanted to hire anybody that came through that system. That put him on the fast track but I'm not saying that's the reason he got to where he is so quickly. Also, he is a people person and he was well known around the league even though he was just a lower level assistant and then a coordinator. He was extremely well known by people all over the place because he would sit and talk football with anybody who would talk football with him.

One of the funniest stories I saw was about Jon and Monte Kiffin meeting on the beach a couple of years ago in St. Pete when Gruden was still in Oakland and Monte was in Tampa. It was summertime, they were both on vacation and they met on the beach. They sat down and talked football and wound up watching film for part of their vacation together which just shows how dedicated and intense this guy is.

In comparison to the guys I've covered like Tony Dungy, Sam Wyche, George Seifert and John Fox, Jon is the most intense coach in the league. Every coach has to be intense, to a degree. But he is far and away above all those guys. John Fox is fairly close but still, he is not totally consumed like Gruden is. I don't think anybody really comes close to this guy.

One of the most impressive things, I thought, was after he won the Super Bowl. At the postgame press conference one of the first things out of his mouth was a thank you to Tony Dungy for building this team. That scored him a lot of points in a lot of eyes. There are still people in Tampa, fans as well as some players, who hold some resentment about Tony Dungy being fired because he had so much success and was such a class guy. Gruden is smart enough to realize that there is a brethren of coaches and that they should look out for one another. It said volumes about him that he made it a point in all the excitement of the Super Bowl to acknowledge who helped set him up. That's very impressive.

Then the whole Super Bowl week, the way he handled the Al Davis situation. That could have gotten real ugly because there was certainly some behind the scenes things going on there that took place in the past that could have come out that would have cast a shadow over the whole Super Bowl and Gruden, on his part, would not let that happen. He was complimentary of Al Davis and also smart enough not to get too involved in his answers. He said what he had to say and got it over with. That kept a big distraction from coming up at the Super Bowl.

Also, in the aftermath of the Super Bowl, all the appearances he's made on Letterman, going out to the Tampa Bay Lightning games and things like that. Those things are only going to help his image and help his reputation and Jon is smart enough to realize that. But I don't think he's doing it for image. He's probably doing most of those things because he was asked or he would do those things anyway if he had some other occupation.

There was some media reaction to Jon showing up late Super Bowl week. Nobody would say at first if he was violating NFL rules. The first rumor was that he wasn't going to be out there until Wednesday, that he was going to miss Media Day. But then when it came out that the league said it was okay as long as he showed up in time for Media Day, the issue died down a little bit. But the initial reaction was, "Wow. This guy is arrogant. He's stickin' it in the NFL's face and he thinks he doesn't have to be a part of the show." To his credit, Jon wanted to do his game planning back in Tampa like he does every week and he was savvy enough and smart enough to do that yet still figure out a way to get out there in time for Media Day. Bill Callahan heard about it and wound up doing the same thing. I wouldn't be surprised if, in the future, you will see coaches doing the same exact thing that Jon did.

As for his working with the media at the Super Bowl, normally, the team comes in on Monday. With it being a West Coast Super Bowl, you've got writers on the East Coast who are facing some pretty tight deadlines. Those press conferences were around six o'clock Monday night California time which is 9:00 eastern time. Basically, what you're looking at there is a quick turn around where you go in, you get your interview and you quickly go back and write. You probably have about an hour, maybe an hour and a half, from the time the interview is done until the time the story is filed. You've already told your editors back home that, "Hey. I'm going to do a Jon Gruden story today or Jon Gruden talking about whatever." Then you get in there and you don't really know that he's not there until they all show up and Rich McKay is standing where Jon Gruden should be. Suddenly you've got to change-up. It's definitely a major headache. I think a lot of writers were scrambling that day.

Having covered the Buccaneers through the Dungy years, I still keep a close eye on them. At the start of the season, I was watching Bucs games as much as I could in the press boxes between time outs or, if they were playing a late game, I'd watch it in its entirety. At first, I didn't see much different at all between his team and the Dungy team. It was great defense but no offense.

When they came up to Carolina in mid-to-late October it was still the same. They had a great defense and no offense. That game wound up being a field goal battle. I thought at that point that this whole thing wasn't going to work out for the Bucs. They had brought in Gruden to win a Super Bowl and to jazz up the offense but from what I saw it was still a Tony Dungy team. Then the second time, when Carolina went down to Tampa which was in mid-to-late November, the Buc offense played a much better game. Brad Johnson was coming back healthy at that point. That's right about the time that they really turned their offense on.

Then watching their offense in the playoffs in the Super Bowl it was incredibly impressive to think back at the start of the season and realize that it was the same team and the same personnel. They were just so much better than they were at the start of the season. They are only going to get better offensively because Jon didn't have a chance to really bring in his type of personnel for this year. He'll still make some adjustments on that offense to jazz it up even more.

Jon would like to get a little more speed at wide receiver. He certainly has some big possession-type wide receivers but he wants at least one guy who can stretch the field a little bit. That's probably a big priority. Also, the offensive line. They were terrible at the start of the season. They came on pretty strong but Jon probably wants to upgrade there.

Perhaps most important is the running back situation. Michael Pittman had a nice Super Bowl but overall, he just didn't have the big year that they were expecting of him. Michael Pittman can be successful behind a better offensive line. Looking at the past, everyone talks about what an offensive genius Gruden is and how good his passing game always was. He also has had some pretty darn good running games in Oakland that were a key to setting up his passing game. That's what he wants to establish in Tampa—a better running game.

Defensively, I don't think he'll touch a thing because they are already so great. He's got Monte Kiffin over there to handle that side so I don't think they'll mess with the **defense** at all.

> Most of the time the "prevent defense" works.

Gruden got in the heads of the Raiders for the Super Bowl. The first response from players was always, "This isn't about Jon Gruden. He's not the coach here any more." But, it totally was. There were some guys who broke down and admitted that. Lincoln Kennedy spouted off and took some shots at Gruden as did a couple of other guys which just shows you that he was definitely on their minds.

The Raiders also had a strong indication or a strong fear, perhaps, that what actually happened would happen—that Jon Gruden knew so much about their offense that he could pass that information along to his defense and shut them down. That's exactly what happened. Gruden is the guy who built Rich Gannon into an MVP-type player, a steady Pro Bowl player. This guy was a journeyman all his career. Gruden comes along, makes him into a star and then, for one night, he tore Rich Gannon apart and made him look like a journeyman again. In that game Jon Gruden was a huge factor. I wrote a story where I called it the Gruden Bowl. That's exactly what it was because this game was all about Gruden. Indirectly, he's the first coach in NFL history to get two teams to the Super Bowl in the same year. He built the Raiders to the point that they got there and then he took the Bucs there by himself this year.

In a historical sense, this is the first time that a coach has had that big of an impact in a game. Nobody has left one team, gone to another, and taken the new team to a Super Bowl against his old team in that first year. It was just a tremendous, tremendous story. I don't know that you'll ever see anything like it again because now the NFL is cracking down on trading for coaches and that sort of thing. So this might have been a once in a lifetime deal.

I started covering Tampa during the really lean years. I started in the Sam Wyche years. Considering the way Tampa was back then, I don't feel this event could have been foreseen. I've thought a lot about it during Super Bowl week, I don't believe anyone could have imagined it. Those teams were horrible. You could never see any time where they were getting better. That's mainly because of the management there. They weren't going to spend the money, at that time, to bring in anybody to make them better. I remember how close the Bucs came to leaving Tampa when the whole stadium thing was going on, the rumors about Baltimore, Cleveland, Sacramento and Orlando. Those were more than rumors. Malcolm Glazer was ready to move that team. We could have been watching the Sacramento Bucs in the Super Bowl instead of the Tampa Bay Bucs.

Tony Dungy and Rich McKay, deserve a ton of credit for turning it around and getting them to that point. Jon Gruden came in and took them over the final hump. He was the final closer. This is tough for me to say because I respect Tony Dungy perhaps more than anyone in the NFL and I was angry when he was fired. I was also hopeful that he would end up here in Carolina so I could cover him again because I think the world of the guy. I respect what he did in Tampa in taking the franchise from nothing and making it something but I don't know that Tony Dungy was ever going to get the Bucs to win a Super Bowl. He was going to get them very close every year. Jon Gruden came in and did what Tony hadn't been able to do. He put together an offense that was respectable and kept that great defense intact. It was a smart move by Jon to come in and realize that a great defense was already in place and to just leave it alone. Let Monte run things and focus on improving the offense.

In fairness to Dungy, sometimes you just need to change a coach to change a team. Sometimes people can just get complacent. I'm not saying that's what happened with the Buccaneers but it does happen in the NFL. The Buccaneers under Dungy had a nucleus that had been there together forever, players and coaching staff. Sometimes, one personality or one player can be enough to put you over the top. I think that the Glazers knew they were very close to being very good but they needed something drastic to happen to get them to that point. It was a tremendous gamble on their part. They certainly gave up the farm to get Jon Gruden but, in the end, it was worth it because they got the Super Bowl.

Indiana Football ranks twelfth in winning percentage in Big Ten football history...behind the University of Chicago.

GRUDEN IS JUST A REGULAR GUY WHO SOMETIMES WEARS A CAPE.

JEFF HOUCK

Jeff Houck, 38, first came in contact with Gruden when he covered sports business for Fox-Sports.com, the online version of Fox Sports. Since April 2002, Jeff has been the leisure team leader for the Tampa Tribune. He reported on Gruden's early days during his first training camp with the Bucs. Jeff lives in Valrico, Florida.

I was doing a story looking at how the fans interact with players. I wanted some questions answered from a fan's perspective. Why someone would go out to a practice in the middle of the week in ninety degree weather and bring a Chucky doll that's dressed up in Buccaneer clothing? What are some of the things the propel them to do that? How do players react to these fans? And, how do they react to the players?

I had seen Jon Gruden on TV but this was the first time I'd seen him in person and it was interesting because....Well let me back up for a second. I had gone the weekend before with my seven-year-old son. The thing that impressed me then was that I was sitting probably fifty yards away and I could hear Gruden's voice clear as a bell and out of all of these guys grunting and groaning and yelling and screaming, he just has this bullhorn of a voice. You could tell he was clearly in command of whatever was going on.

He was dressed in all black. He had a black sort of thermal shirt on and black shorts and you could just find him immediately just by his voice. My son was transfixed by him. He liked **Tony Dungy** a lot and

Tony Dungy, Indianapolis Colts coach, is the last NFL player to throw and make an interception in the same NFL game. He was a defensive back and a backup quarterback for the Steelers.

he was a big Bucs fan when Tony Dungy was there. But he just thought it was very cool that here was a real young coach and he thought it was funny that he could hear him from so far away.

Then, when I returned to do my story, I learned that Gruden is one of those coaches you read about now and then who stay until the last autograph is signed. It's true. He stayed until everybody had an autograph, and there were hundreds of people there. It was in the mid-nineties and he'd just been through a two-hour practice and yet he stood there and did interviews and after that he walked to the various groups of people. And not everybody was as polite as they should be. This was really the first couple of weeks of his interaction with fans on a large basis and he accommodated everybody and was very polite to everyone. I was very impressed with the fact that he realized that there was a rabid fan base waiting for him.

He very much appreciates the amount of fan support. He came from Oakland, a place where there was such fanatical devotion and he's worked in Green Bay and San Francisco where he's used to that kind of attention. He was very pleased with the fact that there was so much positive energy here in Tampa. That seemed to really strike him. He said several times that he appreciates the fan support because he used to be one of them. He used to come out to football practices and various places and if he wasn't doing his job he'd be where the fans are. Not that he necessarily has a blue collar mentality but he seems to understand what drives the fans, what their interest level is and where he fits in all of that.

He responded very well to one lady who came back for seconds. It wasn't like he said, "Okay, you've had your shot." He listened to her again and was very understanding. She was very bubbly and very patient. This was a woman who had difficulty walking and yet she had driven all the way from her home, sat in the heat for two hours and then stood in the rope line for a good forty-five minutes before he came over.

She had a Chucky doll. She had gone and made this little miniature clipboard that looked like a coach's clipboard and everything was tailor-made and I think he saw that. He could have had one of two reactions. Warren Sapp would say that's not part of what I am and blah, blah, blah. Then you have a person like Gruden who responds in a way that says "I appreciate your enthusiasm." I was interviewing him beforehand during the media time and I said, "You know, the lady over here, she's standing here with a Chucky doll," and I asked, "How does that affect you?" He said, "Well, like I said, I'd be one of them if I wasn't on this side of the rope."

He's the real deal. He doesn't turn his personality on and off. I get the sense from the guy that he has refined his personality to be a very efficient kind of machine. As such, to change from one to the next would be inefficient. So he's constant all the way across the board. I've never come across him where he wasn't one hundred percent sincere all the time.

He understands what his celebrity is. In talking with the people who cover him full-time and talking to him he clearly relishes the attention that his job brings and not in an egotistical way. Its just like, "I work very hard and I get to work everyday at 4 or 4:30 in the morning. I stay until 11:00 at night. I sacrifice a lot of things. There's a payoff for this and I'm enjoying the payoff." Part of it is not necessarily celebrity, but attention and recognition that his work has achieved something. I get a sense that he's a guy who isn't a Mike Ditka who is going to pose on a cover in a wedding dress and tuxedo with one of his players. He's a guy who, when they ask him to make the Chucky face, makes the Chucky face. He understands what that's about, but it's not like he's going to go out and start Chuckyface.com and market Chucky face. I think he understands that there is a point where you draw the line because it doesn't contribute to what you're doing. I get a sense that some of it is about building up a mystique so that it can be used as a plus on the field to intimidate the other team.

When I saw him it was at the stage where the fans were very much judging his actions. People do that. They have knee-jerk reactions. If you sign three photos and walk away, the people who got the three photos love you and the other ninety people think you're a jerk. He seems very cognizant of that and perhaps that's one of the reasons why he signed as many as he signed. There is a certain electricity whenever you have any athlete or any high profile person who comes into contact with the public. It's very much like spring training in baseball where you can't believe you can get that close to these people. There was a certain electricity to their interactions with him—especially people who are obviously long time fans. The thing I kept hearing was, "We really loved Tony Dungy but this is really exciting. This is a guy who we feel can really improve the team and take it to the Super Bowl." They were right.

I went to every one of the home games as just a fan. The thing that was interesting during the course of a sixteen-game season and then, the playoffs, was that you expect to see some drop off or some pit-falls. Your eye is in tune to seeing variations because some guys get injured and some guys get tired. Some guys don't like that they're not getting the ball. His job was to be consistent and to propel the team. You just got the sense that, if you measured it, his heart rate would have been constant. It was just a constant energy there. That's one of the things that people mention about Tony Dungy—you knew he cared and he was very good, but you wanted him to get upset occasionally. You wanted him to lead by anger on occasion and get emotional about things because it is an emotional game.

The thing that struck me about Jon when I first saw him was his youth and how he used his youth to his advantage. I got the sense that he was discounted because of his youth and as such I got the sense that he positioned himself like, "Okay, well, you underestimate me? You do so at your own peril." He seems to understand what his strengths are at any given period. Like right now, he understands he's a championship coach. He's a **Super Bowl** coach now. Well, how do you build on that? You're not the new guy. You're not the young guy. You're the youngest to win a championship but that's not a novelty anymore. Let's build on that.

> The first Super Bowl, in 1967 at the Los Angeles Coliseum, had 32,000 empty seats even though the most expensive ticket was $12.

Class of 1982

Jon David Gruden: Baseball 1-4, Captain 4; Basketball 1; Football 1-4, Captain 4; Prom Committee 3; Student Council

Jon Gruden, left, at age 11,
Jim, age 14, Jay, age 7

Big Jon Gruden, right, gives brother Jay a hug

**Jon Gruden with girlfriend, Lisa Webber,
at Christmas Dance, 1980**

1981 - Quarterback Jon Gruden relaxes with Clay High School's #1 Fan, Jim Derbin

Clay High School Homecoming King,
Jon Gruden, crowns Ann Atwood
Queen in 1981

**Jon Gruden, Junior year
Baseball, 1981**

Jon Gruden with his high school sweetheart, Lisa Webber, Thanksgiving, 1982

The Brothers Three, 1994

Finishing a round of Putt-Putt in 1992. Sherry and Cindy Gruden are in front. Jay Gruden and father Jim are bookends for Phil, a family friend, and Jon.

From left, Jim Gruden, Sr., Jim Jr., Jay and Jon

Guess which kid is Jon Gruden II?

Jim and Kathy Gruden with son, Jay.

Jon Gruden, Senior year
in high school

Father's Day–1992

Jon and Jay Gruden are doin' the cookin. Did Parcells buy the groceries?

Green Bay Packers Coaching Staff 1992
Front row, left to right: Greg Blanche,
Nolan Cromwell, Jim Lind, Dick Jauron
Second row: Bob Valesente, Sherman Lewis,
Mike Holmgren, Ray Rhodes, Kent Johnson
Stairs: Jon Gruden, Gil Haskell, Steve Mariucci,
Tom LoVat, Andy Reid

The Courage of SANDY KOUFAX

Sports Illustrated

He's Obsessed
And That's What It Takes to
Coach in the NFL

Jon "Chucky" Gruden
gets intense with
Warren Sapp and the Bucs

SEPTEMBER 9, 2002
www.cnnsi.com

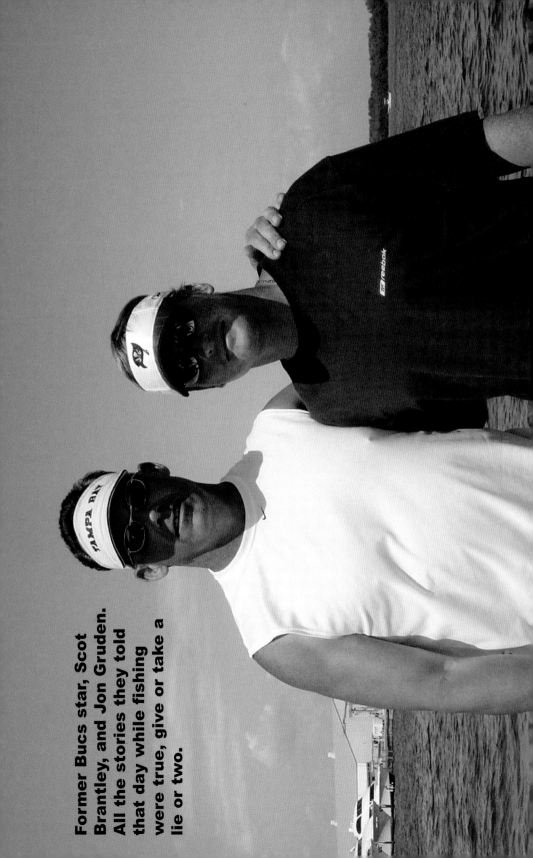

Former Bucs star, Scot Brantley, and Jon Gruden. All the stories they told that day while fishing were true, give or take a lie or two.

Don Zimmer of the New York Yankees: "Jon, we call it a curve, not a quick slant."

"Trust me, Lou. It's not like golf. Low score doesn't win."

Lou Pinella with Jon Gruden, opening day, Tampa Bay Devil Rays, 2003

The Hooters where Jon Gruden once shucked oysters. Picture taken the day after Super Bowl XXXVII

Jon Gruden–Green Bay Packers, 1992

"Ya know, Corey, if Favre had my arm and you had ball bearings in your cleats, we'd be rollin' now."

Jon Gruden as Green Bay Packers Assistant, 1992

Eight is Enough!
Jon and Cindy Gruden
with their three sons
and three nephews

Jon and Jay Gruden with their families

Jon Gruden with mother
Kathy—Mother's Day 2003

The Beach Boys

IT'S 3:17 A.M. DO YOU KNOW WHERE YOUR COACH IS?

IRA KAUFMAN

Ira Kaufman, 48, was the pro-football writer for The Tampa Tribune *during Gruden's first season with the Buccaneers. Kaufman remains the* Tribune's *pro football writer and lives in Lutz, Florida.*

I've covered NFL, on and off, for about twenty years. I remember Jon Gruden when he was an assistant with the Philadelphia Eagles. That was the birth of his persona, the Grinder, the guy who was gonna outwork everybody, the emotion, the passion. I didn't know him on a personal basis really until he moved down to Tampa more than a year ago. I've since developed a very good relationship with him over a twelve-month period. He had to trust me on certain things. A lot of people in this area don't feel that he even knows their names, but I've never felt that way. He gave me the phone number to his direct line last season. That sort of cleared the hurdle. I was part of the "inner circle." I try not to use it too much, but one thing about Gruden, if you need him in a pinch, you know where to get him. Just call that office number, and he's gonna pick it up, day and night. We've got a nice easy rapport. I look forward to working with the guy for a long time.

Actually, Gruden made me laugh a little bit. When they had the big introductory press conference at the swank Tampa Marriott Waterside Hotel, the day after his hiring by the Bucs, one of the first things he said was, "I'm not really deep. I'm not a real deep person. I don't have a lot interests." You chuckle a little bit. You think the guy is just something basic, not taking himself very seriously, which is refreshing. Then as the months grind on, you realize that Jon Gruden was very much telling the truth. He is consumed by football in all shapes and sizes and has been for a very long time. He's just fascinated with everything about it, from practice to training, putting in place, dealing with players, dealing with media. Everything is fresh and new for this guy. Part of that may be that he's not yet forty years old and hasn't worn out a little bit. But you find out quickly that this 3:17 a.m. story, which seemed like a fantasy, seemed like something that he just tells people, is really true. I talked to people on his coffee run at 3:45 a.m., and they can vouch for that. I did get into his inner sanctum this year, the office, which is an experience. I would liken it to a dungeon, perhaps. The whole room lit by just a single dim bulb hanging over his desk. The man watches more film than Martin Scorsese. He never gets tired of it. He breaks down players. He breaks down plays. He asks, "What are other people doing?" "Are we getting too predictable?" Things like that just consume him.

I've talked to his wife a few times. I met her for the first time at the NFL party two days before the biggest game of Jon Gruden's life, the Super Bowl. Jon Gruden stayed approximately sixteen minutes and thirty seconds at the NFL party. He did make an appearance, but his wife was with him, and this woman, God bless her. The first time all week she spent any time with her husband, and here it is on a Friday night, and he leaves after sixteen and a half minutes to get some more work done with Monte Kiffin and the boys. She's all dressed up to the nines. That's him. She has to be very understanding, a very remarkable woman. She knew exactly what she was getting into because she certainly knows by now that he is all football, all the time. There's no pretense about this guy. In a way, that's very charming and refreshing.

Here is this driven guy, but he's got a pretty darn good sense of humor and curses like a sailor...although not in front of the cameras. He doesn't want fans or kids to see that side of him. He makes fun of himself which is always endearing—"Chucky face." He doesn't mind throwing that out there. I saw him in a very unguarded situation with a bunch of school kids at an elementary school, a very different setting. I was glad I went because I saw him in a totally different light dealing with kids from first up to sixth grade. He was delightful. I turned to the guy next to me, and I said, "Can you imagine this guy going from dealing with Warren Sapp to dealing with a six-year old?" The more I thought about it, the more I realized it's not a bad transition. It's a lot easier than you think. He was telling jokes to these kids, but yet he was getting the message across. "Listen to your teachers. They are your role models." He related a lot to himself—

"Don't let anyone distract you from what you want to do. I love football. I do what I want to do. I didn't let anyone talk me out of it." He was great with these kids. That was a side of Gruden that I had never seen before. I'd only seen him deal with grown men and with Warren Sapp. It was nice to see that. He was very relaxed. He was himself. He thoroughly enjoyed himself.

He's got three young kids that he talks about all the time. He regrets a bit that he doesn't have more time to spend with them, but that's his choice. If you would encapsulate Jon Gruden in a short phrase it would be "max out." "Max out" is his big message for everyone. He feels he's on this Earth for X amount of years, and he doesn't want to leave anything behind. Every day is a new challenge to this guy. If you're not ready to match his intensity level over at One Buccaneer Place you may not be there very long.

I was in New York and covered Bill Parcells for a while right after Ray Perkins left to take the Alabama job. I'm not sure Parcells matches Gruden's workaholic nature. I'm not sure he puts in the hours that Gruden does. He's a lot more calculating and sinister, at least on the surface, than Gruden is. He will lie to your face—he's done it many times. Everything is like a master plan, Machiavellian—that's Parcells. You never quite know where he is on any topic. He wasn't even at Emmitt Smith's press conference when the **Cowboys** dumped him, and Parcells was conspicuous by his absence. Let Jerry Jones take the fall! I don't find Gruden calculating to that degree. Parcells will not let coaches talk to the media. Gruden did close practice, which we found a little bit disconcerting because we were used to certain freedoms under Tony Dungy. He has absolutely no problems with his assistants talking. He has no problems with his players' talking, where Parcells wants to be totally in control.

Having said that, while Gruden's ego does bubble to the surface once in a while, there are some problems between him and the general

It is true that NBA Coach Pat Riley never played college football, but was drafted by the Dallas Cowboys. His brother, Lee, played seven years in the NFL. It is not true that Pat Riley combs his hair with a pork chop.

manager, Rich McKay, over some issues. One thing everybody has to look out for in the future is that Gruden's agent, Bob LaMonte, a pretty powerful agent, has about six coaches under his wings, and a lot of his coaches have a dual title like general manager, vice president of football operations. Mike Sherman is Executive Vice President/General Manager/Head Coach of Packers; Andy Reid is Executive Vice President of Football Operations/Head Coach at Philly. Gruden doesn't have it yet, but I think that's something to keep an eye on. He wants more power, not to the extent of a **Bill Parcells**. There's no question who is in command of a Parcells' team. That's what going to make the Dallas situation so interesting. Gruden doesn't want any part of the salary cap issues. He doesn't want any part of the negotiations. He doesn't want to deal with agents. Yet, he wants and wants and wants players. So he wants final say, he's out of Oakland, he's out of Al Davis's shadows. So in that respect, he's gaining on Bill Parcells a bit, but I don't think he is ever going to demand it as a prerequisite. I don't think he's going to try to force McKay out. I think he respects the job McKay has done in acquiring talent and with the draft. But, having said that, there's a similarity with Parcells in that he wants input. He knows what he wants out of certain players at a certain position, the type of players, and it's not gonna be like it was with Tony Dungy and Rich McKay any more. There's a new sheriff in town. If the Super Bowl did anything, it validated Gruden's idea that he should be more involved. He knows he has the full backing of ownership, and McKay may or may not have that full backing. Everything has been vested in the coach here—the draft picks, the eight million dollars, and it paid off with a Super Bowl. So that cemented Gruden's foundation even more here. He can literally get what he wants. The question is how much does he want?

I think everybody was prepared to hate this guy in February of 2002. That might be a harsh word, but such was the extent of Tony Dungy's popularity in that locker room that people were very prepared to dislike Jon Gruden. And if the Glazers did anything right in that madcap

> Patriots player personnel director, Scott Pioli is married to Bill Parcells' daughter, Dallas.

search, it's that they finally ended up with a guy who was a hundred and eighty degrees different from Tony Dungy. That was very important for the acceptance factor. If you're going to get a Dungy clone, stick with Dungy.

Here comes this guy, passion bubbling, emotion at the surface, cursing like a banshee, out there challenging players, hands on, ripping players down to their foundation saying, "Can't you do better?" Shaking up the whole comfort level of everybody in that locker room. It didn't take very long to win people over. He was smart. You win Warren Sapp. You win Derrick Brooks. You win John Lynch. You win Brad Johnson. You pretty much have the Tampa Bay Buccaneers. Keyshawn Johnson is always a wild card. He's not going to like anybody unless they've got him as the focal point of their offense. He's a whole other issue.

But Gruden was masterful. Some of the things he did, some of the techniques—he gave credit to Dungy right away, right off the bat, for laying the foundation. That was important for the players who had been around this team. They were looking for somebody who would give Dungy his due and his respect. Gruden was excellent at that. The Glazers were conspicuously absent on that issue. And he kept it up through the year, even through the Super Bowl. He always gave the previous coach his due. Maybe that's not so important, but with Tony Dungy it is because he's such a uniquely beloved figure around the Bay area. He won over the players who were critical and challenged the **defense** to play even better.

The greatest accomplishment Gruden achieved with this Buc team is that he slowly won over the defense and had them believing in the offense. That had never happened in this town since before I came to Tampa in 1985. You'd have to go back to the early 1980s—the Doug Williams era—when the defense of the Bucs really had much confidence in the offense. It's always been a defensive oriented organization, always. By the end of the Super Bowl, certainly by the advent of the playoffs, guys like Warren Sapp, Derrick Brooks,

The best defense is the one standing on the sidelines.

Ronde Barber, John Lynch and Simeon Rice all couldn't wait to put the offense back on the field. They didn't feel they'd have to pitch a shutout to win. They no longer thought they didn't have a chance of winning if they gave up more than ten points. That was a huge difference. In effect, it actually turned the defense loose to play even more aggressively and with more confidence. They were not worried that every little mistake would be fatal, whereas Buc defenses in the past did have that mind-set.

Midway through the season, the Bucs were still winning with defense and everyone was wondering, because the numbers were similar to their numbers under Dungy. All of a sudden the offensive line got a little bit better. Brad Johnson really came on the second half of the season. The running game was better, especially in the playoffs. They cashed in with touchdowns. The old Buc bugaboo was scoring three points at a time. That ends up getting you beat. When the touchdowns started to flow, the defense went along with the ride, played with a tremendous amount of confidence and actually had a lot of fun watching that offense take the field.

Gruden said, "Give them some time," and nobody believed him. Everyone thought they were the same old Bucs but in the end, he was vindicated. By the playoffs, they were a very accomplished offensive team. No one can deny that by Super Bowl Sunday the Bucs were the best team in the National Football League.

I was a little surprised with the way Jon handled the Keyshawn Johnson thing on the sideline. I wasn't sure he'd be able to turn the other cheek. I've talked to Gruden about this subject—Keyshawn just sort of wears on you. He just grates on you. I remember in 2001 I used to get a big kick out of watching Clyde Christensen, the Buc offensive coordinator, on the sideline. He was a little bit out of his league at that point. I would watch him when the Buc defense was on the field. He'd be standing off by himself trying to talk to the guys up in the booth, and Johnson would always be there—always. It was just infuriating. He was always getting his two cents in. You know his remarks were akin to getting the ball

> The NFL has had nine sets of identical twins. Ronde and Tiki Barber in '97 are the latest.

more. Sure enough, Gruden comes in, and they have their own flare-ups on the sideline. Look, these guys are never gonna be big dinner companions at Keyshawn's restaurant—Profusion at International Plaza. However, Gruden said they got along better as the season progressed. I think that Johnson has more respect for Gruden now than he did before.

What helps Gruden, is being around some great receivers like Jerry Rice and Tim Brown, at Oakland. He hung around Sterling Sharpe one or two years in Green Bay. He's seen the personas of the great wide receivers, and Keyshawn's not alone in this regard. They all want the ball. They all think the path to victory leads through their hands. Johnson's problem is that he ain't Jerry Rice and he ain't Sterling Sharpe. He's not as good. If there's any resentment, that would be it—that Gruden maybe thinks Johnson is not the elite receiver that Keyshawn thinks he is. He's come from Jerry Rice who's just the best that ever played. He's got a point there. He goes out and does it. Johnson has not won Gruden over totally on the field. But, they managed to co-exist. They had the one ugly blow-up, but not much the rest of the way. Both guys came to an understanding two-thirds of the way through the season. With Keyshawn, you can never say there's never gonna be another blow-up, but they're at peace right now.

I was a little taken aback that Gruden handled himself with the grace that he did, especially the first half of the year. Even though they were 6 – 2 at that point, the offense did not look very good. The running game was poor. I would have the same question for this poor sap every week, after each practice, "Why don't you have more of a commitment to the running game?" He'd give me those beady eyes, and I could tell I was irritating him a bit with these questions about the offense. He would say, "It's tough to have the commitment to run thirty-five times when you're averaging two yards a carry." It was a heck of an answer, and I understood it. At the same time, some of us didn't think he was giving the running game enough of a chance. It's all part of the unreasonable expectations.

He didn't like to speak about it very often, but by the time he was hoisting the Vince Lombardi trophy, he let his guard down a bit, and as he and his agent both told me, he felt the weight of the world on him from the moment he came to Tampa because of the circumstances of his joining the Buccaneers. It's understandable. They sacked a good man in Dungy. They took thirty-five days to find a replacement. They paid exorbitantly for this replacement. It was a veteran, seasoned team that was already a playoff perennial so there was only one charge for Gruden, which was to get to the Super Bowl and win it.

In retrospect, getting there was the key. The Philadelphia game was *the game* along the way. That was the game that Gruden was brought in to win. He couldn't have scripted it any better. If there was one match-up, one date, that the Glazers felt that the eight million and the draft picks were worth it, it was having Gruden go into Veterans' Stadium that day, in the cold, final day for that God-forsaken place, fan base screaming. Not many people gave the Bucs a chance. I'll admit it…neither did I…especially when the game started the way it did. That was Gruden's finest hour—that game in Philly. He out-coached Andy Reid every which way. Of course he followed it up the next week with another masterful performance.

He felt so relieved at the end of the Super Bowl. Beating his former team, humiliating Al Davis in the process, and shutting up some of the Oakland players who were very vocal in their criticism of him. He didn't like that one bit. If I ever saw him lose his temper this year, it was when I would ask him about some of the comments that came from the Raiders during the season about how demanding he was, relentless, didn't allow any fun, how much looser it was under Bill Callahan. He really chafed at that stuff. He almost felt it was a betrayal because he felt pretty close to a lot of these Raider players after four seasons. He didn't hold it against Bill Callahan, but he certainly held it against some of the Oakland players. Any references coming out of the San Francisco Bay area suggesting that the Raiders were in better hands with Bill Callahan really got him mad.

My paper sent twenty-three or twenty-four people out to cover the Super Bowl. When we realized Jon Gruden was not there that first day, it was a scramble. It was very much against NFL protocol. I don't think the league was happy. We weren't happy. Gruden is always going to be your focal point. Most of the quotes come funneling through Gruden. But you know what—he put his foot down. He said, "This is the way my coaching staff and I are going to do this." Gruden was not going to be caught in San Diego unprepared and then having to scramble. He loves the way he did it. He's gonna do it again if he gets the opportunity. The league was upset. They could fine him. They could say this. They could say that. That was something that Gruden was adamant about, and he thinks it worked out tremendously. Who's going to argue with him? From a media standpoint, it was an inconvenience. Then, of course, when Callahan found out about it, he said, "To heck with it. If Gruden's not good enough to show, then I'm not showing." So here you've got a little quid pro quo there. I understand that. It's an indication of Gruden's mind-set—that the game is all that matters, and everything else is just an appetizer, including the voracious national press.

They told us in the afternoon that Gruden and Monte Kiffin and the boys were staying back in Tampa and would not be available until Tuesday morning. As a matter of fact, the way everything turned out is another chapter in the Gruden Workaholic Book. Basically, and he told the kids this at the elementary school, this guy operates on two to three hours sleep—on a regular basis. God bless him. It doesn't seem to hurt him. That night, and all day on Monday and Monday evening, they put the game plan in. I believe Gruden and the staff caught a red-eye, and there was Gruden out and about at 9:30 a.m. San Diego time looking fresh as a daisy—this was after a cross-country red-eye flight. Some Don King look-alike was walking around in the crowd irritating everybody, irritating Gruden, trying to get under Gruden's skin. Gruden handled him with kid gloves. He still had his sense of humor intact. Again, it shows how driven this guy is. The guy was basically on no sleep. Yet he showed up at the Tuesday Media Day. That's the key day. That's really when the crazy Super Bowl week really begins in earnest—that mad-house at **Qualcomm Stadium**. Gruden was on time.

> Qualcomm was formerly Jack Murphy Stadium, named after a local sportswriter who was instrumental in helping San Diego obtain the Padres franchise in 1969. Jack Murphy's brother is Bob Murphy, New York Mets announcer for the last 40 years.

That's another thing about Gruden that I have learned to appreciate. He did it that day, and he does it all the time—he stays until the last question. A lot of coaches like their PR guy right there during the Q&A session. And then, I don't know if there's a little bit of telepathy between the coach and the PR guy, but a lot of times, the PR feels like after about fifteen minutes, he's got to jump in and say, "Okay, gentlemen, that's enough." That's not the way it happens with the Tampa Bay Bucs under Jon Gruden. Their PR guy is right there, right behind Gruden's shoulder, just listening, on a need-to-know basis. But, it's up to Gruden to end the interviews, and Jon Gruden doesn't end the interview until the last guy has asked the last question. Remarkable, absolutely remarkable.

It was one season—it was a grand, special season for any Buc fan or any Buc player. They will never forget it. However, it's always what have you done for me lately? They got lucky on the injury front, other than "Booger" McFarland, who's going to be a heck of a player. But, for the most part, guys like Sapp, Brooks, Lynch, and Brad Johnson—although he had the back injury— stayed healthy. Key components like Shelton Quarles and Simeon Rice stayed healthy. You can't always have that. There are X factors around. And, as **Deion Sanders** said, "You know, after a Super Bowl, a lot of guys start smelling their own cologne, their own perfume, a little bit." It was a great way to put it.

Gruden is well aware of the challenge that's ahead of him. For him not to be a one-year wonder he's got to show that he's in this for good. At Oakland, he just kept getting better and better. There's only one

John Elway, Deion Sanders and Billy Cannon, Jr. were signed by George Steinbrenner for the Yankees and given $100,000+ bonuses. All three quit baseball for the NFL. In the 1979 Major League Baseball draft, the Kansas City Royals drafted Dan Marino in the 4the round and John Elway in the 18th round.... Also, in the same year, the Royals hired a Missourian for their Group Sales Department. He left five years later for a job in the radio business. Say hello to Rush Limbaugh.

way to go now in Tampa after a debut year like that. We'll see. You can't be sold that the Bucs are gonna have the staying power of some of the great organizations in the past over a long period. We will see. Free agency generally does a job on that. If you're gonna knock Gruden, it's that like most coaches, he is focused on the here and present. He wants to win the next game, the next season, while the administrators in the front office try to look three, four, five years down the road, and that's their job. That's the classic clash between coaches and personnel, GM types. They share different visions. They have to form compromises. We will see if Gruden is flexible enough to form those kind of compromises with the people who are charged with the job of keeping the Bucs good for a long period of time. That will be the crucial battle. It will not be whether Jon Gruden can coach and motivate. He's always going to be able to do that. To win in the present, while you're staying fertile for a long run is a heck of a challenge for any coach. That task lies down the road for Jon Gruden.

A large reason why Jon Gruden has been able to get closer to his players than some coaches do is his age. I think Steve Mariucci might be that way. Some of the younger coaches in the league like Herm Edwards, tend to be more hands-on. They don't socialize necessarily with their players, which I don't think Gruden does, but relate a little bit more personally to them rather than stay more aloof like a Bill Parcells would tend to do. Maybe a Marty Schottenheimer would tend to be a little bit above the fray. As the years go by, Gruden will lose that personal touch a little bit. He won't want to, but it will be a natural progression. You know what, that could be a significant situation for Gruden. The interaction with the players keeps both parties stoked toward that common goal. It will be very interesting to see Gruden in his fifties—would he relate to players on the same level? He says the passion will not wane, but I remember a guy named Dick Vermeil who also said his passion would not dissipate, and he ended up sleeping on a couch four days a week in Veterans' Stadium, and then one day he didn't want to go to work anymore. There's a danger there. Gruden says he is well aware of it. He can't help himself. This is the way he's going to go. He goes one-twenty down the straightaway in this game of football. It's the only way he knows how to do it. Judging by his track record, if he does burn out ten years down the road, he'll have run a heck of a race, and none of us can really jump on him.

Right around Christmas time, I knew it was the end of the season, but I made an arrangement for Gruden to come into the press trailer around five or six o'clock on a particular night, I think a Wednesday. I asked him come in and meet with the guys, just the beat people, not the TV people, just five, six, seven of us in this trailer that we work out of all year. It was to just sort of break bread, cheer the holidays—we brought some brew in. A couple of guys brought some covered dishes. We were all looking forward to spending half an hour with him in a relaxed setting—no notepads, no nothing. PR scoffed at me at the time because I did not go through protocol, which means I didn't go through PR. I went directly to Gruden. I reminded him the day before, and he said, "No problem." So now the day arrives. I brought in an appetizer. Somebody brought in banana nut bread. We had the refrigerator well stocked with plenty of beverages. We were going to salute the holidays for maybe half an hour, just let our guard down a little bit after a long grinding season. It's almost like your second family at that point.

Well, five-thirty was supposed to be the time. Five-thirty comes and goes. Quarter-to-six. Six o'clock. Now I'm starting to hear it from my peers. "Hey Kaufman, where's Gruden?" The dishes are getting cold, and we'd put them back in the microwave. How many times can you microwave it? I go, "Aw, he'll be here. He'll be here." Well, at six-thirty, I had to face cold reality. I called the office, called PR, "Hey, you seen your coach?" He's gone. Nothing we could do about it. Reminded me of that scene out of *GoodFellas*. He's gone—there was nothing we could do about it. It was when Joe Pesci got whacked. We all ended up eating the banana nut bread and drinking the beverages and having a fine time, but the guest of honor was not there.

The next day the interview is just about over. Gruden says, "What's up?" I said, "Hey, you stiffed us yesterday." "Oh man, I forgot all about it. I had to take my wife and parents out to dinner." I said, "Wife and parents? You see them all the time." Well, he gave me that arched eyebrow from the Chucky eyebrow, and he goes, "Bro, first time I've seen them in about a month." I knew I couldn't go any farther because he was probably telling the truth. With anybody else, you'd say, "Ah, come on." With Gruden, it was, "I understand."

So it slipped his mind. I didn't go through PR. And I learned my lesson because this is a structured man, and you'd better be on his to-do list. Otherwise, it's no-can-do.

I was on a mission Super Bowl week in San Diego. One of the things I wanted to ask a lot of people on the Bucs—players, assistant coaches, administrators—one question, "Does the little man get too much credit?" Everybody was focusing on Jon Gruden. So my question for these people was "Hey, are we obsessing about this guy? What about everybody else in the organization? They all played a role." And I've got to tell you, I was astonished. Craggy veteran guys like offensive line coach Bill Muir, who's been in this league twenty-five years, and defensive line coach Rod Marinelli, who's been around forever looked me in the eye and said, "You can't give that guy enough credit." He re-energized this whole organization down to the guy who sells the tickets at the window. Here I am going out there trying to see if I can get a little germ going that "hey, people are too focused on the head coach." Then by the time I finished my interviews, I found the opposite. I found that the players couldn't stop talking about him so, hey, give him his moment in the sun. The 2002 Tampa Bay Bucs were Jon Gruden's team. He got the job done. He knows it's going to be a heck of a challenge to get them back there, but he's going to keep getting up at 3:17 a.m. You're not going to out-work the guy.

John Madden lost his long-time partner after Super Bowl XXXVI when Pat Summerall retired. Pat Summerall's real first name is George. He is called Pat because when he was a kicker with the New York Giants football team, the newspapers would print: "P.A.T.-Summerall." P.A.T. stood for "Point After Touchdown." Summerall played minor league base-ball against Mickey Mantle.

SO SAY YOU ONE,
SO SAY YOU ALL

We had known for several weeks that the team would be coming to the Celebration Hotel, and we were all very excited about seeing them and meeting some of the players. I've been a fan of the Bucs for almost twenty years. I was real excited and could hardly wait until they got there, but I was a little nervous about meeting professional athletes. I wasn't expecting Jon Gruden to be the first to arrive, but, all of a sudden, this white Mercedes pulls up. I recognized him right away. I opened the door for him. He was real friendly, shook my hand, introduced himself formally to me. I wished him good luck right then.

As I helped him upstairs with a bag, we had light conversation about the season. He told me about Michael Pittman. It was the first thing he brought up, and he said, "We're excited about this Pittman guy."

About twenty minutes later, he came downstairs and told me he had left something in his car and asked me where it was so he could get something out of it. I told him it was just right around the corner, just walk down the pathway, and he'd run right into the lot. He said, "Why don't you walk me down there?" I said, "All right." We started walking down the pathway and were just shooting the breeze. I asked him if he was excited to be here in Tampa. He said, "Yeah, this is where I grew up. I'm excited to be back here with my brother." I had no idea that he was from here. We got out to the car, and all he left was a pair of sunglasses. He got them out and we started walking back to the hotel. We got back to the hotel. He asked me what I was doing that night. He said, "My brother's got a game this evening, a Predators' game, and I'm going to go out there and check it out. I can get you a ticket. Would you be interested in going?" I said, "Oh, man, I'm more than interested in going." He said, "I'll see you later this afternoon and I'll let you know about it."

He was just like a regular person. I was expecting maybe an arrogant person who treated others like they were below him, but he wasn't like that. He seemed right on my level. It was awesome I thought.

——MICHAEL RIZZO, valet at the Celebration, Florida hotel
where the Bucs stayed during summer camp

Chapter 7

There's More to Coaching Than Ignoring Your Best Player

A MAJOR, MAJOR BOOSTER
FROM GOOD OLE ROCKY TOP

JOHNNY MAJORS

Johnny Majors, 68, is a long-time coach and was head coach at Tennessee when Gruden worked there as a graduate assistant. Majors has retired from coaching and lives in Knoxville, Tennessee.

Jon Gruden was a coaching assistant for me. That job would be to do just about anything the head coach and the assistant he was responsible for asked you to do. That's the way you have a chance to break into major college coaching, whatever division it happens to be, or even high school—it's a great learning experience. Jon came right out of college to the University of Tennessee, after graduating from Dayton.

I forget how we first made contact. As a head coach I got a multitude of letters each year from aspiring coaches of different ages to apply for graduate jobs. You hired according to what your budget could handle, and it's different at different schools. Our budget was pretty liberal at Tennessee. We had part-time coaches at one time and volunteer coaches. The NCAA has limited all that stuff now, to two graduate coaches, I think. But they can also have a job at another place working half a day or so many hours a week and can be part-time coaches, graduate coaches and volunteer coaches. Volunteers coaches would volunteer to work for nothing. But now there's only one job as a graduate coach. They do "gofer" jobs. They may have to run errands for the head coach or staff members.

The main thing they have to do is break down films and do a lot of the necessary work for analyzing films and a tremendous amount of video work. I still refer to it as film work, since it was that for so long, but now it's video work. They make analyses on opponents, and also analyze our own team—self-scouting, self studies so we knew what our tendencies were that other people who were playing against us could get from analyzing the films. Where it is on the hash mark, or where it is on minus twenty or plus thirty five, right hash mark, middle of the field, right middle, which is between the middle and right hash mark—what people do from certain parts of the field. They analyze just about anything you could imagine. They spend a lot of time on the preparation squad, as we call it, the down-the-liners, who were third- or fourth-teamers, that we would put on the opposition plays each day, our opposition defensive schemes. They'd line up and try to use the same cadence, the same formations, the same plays, and the same defensive stunts as the opposition did. They were in charge of putting that on the field, as well as preparing and helping the coaches on a scouting report. They did a lot of the breakdowns. It saves valuable time for the head coach and the assistants in charge of game planning. Some assistant coaches are involved, of course, but the graduate coaches—one on offense and one on defense now, but in those days we had maybe three or four or five—did the bulk of the detail work from the standpoint of tendencies.

I'd say Gruden was as good as he could be. He wasn't pretty good at it, he was as good as it gets. There is none better than Jon Gruden was, and we knew it at the time. I'm not surprised that he's so outstanding at what he's doing today. He had all the makings to be superb. He is deeply driven. He demands very little sleep. He would be there till two or three o'clock in the morning many times. There have been times that I've had staff members, and I worked late— when I first started coaching, I'd work sometimes until midnight, two or three days a week. I'd cut back on Sunday, Monday and Tuesday and usually stay only until ten o'clock, unless there was an emergency or there were tough times. Sometimes assistants will stay a little longer, but Jon would stay there until two or three o'clock in the morning if he had a project to do, and he would break it down. He'd be back there at five or six the next morning. We normally got together at seven in the morning, and we'd work till ten at night three days a week, and sometimes the assistants would work on Wednesday. I very rarely worked on Wednesday and Thursday nights. I was with the team Friday night.

Gruden was up early and stayed late. He was driven. He had tremendous enthusiasm and tremendous drive. He is a good-looking guy, not large in stature, but he's large in spirit and large in intelligence.

He's smart as a whip. He's sharp as a tack. He just has excellent intelligence. He also has a good healthy sense of humor, a devilish sense of humor, and he's fun to be around. He's certainly no dull guy, even though he is a working dude. He is a working "son of a gun," if there ever was one. Nobody can outwork him. He also has a good sense of humor, and you'd have fun with Jon.

We were limited, and there were NCAA regulations, but I would have to believe he had the equivalent of a full scholarship when he worked for me. As a graduate assistant, he had to take some courses. He was in Knoxville two years, and I'm certain he would have to pass a certain amount of hours, and he'd have no trouble making outstanding grades if he applied himself strictly to academics, but he was doing both. I have no idea what his grades were. The scholarship should have included room, board, books, tuition and fees.

He just jumped in feet first. The graduate coaches, unless we had them on another project at the time, were always at our staff meetings. I would ask them their opinions on numerous occasions. They were always part of the staff meetings unless we said, "Hey, Jon, you can skip staff meeting today. Go and break the films down, or whatever." Most of them don't have a lot of input. If I asked, "What do you think about a certain thing?" most of them will answer what they think, but the majority of them do more listening than speaking up. Occasionally, some of them will speak up with a good idea because I had an open meeting.

Walt Harris was my offensive coordinator and quarterbacks coach, and Jon worked directly under him. Jon was primarily responsible for the quarterbacks under Walt—doing the breakdowns, analyzing and researching for offensive preparation, and doing some self-scouting and opponent scouting. Assistants did most of the game planning, but sometimes a sharp graduate coach or part-time coach would come up with a good idea that would certainly be worthwhile. Jon was outstanding from every standpoint. His suggestions were positive and he was a great coach on the field for a young person. Walt mentioned to me on several occasions during his two years there what kind of job Jon was doing, and even after he left, Walt refers back to how well he did and how special he was when he was here. I'm not surprised at what he's doing.

I was really pleased and honored, about three years ago, to be at this fabulous banquet—one of the most outstanding dinners I've ever attended—I think it's called the "One Hundred Club" in Kansas City, black tie, formal dress, and there must have been about a thousand people there. They honored certain Kansas City Chiefs, Hall-of-Famers, and recognitions for whatever. They also honored the coach of the year, player of the year and most valuable player in both the AFC and the NFC. I was asked by Reggie White the year before to be presenter to him for Player of the Year for the Green Bay Packers. This particular year, Jon Gruden was the AFC Coach of the Year, and he called me and requested that I be his presenter and introduce him. I changed my schedule, I had something else on my calendar, but I was so honored and very pleased. He's a favorite of mine for certain.

I was talking to his wife Cindy and she was telling me two or three things. He sets his alarm for 3:17 in the morning, not 3:15 and not 3:30, not 3:45 or 3:00 o'clock, but 3:17. She says at times he would be eating breakfast with her, and he would move and take his cereal or plate to another room because he could hear her eating her cereal. Cindy is delightful, and evidently they have a wonderful marriage. She's as pretty as she could be. She was a UT cheerleader, and she has a lot of common sense. She's from way back up there in the mountains of East Tennessee. She's got this East Tennessee twang, but she's very smart, beautiful and has common sense. Cindy knows how to handle it. She is a high-quality person from every standpoint. My son, John, who lives at Knoxville, dated her for a year to year and a half. They had broken up before Jon Gruden and Cindy began dating. Cindy was in our house many times. We loved her very much and still do.

I've known Jon's dad, Jim, since I was in Pittsburgh in the 1970s and I've seen him many times. He's been with the San Francisco 49ers for several years now. I met his mother but haven't been around her as much as his dad. His dad was an assistant to **Lee Corso** at Indiana. In 1975, I was the featured speaker for the Indiana High School Coaches'

Former IU football coach Lee Corso and Burt Reynolds were roommates at Florida State in 1957.

Association Summer Clinic on the campus of Indiana University. Lee had assigned Jim Gruden to be my host for the two or three days that I was there. We played in a golf foursome together and he drove me around, showed me the campus, took me to the hotel and back and forth. We got to know each other very well on that weekend, and we've been friends ever since. I don't recall that being any factor in hiring Jon. I don't remember if I talked to his dad or not; I just don't have any recollection. I think Jon pretty well got that on his own. He was an aggressive person.

Like I said before, I get a multitude of letters every year. I kept a file, and I always responded to everybody who wrote. Some were young and some were middle-aged looking for a chance to maybe get out of high school coaching or go from junior high to college or to a better high school. I'd categorize them and any time we'd lose a graduate assistant or part-time coach, whatever we had, I would get out the file and would have the coordinators and my administrative assistant go through the letters and see if anybody was special and also canvas the staff to see if they knew anybody. How Jon was picked, I could not recall. I went through them all and kept a special file and threw some of them away and kept the ones I thought would be more to our fitting.

Most graduate coaches will take any full-time job that comes along just to get into college coaching—whether it's at Allegheny A&M or Podunk Tech. Some of them would even take a good high school job. They're all looking for advancement. That's the reason they come and make the sacrifice—to broaden their education, primarily their football education, and to look for opportunities.

We've had some outstanding people at these positions, but I don't think anybody has ever had better focus than Jon had. He was focused, had energy, enthusiasm, aggressiveness, and confidence. He had it all.

I watched the Super Bowl this year. In all respects, I think Jon did a great job this year coaching. I was very much impressed. I've never bet on a football game, but I told my friends that if I were betting I would bet on the Tampa Bay Buccaneers because of Jon Gruden's knowledge and experience at Oakland and also what he's capable of doing as a head coach. When I read that he got permission to come to the press conference a day late so he could work on preparation back East, I could imagine that he was up all night and working on the plane. I read something where he didn't sleep for twenty-four/ thirty-six hours or something. He did what I predicted he would do—that he wouldn't be sleeping and that he would be prepared. I believe they were a four and a half point underdog, but I said, "I don't care. I'd bet on them."

Jon Gruden is such a quality person, a loyal person, and as great as Cindy is, and knowing them both so closely, my wife and I couldn't be happier for any couple in the country. We've had a tremendous amount of people who've gone on—Dave Wannstedt, Jimmy Johnson, Dom Capers—all worked for us. Wannstedt started off as a part-time graduate coach at Pittsburgh, where he got his start. Jimmy Johnson was on my first staff at Iowa State. Jackie Sherrill, Joe Avezzano, many, many coaches who've gone on to pro football and college football, and Gruden is as good as it gets. We couldn't be happier for them any more than what we are. We're excited to watch what's happened and very pleased. They are a special couple, and they've earned everything they've got.

To go further, he won't have to guard against anything. I know what he's made of. He'll stay hungry until he stops coaching. I don't think he's got to be wary or leery or whatever. There's no question he's gonna maximize any place he's gonna be as long as he coaches. Only he will decide when that will be over, and that may be several years down the road. He's gonna be up earlier. He's gonna be alert. He's gonna be ready. He's going to be ready for any eventuality that could possibly occur.

VANDALS DID $500 DAMAGE TO GRUDEN'S CAR...THEY STOLE IT

GARY HORTON

Gary Horton heads up The War Room, a team of football scouts that analyzes NFL and college players, coaches and teams exclusively for The Sporting News. Horton spent 10 years in the NFL as a scout with Tampa Bay and Cleveland, and another 10 years at the college coaching level with Arizona State and the University of Illinois. His extensive NFL experience and the close relationships he maintains with front-office personnel staffs and coaches around the league allow him to maintain daily communication with virtually every NFL team.

In 1987, I was in the scouting department for the Tampa Bay Buccaneers, and Jim Gruden, who was director of player personnel, was my boss. At the time, Jon was a junior in college at the University of Dayton. He was actually a back-up quarterback, so I got to know him well in the off-season. He was a guy who was very interested in personnel. You got a feeling that coaching, or scouting, would be the direction he went in. He had a tremendous feel for it, even as a college player. I became pretty close to Jon because I was a single guy and I had an apartment over on St. Pete Beach, and he used to come over and hang out some on the beach. On a couple of occasions, while I would go to training camp, he would come over, camp out at my place and just relax in the summer before he went back to school. I got to know him very well because of his dad and his family. It was a natural friendship.

He did have fun times. Ironically, I got him a job one of the summers, while he was still in college, working at Hooters, and he was actually shucking oysters. Like everything else he did, he became probably the best 'oyster shucker' that Hooters ever had. He worked at it and was very intense. He looks today exactly like he did then. He had a tremendous, great, great work ethic and he had a tremendous hunger to know how everything worked. He would be the kind of guy who if he were shucking oysters, wanted to know the whole process and what went behind it. He was very, very curious.

Jon worshipped his dad and his mom. He was tremendously, tremendously loyal and thankful to them. I think that he had a great feel for the coaching profession because he was around such positive atmospheres growing up near Notre Dame in Indiana. He was an intense guy then. He really worked at it. He was an overachiever as a football player but he trained hard and worked out hard. He was a fun guy. He loved the beach.

Even when Jon was head coach of the Raiders, he used to come back every summer and spend a month here in Tampa. He had a place at Indian Rocks Beach. When he does relax, he is a beach guy, but he is not obsessed with it. Like a lot of coaches, when you work, you work, and it doesn't matter where. It is always amazing to me how many people say, "Well, a coach wouldn't want to go there because he won't like it." With what these guys make today, it doesn't matter where you live, because when you are working, you are working, so you don't have a lot of free time.

Jon is a real grinder. Even as a young guy he always got up real early, which is unusual for college guys. He had a tremendous work ethic and tremendous energy. He didn't require a lot of sleep.

Jon is always thinking football but, even as intense as he is, he can divorce himself from it. When he shuts it down, he really knows how to shut it down. For Jon, shutting it down may be sitting out on the cabana talking football. He has learned to do a better job of relaxing, but this isn't a guy who is going to leave the office at three in the afternoon and go play golf. When he sets time aside, he sets time aside for family. He loves the beach—get up, walk on the beach, get in the water, play with the kids, that kind of thing.

He legitimately likes to work. Given a choice between sitting in a room watching film, or out playing golf, Jon is probably going to sit in a room and watch film. He realizes as he gets older, and especially with family obligations, he has to be able to shut it down. He is always around the game. I am not saying he would watch film on his vacation, but, when he would come to Florida from Oakland on vacation, he used to meet with Monte Kiffin, and they would pick each other's brains.

He had those matinee idol looks, and he always had the Hooters Girls chasing him. He was the guy they all thought was absolutely gorgeous. He was a fun-loving guy but he was kind of above that. He was very focused, even in college. He didn't party a lot and he knew exactly what he wanted to do. There are some stories I'm not gonna tell ya. He looked forward to when training camp started and I would stay at the team hotel near the complex in Tampa. Then, he could come and use my place on the beach as kind of a bachelor pad. As I said, he loves the beach, that whole strand up there from Clearwater down to St. Pete.

When Jon graduated from college, he decided he wanted to be a graduate assistant. Walt Harris was offensive coordinator at the University of Tennessee. Walt is a dear friend, and we were together at University of Illinois on a coaching staff so I called Walt and said "I've got a guy I think is really gonna be an outstanding football coach." Graduate assistantships were very, very competitive in those days and were very tough. I said, "This guy has an offensive mind. He wants to coach quarterbacks. That's his expertise." Walt, who's now head coach at the University of Pittsburgh, was a great offensive guru. He hired him as his graduate assistant and let him coach quarterbacks at University of Tennessee. That's where Jon met his wife, Cindy, who was a Tennessee **cheerleader**. That's where it all started.

Jon jumped in at a hundred miles an hour and did a tremendous job. You knew he was going to be something special. He is a real funny guy. Obviously, there are a lot of trappings that go with the job now, but, earlier in his career he was the ultimate grinder. You give him a bed to sleep in and he didn't care about any material things. He didn't care if he had money, and he went through a couple of jobs where he didn't have much money. "I'm learning my craft. I don't need a lot of

> When the Dallas Cowboys Cheerleaders started in 1972, each earned $15 per game—the same amount they receive today.

fanciness. I don't need the social thing. I'm gonna get up at six in the morning, and I'll work till ten at night and I'm not going to have a lot of luxuries because I am laying the foundation of this career." Then, he was at Southeast Missouri for a year. He was there with Billy Maskill, another friend of mine. At University of the Pacific, he was the tight ends coach and did some recruiting.

At San Francisco, Jon was an entry level guy. Then, he was just trying to put it all together at Green Bay. This was a guy who had a tremendous work ethic, but he had a lot of low-level, non-glamorous jobs early in his career, when he was bouncing around places. That probably had a great deal to do with forming his work ethic. It is his tremendous work ethic that distinguishes Jon from a lot of other people.

This is not a guy who just all of a sudden says, "Okay, now I'm an offensive coordinator." This guy has had to go get coffee, carry out the trash, and do it all. I started the same way, as a graduate assistant for Frank Kush at Arizona State, back in 1973. I remember, as a graduate assistant, checking with the secretary to find out what time the head coach was going to come in, and if he was going to be in at 7 a.m., I was going to be there at 6:45 a.m. Jon had that same attitude. Everything else comes second. If this is going to be my career, then I am going to learn, I am going to soak up every learning experience I can. People don't realize what tough jobs he had. He hasn't always had it glamorous.

He was probably spoiled a little bit because of his experience with Walt Harris. He still thinks very highly of Walt. Walt was a great mentor to him. He gave him a lot of responsibilities, and I think that is where Jon really got his taste for coaching. Walt basically let Jon work with the quarterbacks at Tennessee where they had a very solid program. It was a great starting experience because some of his experiences after that weren't as glamorous. When he went to San Francisco, if I'm not mistaken, it wasn't a very glamorous job. It was basically bottom-of-the-barrel stuff.

Jon has tremendous respect for the game, but he has that same respect for his mentors and other people. If I had a problem tomorrow, there is no doubt in my mind that he would come to the rescue, or be there for me. It's because he grew up around football and his dad was a coach. He really, really respects the profession. Jon has a tremendous, tremendous allegiance to coaches and a lot of his mentors are his dad's friends, guys that his dad worked with. Jon is a young guy and most of the people who influenced him are older guys, like Monte Kiffin. Jon's recent success has come at a very young age, although he has so much more experience for his age than people realize. Like I said, this guy has never had a silver spoon.

When he was at the Raiders a couple years ago, he said something interesting to me: "You know what, sometimes I'd love to be in Tampa or St. Pete coaching a Pop Warner team or a high school team." I asked, "Why?" He said, "You know what—it's football at its purest. There is no salary cap. You don't have to baby players. You can go out there and coach the kids just for the love of the game." I really think Jon Gruden is the kind of guy who could go out and coach a Pop Warner team and absolutely be fulfilled in terms of "this is coaching at its purest." Of course, that's never going to happen.

Jon is absolutely at the core of his being. He is a football coach and he loves the game plan. He loves to watch film. He loves to pick people's brains. I think a relaxing day for Steve Spurrier might be to play eighteen holes of golf. A relaxing day for Jon Gruden might be to sit down on a lawn chair at the beach and diagram plays with somebody. When he would meet with Monte Kiffin, he would get rejuvenated just talking football—he is one of those guys who loves to do that. It doesn't have to be in an office. He loves to study the game. I guarantee you he will be energized in the off-season trying to figure out new ways to play people.

I think Jon and Cindy went through some trying times early because all of the jobs weren't glamorous, so it wasn't like they were rich, although he was past the struggling point when they got married. He was driving around in rat-trapper cars and stayed in four hundred dollar a month apartments, but again, early in his career, when he was learning, those things weren't important to him. It didn't matter. If he had to sleep on a couch, so be it. Material things have never been that important to him. I think that is what is amazing. Maybe he's changed now that he can provide for his family, but they are still a very simple family.

His parents provided great role models for him. His dad did a tremendous job of coaching, and his mom is a teacher. They provided a very, very strong image for him growing up. He knows how tough a coach's wife's job is. He knows the time it takes.

His dad is a non-ego type, absolutely the most regular guy in the world—they are a regular family. Their phone number is still in the phone book, and they still live in the same house they lived in forever. His dad is going to retire this year. They are still tremendously close. Jon still not only idolizes his brother Jay, but has tremendous respect for him. The feeling is mutual. Obviously, Jay was a better college player than Jon. They are just a very, very close-knit family, and I think Jon absolutely worships his parents and their value system and everything that they basically provided him. It is probably as loyal as you are going to see in a son to a father.

He shows up early in the office and he does it not to impress anybody but because he likes to. I don't think any of that stuff is for show. That is why he and Billy Callahan were very close—they had the same work ethic. They both have similar backgrounds—Billy was a college quarterback over at Illinois Benedictine, studied film, and worked his tail off.

I think Jon will be the best coach ever, because he will never get lazy. He will never get to a point where he says, "Okay, I've made it." Because he loves the strategy of the game, he will always keep up with the times in terms of strategy and changing things. I sometimes wonder if his intensity can keep him in one place forever. Sometimes, when a guy is that intense and gets in your face it eventually wears out players over time. Sometimes, guys like Bill Parcells and **Bobby Knight** have to move on. But I think this is his perfect job

Ironically, at the very hour that Indiana University President Myles Brand was announcing Knight's firing, Gruden was leading his Raiders from a three touchdown deficit to a victory over the Colts at the Hoosier Dome, just a few blocks from where Brand's press conference was being held.

now. If he could be anywhere in the world, it's Tampa. He loves it there, his folks live there, so for him I think this is probably his dream job. I think he will stay there as long as he can, because he will never change in terms of work ethic and what got him there.

His relationship with the players is very interesting. I don't think that he is buddy-buddy with them. He has earned their respect because they know he works so hard to prepare them. That is where the assumption he is really close to his players comes from. When Warren Sapp goes in at eight in the morning, he knows Jon has been there four hours. He knows that Jon is working for an edge. Players really respect that this guy is in the trenches with them. He is working on both sides of the ball to give them the best possible way to win. It's not because he is young and identifies with them. It's the fact that they respect him—"Hey, this guy has the same goal as we do, and he is not going to let us fail." That's part of Jon's charm.

Jon can be a little abrasive. He can be a guy who can embarrass you, but I think his work ethic and preparation and his "we're gonna do this the right way" approach is so intense that players who really want to win are drawn to him and are loyal to him. I think he will keep that. He will always prepare. He will always put his players in the best situation to win, and if you are around winner-type players, that is what they want.

It was clear in high school that Jon wanted to coach football. He wanted to be coaching with his dad. They talked a lot after the games and you could see that he thought a great deal of his dad.

What I really saw from Jon was his leadership. There were times when Coach Elmer Britton would call a play and he wouldn't run it because he didn't think it would work. He'd flat out tell Elmer that that play wouldn't work, or if Elmer would send somebody in and he knew that the guy couldn't carry the ball or run the ball, he'd say so. Elmer would take him back out.

——**DAN KASPER**, 51, Former Asst. JV Coach, South Bend Clay HS

GOIN' TO STOCKTON WAS A FOOLPROOF PLAN AND THEY WERE THE FOOLS WHO PROVED IT

WALT HARRIS

Walt Harris, 52, is a close friend of Gruden's and worked with Jon at Tennessee and the University of the Pacific. Walt is currently the head coach at the University of Pittsburgh; he lives in Pittsburgh.

The first time I saw Jon Gruden was on our practice field at the University of Tennessee when he came down from Dayton. We were at spring practice, and Jon came in wearing shoes that made him about two inches taller than he really is. My first reaction to him was, "Damn, where'd you get those shoes?"

He looked like he might have been a little different, trying to look like a dude, you know, Midwest dude, typical, from the city of Chicago. But that's the last thing he was. He was hard-nosed, hard-working, and talented. Football meant everything to him.

A good friend of mine, Gary Horton, who now heads up The War Room, a team of football scouts that analyzes NFL and college players, coaches and teams, recommended Jon real highly. Gary and I coached together at Illinois. He was the recruiting coordinator and we became real good friends. Gary met Jon's dad, Jim, when he worked for him at the Tampa Bay Buccaneers. At that time Jim Gruden was the Director of Pro Personnel, I believe. Gary was the scout for him.

What was great about Jon was that he was really smart. Jon really picked things up real fast. A lot of people don't realize how smart he is. His brother ended up graduating number one from the University of Miami Medical School, which is pretty impressive.

I remember two things about Jon. First, every time you gave him an assignment, he always looked at it. You know some guys might have thought it was busywork, but it was something I asked him to do so he could better understand what we were doing. When he looked at any assignment he never made me feel like it was busywork. He looked at every assignment as an opportunity to improve. That's the feeling he gave me.

The other thing I remember about him is that on Thursdays he and I would go for a jog. It was like jogging with my little brother. He really gave me an opportunity to kind of unleash myself of inhibitions and a lot of pressures. He was just a great friend, a great friend.

Jon was obsessed with football. But he's really good with people. He gave me someone I could vent to, and I knew it would stay with him. I don't know if he really understood how much peace he gave me. He gave me someone to talk to, someone I could trust, and someone I felt real good about.

I don't have the capacity to work on limited sleep hours that he has but I have the same intensity he has to become a better coach. If you talked to him, you would have to ask him what he thought I gave him. I always thought his intensity was great, and that was the kind of guy I wanted. When I became a head coach, he was the first guy I hired at University of Pacific.

When Jon was a graduate assistant at Tennessee, he would get all the jobs done quickly and always had a great attitude about it. When you've got a graduate assistant, you're not sitting there analyzing them, you're analyzing your players. You don't spend a lot of time thinking about your graduate assistants in terms of what kind of talent they've got. What you're focusing on is your guys, your coaches, because they're the ones who are going to make a big difference.

The thing I remember about Jon is that he loved it. He went right to it. You couldn't wear him out. He always wanted to get better. After a while, some get worn down. It's a hard profession. In those days we had a lot more graduate assistants than we have now. I can't remember exactly what the rules were when Jon came in, but I know at one time when I was at Tennessee, we had a grad assistant for each coach so there were nine graduate assistants. Now you can only have one on offense and one on defense. Each year they kind of knock you down lower, so I don't exactly what the rule was at that time. We had a lot of them. He left after two years as a graduate assistant and one year as a volunteer coach.

He went to Southeast Missouri State and coached for Billy Maskill. He was the quarterback coach and offensive coordinator there. In some ways I thought he didn't want to go, but it was a chance to make some money. It was a chance to get off his dad's credit card, and that was always important to Jon—to have his own identity. I hated to see him leave because he did so much for us. He was so much fun for me to be around. He was like the little brother I never had—that's the way I looked at him after a couple of years. Then when I got a chance to be a head coach, he was the first guy I hired. He is the first guy I picked.

When Jon came to University of the Pacific, in a way I might have broke his heart a little bit, but I thought so much of Jon that I made him my tight-end coach and not my receiver coach. I always coached quarterbacks. I don't just want to be a head coach; I liked actual coaching. I figure he probably wanted to be the receiver coach, but I hired him as a tight-end coach because I believed in the long run that was going to be better for his career. What happened is he would get a chance to learn—tight ends are tackles in the run game and wide receivers in the pass game. I thought in the long run, it would improve him as a coach more by being a tight-end coach in that he would really get a great background. I thought that was important to give him an understanding of the game, and all the details of the game.

I have a tendency to take over programs that are hurting. University of Pacific was my alma mater and its program was really in bad shape. Being a Pacific graduate, I was very appreciative of the scholarship they had given me and all the friends that I met. A lot of the key guys in my life came out of my college days. The three guys, to my knowledge, who were up for the head coach job, were Pete Carroll, Greg Robinson and myself. I was really not much of an egotist, but I just felt that because I'm older than those guys and had a few more experiences that I would be the best candidate to come back and try to rebuild that football program.

I believe Jon was there six months. Our opening game was against Pittsburgh and our second game was against Auburn. Jon was coaching the tight ends. We were dropping out the tight end against Pittsburgh. The first pass that we threw to his tight end was at Auburn, second game, a really tough place to play. The guy wasn't even looking for the ball— it hit him in the butt. That was the funniest thing. We were sure teasing him about his first great job of coaching. The first pass you guys have thrown, hits your man in the rear end.

I had Jon and two other guys come out and become part of my staff. One of the guys was Charles Davis, who is now working as a sports reporter for CBS Sports. He was an outstanding defensive back at the University of Tennessee. I had Jon and another guy by the name of Brian Williams, and we were flying to California to get our first job. We were riding out on a plane that had three seats on either side, and I have these big wide bodies out of Atlanta. We're all in the middle seat. We get to California out where it's supposed to be hot and sunny. In January that year they had that ground fog—really low on the ground. You can't see one foot in front of you, but you can see the stars through your window. And it's frigging cold, and they say it's sunny California.

As we drove to Stockton Jon said, "—— California! Isn't this great?" It was so cold and so foggy. It was a riot. All four of us got an apartment right on campus where the other students lived. That's when we first got wind that Jon's sleeping pattern was different. All of a sudden I'd hear someone getting up about two or three in the morning. I'd hear this puffing and I didn't know what he's doing. The next morning, I asked him and he said, "I couldn't sleep. I was doing sit ups." He doesn't sleep. He's really a health-food guy. He eats tuna out of a can and he really watches his diet. He has always worked out and lifted weights and always was a well-built guy. Then he decided to move downstairs and sleep on the couch so he wouldn't bother the rest of us. We lived there about a month and then all moved out to our own apartments.

Jon's a good athlete. He and I played hoops one-on-one all the time. I always wanted to get a workout and I always loved playing basketball. My day as a head coach is that after our first staff meeting we get our whole staff together we go down to the court and play hoops, which is what we did. That summer we were playing almost every day, and I think he beat me three times out of maybe a hundred. One-on-one, he couldn't beat me—could not. I remember when we were at Tennessee, we played every day, too—one-on-one whenever we could. There were a group of guys who played basketball almost every day, but then every once in a while, we'd play one-on-one. We played a game called Tennessee, and I hit one from Morristown, which is almost half-court. He could not believe that. He was really in the tank getting beat so bad by me so I told our starting quarterback, Jeff Francis, "You'd better go see Jon. He's got problems." Jeff asked what the matter was. I said, "I don't know, man, he's got real problems." All I'm trying to do is build up about him getting his butt beat.

Jon's a very unusual friend. He's not big on talking on the phone. If you don't make the effort, he ain't calling. The guy I talk to regularly is Bob LaMonte, his agent, who is also my agent. The Raiders came here to Pittsburgh three years ago to play the Steelers. Jon had coached at the University of Pittsburgh in 1991. I talked to Bob to arrange to come and pick Jon up and show him our new facilities and promised to get him back to the hotel by ten. Bob said, "There is no way you'll get him out." But he did come, and I got him back in time for his meetings. The funny thing was that he actually got out. Most of the time Jon is a recluse and LaMonte thought Jon would never get out and would never leave before a game. He got a chance to see what we have, and he was impressed. He's been a great friend that way in a lot of ways.

He's quite a guy. The success he's had is tremendous. It's great to see someone who is as committed as he is to have the success that he has. He's learned from everyone. Nothing he has gotten has come easily to him. He's always worked for everything he earned. It's just great to see somebody make it. It's great to see what he did with the Raiders even though he was hamstrung by Al Davis. In the NFL you don't want to have 'no' years left on your contract or 'one' year left on your contract. Jon wasn't getting the respect. He did a wonderful job out there. It would make you wonder why Al didn't try to sign him. What is still so sweet is Davis let him go, obviously he got a lot, and then they play in the Super Bowl and Jon beats his ass. It's amazing, really.

It was a great game. The Bucs dominated Oakland. It was no fluke. The great thing for Jon is that he came into a place with great defense. I know Monte Kiffin. Monte is a great coach, a great motivator, and that's a great defense. You always want to have a great defense over a great offense. That's the one thing I try to do here at Pittsburgh—take care of defense first. Jon had to put his offense together with not a single coach of his own. He had to teach everybody his system, which makes the job he did even more remarkable. He tried to coach everybody and develop coaches, and they had to overcome **Brad Johnson** getting injured. It was a great example of a team getting better as the season wore on.

Jon and I visit every two or three years and we talk football. He's smart. He does a great job of utilizing his talent. He's not easy to prepare for. He's a "run the ball" type guy. The more you run, with that defense, the shorter the game is. It doesn't matter whether you win ten to seven, or forty-two to forty-one, it's winning, so Jon doesn't really care. You run the ball and have a ball-control passing game. He's branched out from his 49ers uproots, which is what my uproots are. His first example of a good offense was when he went with the 49ers. He was with Holmgren then. And then his own job there at Philadelphia in the 2002 NFC Championship Game—I think he's grown into his own direction. The bottom line, though, is he does what he's got to do to be successful.

Jon and I are both football-junkies. We can talk football for hours. We can talk forever because there's so much to a game. People don't realize when you have a week between games how much strategy goes into it, how much X's and O's goes into football. If you got a chance to sit down in a meeting, you would be shocked to learn just what the quarterback has to do in order to get the football, how much verbiage he has to know in order to call a play in the huddle. It's tremendous.

When I met with Jon, I brought in a bunch of questions that I wanted to ask about how they do things. We had a take on it, and I wanted to

> Brad Johnson started more basketball games than football games at Florida State. He once made 147 consecutive free throws in basketball practice…The Vikings drafted him in the ninth round of the 1992 draft—the 14th player picked. He did not start an NFL game 'til his fifth season…He is the only NFL quarterback to complete a touchdown pass to himself.

see how much he involved. One of the great things about playing pro football is you're going to get the best. You've got the best, and you're going to get the best. I wanted to see how much he's involved through his experiences so I brought a battery of questions that I wanted to get answered. We had a shared-existence. It wasn't just me asking questions of him. We traded. We exchanged. That's what makes it fun to mess with. I don't like just hearing a guy talk football. I like to exchange. Jon and I go back far enough that we have a lot of common ground, and that makes it fun.

I think Jon's first exposure to real 'X and O football' was probably what we had at Tennessee. He wasn't a "yes man", but that's the way he grew up so that's what he believes in. When he took that offense to Maskill at Southeast Missouri State, Maskill might have grown up in a different way and Jon was a believer in what we did. When he left Tennessee, Jon was a believer in what we did. I think his focus was more "What do I have to do to get this thing coached properly?" than, "Coach, I don't think you ought to do it that way." Jon and I grew up from the same cloth so we're very similar. We have the same background.

You can hear Jon talking about Dungy. You can hear him talking about Al Davis. He's so much into it that he's taken something from everyone. He has the desire to be great and to be special. When you're smart, you don't come in thinking you've got all the answers. That's one of the things I tried to help him with—it's a great game and I'm learning all the time. It's a challenge. It's hard. You can't stay the same—you either get better or you get worse. So you'd better be learning, and Jon is. He's learning, and he's getting better, based on his personnel, and he uses his personnel extremely well. I think he'll be back at the Super Bowl again. When? Hopefully, next year.

He won't get tired of it. He's got a wonderful wife, Cindy, who is just a great gal, and that really helps. He loves his three boys. They're very important to him. He grew up in a family of three boys. He loves what he's doing. He's not going to burn out. He's not a Dick Vermeil type. He's a competitor. He talks about himself as a "ham and egger." I'm sure that when he takes the time to think about it he's real proud of what he's accomplished. He should be. Everyone associated with him is real proud of him.

A COACH IS A TEACHER
WITH A DEATH WISH

ELMER BRITTON

Now Head Coach at Logansport High School, (IN), Elmer Britton, 62, was Head Football Coach at Clay High School in South Bend, Indiana when Jon Gruden attended high school there and played quarterback.

I was the head coach at Clay High School for nine years and I coached Jon Gruden. Jon was there at a time when he didn't start until he was a senior. We had a kid who was a returning starter his junior year and I had a difficult decision to make. Jon really didn't start until he was a senior. He was 5' 9" and 160 pounds when he played as a senior. He may have been small but he always had a twinkle in his eye and he was the kind of kid you just really like to coach. Everyone would love to coach a kid like Jon Gruden.

Jon was the kind of person who got along with everybody. I'm sure he got into a falling out with somebody some place at some time, but I really believe he knew what he wanted to do. I predicted that he would be a coach. I certainly didn't predict he would do this and rise this fast. But I thought all along that he was going to coach because he was from a coaching family. He really respected his dad a great deal and he'd been around coaching his whole life.

We knew he was a quarterback and couldn't really think about using him someplace else because he was too valuable. In retrospect, I probably should have played him someplace else as a junior but I didn't. That's a little bit of hindsight.

I knew his father Jim, who was an assistant coach at Notre Dame at the time. The Grudens were a football family and were extremely supportive. They were just really fabulous. They had good kids and

Jon fit right in. I'm sure that I made coaching mistakes that he was aware of. But, you know what…he never said a word.

I don't think Jon was serious about girls at that time because he just thought of himself as being a football player. He loved Notre Dame and I heard that he and his brother built a miniature replica of Notre Dame Stadium in their basement.

I read someplace that he went to the doctor because he thought something was wrong with him because he had all these weird hours. I think he gets up at 3:17 a.m. and he thought something was wrong with him and there really isn't anything wrong with him at all. It's just his physiology and he's kind of a live wire. That's just he way he is.

He had a lot of tools and I think he could have really been successful at a Division III school. He just loved the game. You'd go into a baseball game, for example, and he'd be there with a football and twirling it around in his fingers. You knew that it was a big deal with him.

He understood the game and was intense about the game and I probably respected his judgment. He'd say run a play and I'd often say, "Lets do it." He was intense as anybody I've ever coached. When he was a senior, we won two or three games which we really had no business winning and basically it was just a superhuman effort on his part. I can recall one game where he won just by throwing a touchdown pass. He scrambled everywhere and he always knew where his receivers were. He got a two-point conversion. He was really a good high school quarterback. What I wouldn't give for quarterbacks like that every year!

He was tough minded. He could get angry if somebody couldn't get something. He understood the game so well and he could get angry. I wish I had a player like that now to get angry when things went wrong.

There are two plays that I remember. One occurred when we were playing against Penn High School and they had really a good team. We were running a play and the tackle came through absolutely clean. Nobody touched the tackle. Jon just sidestepped and he stood and threw a strike thirty yards down the field. Normally the play should have been blown up completely. He turned a blown play into a touchdown.

The other time he won a South Bend Adams game where we scored with less than a minute to play and then he made the two-point conversion for us to win by one point. We were behind by one. He scrambled to the right and then he scrambled back to the left and found a guy wide open and put it in there. So we called ourselves the most exciting team in the state.

Above all, he was a leader. He would organize seven-on-sevens against an opponent school. The rest of the team really believed in him and he really won the hearts of the coaches and the team. Without him, we would have been up the creek…really up the creek. He didn't have a fantastic arm but he had a more than adequate arm. His speed was pretty good. He always knew what would happen when the play broke down and what he was going to do. He knew what was going on all the time. He was the "little general" out there.

I can't imagine what it would be like to be in his position with everybody in the world trying to get a piece of him. I think that's something he grew up with. He was in a coaching family and had a coaching background his whole life. He knew what was expected of him and that's exactly how he behaved.

The best game statistically that I ever saw Jon play was the Mishawaka game when he threw for 256 yards—which was a school record for years—and four touchdowns. Steve Radde caught all the touchdown passes. Mishawaka was ranked fifth in the state and that's before we class football. So they were one of the top teams in the state. We were a very nondescript 3 and 6 coming into the game. We had lost a number of very close games, including the one to Penn High School—a rival school—16-14. We lost to Penn on a dropped a touchdown pass in the end zone right near the end of the game. Otherwise, we would have won that game.

Penn knew that he was the guy who was going to be the difference in the game, so they put all kinds of blitzes on him. To Jon's credit he ran around back there and stayed out of trouble and impressed the hell out of the Penn head coach, who said "That's quite a quarterback you got back there."

——DAN KASPER, 51, Former Asst. JV Coach, South Bend Clay HS

Chapter 8

One Man's Family

MAYBE THE PSYCHIC HAD ESP, MAYBE THE PSYCHIC HAD ESPN

SHERRY GRUDEN

Growing up, Sherry Gruden divided her time between Charlestown, Indiana and Louisville, Kentucky. Her husband, Jay, once a star quarterback at the University of Louisville, is an assistant coach with the Tampa Bay Buccaneers, and head coach of the Orlando Predators in the Arena Football League, as well as their star quarterback.

Jay and I met the very last day of my freshman year of college, and he was a junior. Our campus was very small. The only people who lived there were the athletes and the students who were in a fraternity or a sorority. I was a resident assistant for one of the dorms there, and the last day, we were having an end-of-the-year party for everybody who lived immediately on campus. We met through some friends at that campus party. Jay was going back to Florida the next day, and I was staying on for the summer, going to summer school and working.

I'd heard of Jay around campus but had never met him. I was the RA for the basketball dorm for both the girls and boys teams so I really wasn't up on football at that point in my life. I'd heard a lot about him, and only good things because nobody ever had a bad thing to say about the guy. It was amazing. He had no enemies at school.

When Jay came back for the last session of summer school before the fall term began again, we got back together. He'd had a knee **injury** his sophomore year of college, and he was going to be back playing

> Almost every good football team at any level in America is one play away (injury) from being average.

his junior year. We never actually dated until he finished playing. I was engaged to a guy my sophomore and junior years of college, a guy I had dated off and on from high school on. At that point Jay and I were just friends. We met and remained friends through most of college. This was probably a good thing. He dated lots of different girls and ran around with the football players.

There were always "Derby Eve" parties. The football players had to actually drive the dignitaries around on Derby Day. Jay, in his junior year, drove George Steinbrenner around at the Derby. Jay was driving his car. Steinbrenner actually gave him two tickets to the Derby that day. Mr. Steinbrenner still remembers that. We ran into him when Jay was playing at Tampa that first couple of years. Steinbrenner goes, "I still remember, and I'll bet you don't, but you drove me around the Kentucky Derby." Jay said, "How could I forget that? Of course, I remember it."

I was still engaged, and there was kind of a joke, because Jay and I got along so well, and for about a year, he would ask me out. I always had to decline because I was dating someone. But his whole senior year I never saw him. My fiancé and I broke up toward the end of my junior year of college. So it was two full years before Jay and I started dating, and he was done playing football.

I met his mom and dad first. They flew in for to see Jay, and they took us all out to dinner. I remember my very first impression was that I thought he was adopted. I asked him that, and he went, "No. Why?" I said, "Because you're six inches taller than both your parents." They were both closer to my height, 5' 6", (Kathy is 5' 1" and Jim is 5' 6") and I couldn't figure out where he got his 6' 1" height from.

I remember that Jay was one of the very few guys in college who religiously talked to his parents. If it wasn't every night, it was every-other night. I would go for a week or two without talking to my mom and dad. He would be home every night at a certain time, and he would either get a phone call from them, or he would call his mom and dad. They were really close.

I went home with him for Christmas break one year and met the rest of the family for the first time. Jon was at Tennessee at the time, and he and Cindy were dating. We all went bowling one night. Jon and his dad were so much alike, and I thought Jay was so different. But now I'm seeing that he's becoming more and more like him as he gets older. They are all so high-strung. They always have to be doing something. They can't just sit still. They always have to be on a mission to go somewhere or to do something. Jay could never get a break because they were always, "Do this. Do that," ordering everybody around or making plans for everybody. Jim, Jay's oldest brother, is real laid back.

Jon had this little white **fishing** net, and he would walk out in the water and would stand there for hours and just throw this net in and out of the water. Two of his boys just think it's pretty cool to do that. He may throw it a hundred times and there'll be nothing in there, but after an hour, he might have two of the smallest fish you've ever seen, or a piece of shell or something. Now my kids get bored just standing there watching so they don't do it for long. I asked Jon once what he was doing and he said, "What the heck do you think I'm doing? What does it look like I'm doing here?

Jay and Jon are nothing alike. Life is never dull in our family. I would love to say that we could have one free day to do nothing, but it just never happens. It goes straight from the Arena Football in the summer to being involved with Jon's season. We never had a moment off. Now this year for the first time, we are going to have three or four weeks off in the summertime before the football players report. Really it's a lot of fun, and I don't know what we'd do without it. Thank God, we have three boys, and they love it because we go from one game to the next. If it's not my kids playing, we're going to Jay's game, or we're going to the Bucs game.

Last year was the first time Jay and Jon coached together. It was great. It's harder on Jay because he's so used to being the guy in charge, too. They're both very competitive. Jon is more a mental competitor, at least since I've known him. I know he played, but I've

> Ted Williams is enshrined in two fishing Halls of Fame. Williams once said that fishing was a great way to hide a drinking problem.

always known him as a coach—to always be thinking ahead, to doing the game plan or looking at talent. Jay's always been the on-field leader, making things happen with the people he has around him. Jay doesn't realize it, but he's such an effective coach because he was a good player, and he knows what's going on out on the field. He's got all these guys round him that look up to him. He's like a director. Jon is more a producer. When Jay's not in that role, I've seen that it has been really tough on him. When he's been a head coach, he's hated not being a player coach. He loves the camaraderie with the fellows and being out there. He loves to be able to one of the guys, and it was difficult for him last year to not have as much say and have to take more of a back-seat and a learning role.

Jay has been so fortunate because he's been able to be a head coach in the Arena League at a young age and be the offensive coordinator and call all his own plays as a player. He's been a leader, but he's been able to control it all. He's had a direct impact on their winning. Whereas with Jon, Jay's role is more limited to having to learn, which he would anywhere, but I think that's been the hardest thing for him. He feels like more of a grind to him doing that than being able to be an Arena player and coach.

He's just really torn with deciding if that's what he wants to do with the rest of his life.

I think that being in football all their lives is one tie that binds them. In growing up they've always gone to their dad's games. Both Jon and Jay, being athletes, have just grown up with that—it's just been their way of life, all their life. Whether it's going to work with their dad, or being on a field with each other, they got to grow up playing on the same ball teams, and being All-Stars together. That's brought them real close growing up. They've always just had that as an interest and a desire. Jay was able to play through college a little longer than Jon.

Jon has always been the guy that soaked in knowledge from every-thing. He can probably tell you every player that played with Jay in college. He can go back and remember games and stats, and from that regard, he just loves every aspect of the game itself. He's always watched Jay play, and they've always talked on the phone about it and about things that have gone wrong. Jon has always been there to give advice or to tell him things that might work, from a coaching and a bystander point of view. They just always had that to bounce off of each other growing up. I think that has been the big thing that has brought them together, and then their dad coaching, then on through the NFL, and going to Buc games, and then being a 49ers fan. Their love of sports is the biggest common tie they have.

As soon as Jon was named head coach at Tampa Bay, people started calling us from everywhere looking for jobs, wanting Jay to put in a good word. People we hadn't heard from in twelve years. It was our first year playing arena football, and it would be like "Great job with your brother." We had to screen our calls and not even answer most of them. Jay didn't have any input there, anyway, but people thought he could help.

Then ticket requests started to flow in, even before the season started. That was easy to control. The Bucs sold out after Jon came, so we'd say, "It's a sell-out. We don't even have tickets. If we're lucky enough, we get to sit with Cindy up in the box."

It even amazes me about Arena games how many people we know who ask us for tickets. It's the cheapest thing in town. You can get tickets for five bucks, cheaper than a movie. It just kills me the people that ask you all the time over and over and over again for tickets. We're fortunate that there are seats in the Arena League, and he can usually get them for people. So we do that.

We have three boys, Jay, Jr. who is twelve, Joey who is almost nine, and the youngest is Jack who is six-years old. Our kids' friends see Jay or Jon or see them on TV and they are just awestruck, which my kids don't even get. They'll say, "We saw your dad on TV!" My kids are just immune to it. I guess it's just their way of life. It's just dad and Uncle Jon to them when they're around them. They do love the Buccaneer games. The thing they like is not so much the game, it's being up in the box with their cousins and having food. They're happy as long as you feed them, and they're just there and hanging out with their family. It's not so much the game but what's going on around them.

With Arena their very favorite thing is getting to go out on the field before they open the gates. They beg me to get there really, really early so we have to go an hour and a half early so they can out on the field and play football games there every week. Then when the game is over on the Arena field, they let you on the field. They're in the end zone, and they've got forty kids and they're playing a tackle football game. That's what their highlight is. They think it's kind of neat that their dad plays, but they're not as into it as getting to get onto the field themselves and play.

My kids love to play football. Jon's kids are not big athletes. They would rather be fishing and picking up lizards and things down by the lake. They are really outdoorsy. My boys live for sports.

Everyone in my family back home has become the biggest Buccaneer fans. It's scary. My mom is probably the worst. She e-mails Jay's mom every day. They send articles back and forth, and she gets pictures signed for people. They hound us for Buccaneer and Super Bowl clothes, whatever we can get for them.

We were all excited when we realized Jon would be here in Tampa Bay as coach. How cool is that to have your whole family that close together for the first time in fourteen years? Jon has either been in Philadelphia, Green Bay and San Francisco, and Jim's been in New York and San Francisco. Jim is in Atlanta and that's farther away than anybody, although he gets home quite a bit. I grew up around all my cousins, and every holiday we were all together. We were very close. My boys really had not had that before. So now it's really nice. During training camp, Cindy and I took all the kids, and we stayed out at Disney's Animal Kingdom Lodge and did the Disney thing with all six of them. Now they can sit together at the games, and they got to go to the Super Bowl together. It's been really nice that they can grow up together a little bit.

A funny thing happened when I was working at my old job in real estate. A friend had me to go to a psychic with her. She said her friend had gone and all the stuff had come true. At this time we thought Jon was stuck in Oakland and wasn't going anywhere. So I called Elizabeth, the psychic, and made an appointment but I didn't give her my last name. When I walked in, my friend hadn't arrived yet, and she told me to come into her living room. She's an older lady, from England or Scotland, and she was just like a grandmother. We sat at a chair, and I told her I had just come for entertainment, that my girlfriend was coming and wanted me to come with her. We sat there, and she said, "Well, I'll just tell you things as they kind of come to me. If I'm rattling something, it's just things I'm getting from you or things that might be on your mind."

We started to talk and right away, the first thing she asked me was, "Who is Jon?" I said, "Jon?" I wasn't thinking of my brother-in-law at all. "I don't know. My husband's Jay." She said, "No, there's someone Jon, and it's someone you are close to. Something really big is about to happen with him." I said, "Really." I thought maybe my brother-in-law? In the back of my mind, I was thinking about a job because we had talked about it before, but we thought that chance had passed. She said, "I see papers, contracts or something with Jon." This really freaked me out later. "Something big is going to happen to him very soon." At the time I didn't think anything of it—this could be years down the road, I was thinking.

She figured out, too, that we were all 'J's'. She asked me about Jim and she said, "And your husband is a J?" I said, "Yes, his name is Jay." She asked, "What is Jay doing at this time?" I'm thinking maybe because he's getting to be a player, maybe it's a player contract. She had kept talking about contracts. She just kept saying, "Something big is going to happen with Jon." I said, "Okay." And that was it with the psychic that day.

Then she moved on to other things. She talked about my having three boys and how different they all were. She pegged every one of them in everything. She even said something about my father who was in Indiana at the time. I hadn't spoken to him in about a month. She said, "He's been really sick. Something with his ear and his chest. He's having something with his ear. You might want to call him." So I called my dad and he told me he'd just gotten over a bad ear infection and a case of bronchitis. He'd never even had an ear infection. That freaked me out.

She told me some personal things, too. She said I probably wouldn't be at my job much longer. She said I would be going to work for myself and would be fine financially, that money would not ever be an issue for me that I'd always have enough. Sure enough, I'm doing my own thing in real estate, and I love it. I don't have any complaints about it. I'm not working for anybody, which was my huge complaint.

I left, and I told Jay that night, "I went to a psychic today." He goes, "You did what?" I said, "I know. I just went for fun with Adrienne and she said something about Jon. Something big is going to happen to Jon."

The next night, we heard on TV or radio that the Buccaneers had talked with Jon Gruden, and that Jon was coming there. I just went, "Oh my God." We just looked at each other and got goose bumps. Jay called Jon in Oakland and told him about it. I remember telling Jon that story, too.

Jon has always been so faithful about coming to Jay's games whenever he can. They all drove up for the last game, and they spent Easter here. We had an Easter egg hunt with the kids. Jon just breezes in and out. When they lived away from us, they would always try to come in the summer and spend a few weeks. Now we see them year round and we kind of take it for granted. We do see them at the Buc games.

At Arena football games, people are always coming up to talk to Jon and get his autograph, and he's never been rude or disrespectful to anybody. He'll talk to them and say, "I love ya, man." He doesn't care who they are.

We took our family to a restaurant over by Jon's condo, and the waiter made the comment, "That kid looks like Jon Gruden's kids." We told him he was Jon's nephew, and he said, "That whole family is so nice. They come in here all the time and eat and have a drink." Jon will just talk to anybody there at the bar, and he's got fishing buddies over there now.

THE APPLE FELL FROM THIS TREE

JIM GRUDEN

Jon Gruden's father, Jim, has had a long and distinguished coaching and scouting career in the football world. As proud as he is of Jon's accomplishments, the Cleveland native is every bit as pleased with the efforts and successes of sons, Jim and Jay. Jim, Sr. has been a key scout for the 49ers for years. He has resided in the Tampa Bay area for the last nineteen years, where he sports a single-digit golf handicap.

I still find this past year hard to believe. We have all the games on CDs, and I watch them every once in a while. In looking back at games, I know how hard it is to prepare every week, especially the closer you get to that championship game.

I think the basic goals Kathy and I had for our kids were to make sure they could take care of themselves—be financially, mentally, and socially prepared. Kathy's parents died when she was young, and I was raised by foster parents so they really never had a grandparent. As a result, Kathy and I were the only people they had. It was important to me that when they grew up, they would be able to take care of themselves and be successful and happy in what they're doing.

I really didn't know that Jon was going into coaching until he graduated from college. I asked him what he really wanted to do, and he told me he wanted to be the head coach at Michigan. I said, "Well, that's great. Then you have to not go the way I went. You have to become a graduate assistant at a major university and hopefully catch on with a hot coach and do a good job, and he'll take you with him. Then we'll see what happens after that."

I was a junior high coach and a JV coach, assistant coach and head coach in high school. Then I went to a small college, the University of Dayton, when it was still playing Division I football, and then I was an assistant at Indiana, under Lee Corso, and at Notre Dame, under Dan Devine. I went the whole gamut. But if Jon wanted to be at a major college, I felt the best way to go was to be a graduate assistant. He was single and young and had time to latch on with a good man. I just gave him what I thought was the correct path to take and in the end it has worked out. He worked hard. A lot of guys get opportunities when they're young, and it doesn't work out the way they want. Jon was fortunate to be around good people and good management, and he took advantage of it.

When Jon was a senior in high school, he got a pretty good summer job in a factory, which wasn't much fun. He wanted to quit the job so he could go out every day and throw balls and get ready to play football in the fall. That's about as mad as I ever got at him. We didn't have a lot of money. We weren't making a lot of money at Notre Dame. I did get mad at that, and I made sure he didn't quit.

I really don't know where Jon got his passion for this game. I know he was fortunate to be around some really good guys, good coaches, when I coached at Indiana and Notre Dame.

When Jon was young, he got to watch and learn from Joe Montana and others. Montana was awesome. He was the best when the game was on the line or we were behind in the fourth quarter. That's when he really was good, when he really shined. I don't know what makes some guys like that—that's what makes guys Hall of Fame players. They can bring you from behind. They can raise the level of the guys around them. They have that ability, the John Elway kind of guys who make the people around them play better. I mentioned to Kathy that Rich Gannon was like that. Jon couldn't get him out of the film room. Brad Johnson was kind of like that. I guess that's why I like him so much. These guys really want to be good, and they don't just say it with their mouth, they do everything they can to be good.

After the Super Bowl game, I just stood there, kind of in awe. It is hard for me to describe the way that feels. First of all, I know how hard it is just to be a leader of all those players. He had fifty-three grown men who are pretty emotional people, hyped-up guys, and to be able to lead them all into a game where they come together like they did in the Super Bowl game—it's awesome really.

Jon works so hard. I really don't know where that came from. I'm happy he's like that, but I just wish he had the ability to delegate more responsibility to other people 'cause I think he's going to wear himself out at a young age. I just hope Jon doesn't drive himself so hard, and that he doesn't miss the important things, especially with his kids 'cause they grow up so fast. I think he spends a lot of time with the kids when he can. That's the way it is, though, and you've got to understand that when you get into this profession. You just have to do the best you can do. It's like Bum Phillips said, "There are two kinds of coaches—those who have been fired, and those on their way to being fired."

It was fortunate that Jon and Monte Kiffin had known each other, and he had great respect for Monte. A lot of Monte's respect was the way he handled the defense. All the defensive coaches stayed with Monte, and Jon just left them alone to run the defense. He had great confidence in him because they had been doing a great job, and he was a friend. There was great rapport between the two guys. Now he had to prepare the offensive staff and teach them the offense and to have those players ready and get it all done by the time the season started. It took a long time.

I don't know how this all became such an obsession for Jon. As a kid growing up, he played all the time with his buddies. He played football, basketball, baseball and had a good time and did what he had to do in school. He wasn't worried about being a Rhodes Scholar or anything like that. He was just a normal kid. I don't when Jon decided that he was going to be the best that he could be.

When I go to meetings with other NFL people, they all tell me congratulations for what Jon has accomplished. We all know that fame is fleeting, and nothing is as old as yesterday's hero. You wear a big bulls-eye on your chest. You can be great today, and they'll all congratulate you on doing a great job, and then they start looking at their players for next year. That's why very seldom does anybody repeat.

I don't try to tell my kids what to do. It's their life. Whatever they want to do, as long as they're good citizens and respect other people, I'll be proud of all of them.

GOD SO LOVES JON GRUDEN
THAT HE GAVE HIM THIS MOTHER

KATHY GRUDEN

Kathy Gruden, Jon's mother, was born and raised in Sandusky, Ohio. Her family were big Cleveland Indians and Cleveland Browns fans. She recently retired after teaching the last eighteen years at the Berkeley Preparatory School in Tampa.

So much of this has just been so surreal. We turn on the TV and there's Jon prowling the sidelines of the Tampa Bay Buccaneers. It's just unbelievable. I don't know how to describe it. It's amazing. It's inspirational. It's a gift from God—that's a definite.

I am a simple person of great faith and a strong belief in prayer. You know the verse, "Train a child the way in which he should go, and he will not depart from it." The Bible is a great training manual for parents. Sometimes in a family when one has a strong faith, they rely on you, like, "You're in charge of this department."

Jon's father has an incredible work ethic, and my father had a fantastic work ethic too, which my sister and I both inherited—push, push, push. It's not a thing where you're in competition with anybody else. When I taught school, I did not want to compete with other teachers—I simply wanted to be the best teacher I could possibly be for the children and to satisfy my own goals.

It's a matter of paying your dues and in learning how to deal with things. Everything out there is not rosy. You have to deal with the cards you've been dealt. Good, hard work is not going to hurt anybody. When you get to where you're going, you can look back, and be thankful that you had a hard time getting there. You'll appreciate it ever so much more.

We had always had this thing—if the boys got into trouble at school, it would be worse when they got home. We always tried to teach them that if you do it right, there won't be any consequences. You have a choice to make. You can either do it right or you can do it incorrectly. Always, when you do something wrong, there's going to be a consequence. We preached that all the time. Do the right thing the FIRST time.

We never let our boys quit anything. If they signed up to play Little League baseball, it was like a contract with them agreeing to play. If they didn't like the coach, the kids, or the practices, that was too bad. If they signed up, they were going to finish. Whether it was Cub Scouts, baseball, taking piano lessons, whatever, they were in it for the long haul.

Many years ago, Jim and I decided that I should not teach and stay at home with the boys. With Jim being in the coaching business and away from home so often, we thought that there needed to be one stable influence at home for them. If anybody was going to mess up with our kids, it was going to be us, not a babysitter, or a child-care center. They learned that sometimes you have to do without because we didn't have that second income. Sometimes, you have to work a little harder and a little longer at something and be a bit creative in the process. Those were among the best years of my life...the most fulfilling and rewarding. Over the years, after they became adults, they have thanked me for staying home with them, and for always being there. Some of the most precious words that a mother can hear are, after school, when that front door opens, and a little voice says, "Hi mom, I'm home." Then, of course, they head straight to the refrigerator.

Jim or I always waited up when the boys started to drive and went on dates. They always had a curfew and had to be in at a certain time, depending on the situation. One of us always waited up until they came home to make sure they were in safely, but I prayed them on their dates, and I prayed them home.

Our oldest son, Jim, played baseball as a youngster then played football in seventh grade, and just didn't like it that well. He started to play golf and was on the golf team in high school. He still plays golf occasionally. He was more into individual sports. God led him in an entirely different direction from his brothers where he could not only flourish and be successful, but help others in his chosen profession of being a doctor. His hard work, inner drive, and dedication have allowed him to reach new heights that make us so proud.

Jay has always been a competitor, too. Being the youngest sometimes helps you along life's way in terms of making you better. Jay was always the youngest one in the neighborhood to play basketball, football and baseball. He learned a great deal from his older brothers and their friends. He is so easygoing and so calm—such a special guy. I saw almost every one of his games in Louisville. I would come home Thursday after school, and Jim was traveling at the time, so I would mow the lawn, clean the house, and on Friday I would be all packed and ready to go after school. I'd catch a plane and come back on Sunday. I'd meet Jim in Louisville, as he had the Northeast Region for the 49ers at that time. We have proudly watched Jay's success through the years in the Arena Football League. As a player for the Tampa Bay Storm, he and his team won four Arena Bowls in six years, then Jay won two as a coach for the Orlando Predators. This year he decided to "unretire" and play again. What he'll do after this season is in God's hands, but he has certainly brought us great joy through the years.

My husband Jim has really enjoyed coaching. I think he might retire this year from the 49ers, but I'm not sure. I'm never sure what he's going to do. He may work part-time, I don't know.

Jon is tenacious. He's like a dog with a bone. He's gonna get every last piece of meat off that bone—to reach where he wants to be, to be what he wants to be—it's not to be in contention with any other coaches—not any competition. Jon just has this intense desire within himself to be the best he can be. I don't know where this comes from in a person. Is it innate? Is it something God-given? Is it a trait from a parent, a grandparent? What is it? As an educator, I can't really answer that. It's been tossed around quite a bit, but I don't know. I used to look at my students and see it in many of them. I have a sense about which ones are going to be successful. There will be some who will build along the way, but there is just something about some people who stand out. I don't know how they got that way.

All my life I have prayed, prayed and prayed—when I thought Steve Mariucci was going to get that Tampa Bay job, I went to bed that night and said, "Lord, just lead Jon in the direction of your will," as I had asked so many times before. By golly, the next morning he had the job in Tampa Bay. Miracles DO happen!

It's kind of an unwritten law when you're in a coaching family that you don't interfere with other coaches. I only went after one coach in all of my boys' experiences. That was Jon's flag football coach when he was six. It was in Dayton, and it was so hot when they practiced. The coach and his two assistants would go have a beer when there'd be a short break and drink it right in front of the kids. I went to them and said, "I don't think this is a good example to be setting in front of six and seven-year-olds." That's the only time I have ever questioned a coach—to the coach. Other than that, I have kept silent. But it worked—the next time I went to practice they were holding up a Coke or something and said, "See, here we're drinking Coke."

After Dayton, Jim became an assistant at IU in Bloomington, Indiana under Lee Corso. Lee has always been very good to us, and we keep in contact with him and his family. He's even written Jon congratulatory notes, although he hasn't seen much of him since Jon was a youngster following his dad around at football practice.

People are so critical of Bobby Knight, but when we were at IU, he was so good to me, to our family. Howard Schnellenberger is another one who was good to us. The only way I can judge people is by their relationship to our family, not through what I read in the paper. Jon and Tim Knight played on the same Little League football team. That's how I really met Bobby. I went to a game, and Nancy, his first wife, was there watching the game with me. Bobby came and we talked and had a good time and couldn't help but talk a bit about Ohio, since we were all natives. We did a lot of cheering and yelling. The next Sunday I went to church and got home, and Jim said, "Kathy, you've got a telegram. It came over the phone. I just got it." I read the note that Jim had written, and it said something like, "Due to the fact that you are making too much noise and your behavior is somewhat out of control at your son's Little League football games, we ask that you no longer attend." It was signed "From the

Commissioner." I was appalled. I thought, "Gosh, what did I do?" Then the phone rang, and Nancy Knight said, "Are you going to the game today?" All of a sudden it hit me like a ton of bricks. I said, "It was Bobby who sent that telegram, wasn't it?"

But I was able to get back at him. On his birthday, October 25, I sent him a birthday card. It was a lovey-dovey one, and I signed it "A small-town girl from Ohio." Nancy said it drove him crazy. He could not figure out who sent it. Finally he brought it home, and Nancy said that as she started laughing, he said, "It was that Kathy Gruden!"

After having cancer surgery, the first thing I found at home was a package from Bob Knight. It had two IU basketball T-shirts in it, and a note that said, "It's my understanding that you're doing a lot of walking to make yourself healthy again. Wear these and know that I'm thinking of you." This is the Bobby Knight I know, and he will always be close to my heart for his many kindnesses to our family and to me.

I got a note from Sherry, Jay's wife, who said she ran into somebody who said that they went to the summer training camp in Orlando. This woman was telling her that Jon was so wonderful because he stayed and signed autographs for a good half-hour after practice. Jon was always a big "autograph seeker." He has quite a few of the autographs of the Notre Dame guys. When Jon was six years old, he took a big piece of brown paper and wrote a letter to Leroy Kelly, of the Cleveland Browns, his favorite player, and asked him for his autograph. I have to confess that I never sent it because I thought it was too special, and of course, I still have it. We went to Florida one year and attended a Cincinnati Reds exhibition game. He was busy getting autographs there, too. I don't remember who his favorite baseball player was, but I would guess Johnny Bench or **Pete Rose**. He admired Pete Rose because he was "Mister Hustle."

Jon was always tailing around after his dad—at Dayton, at Indiana University, but I think it hit its stride at Notre Dame. After IU, Jim took a position under Dan Devine as an assistant coach at Notre Dame,

Pete Rose is in the Summitt County, Ohio, Boxing Hall of Fame.

where Jon was around people like Vagas Ferguson and Joe Montana. Our home was always open to any of the players to raid our refrigerator and to come for dinner. And, you know, there are fine athletes at Notre Dame, but they're fine fellows as well. At that time, it really hit home with Jon that that's what he wanted to do with his life.

Dan Devine and his wife Jo, were such good people. Jo was one of the most inspirational women to touch my life. It was almost as though you could actually see angel wings and a halo emanating from her. Dan was admired and respected greatly by our family, and Jim found him a great mentor. I received a letter from his son at Christmas time just before he died. He gave me Dan's address and I wrote him and told him, "The reason Jon had turned down the Notre Dame job was because he didn't think he could coach there as well as you did." He was just a wonderful man, and both he and Jo had a profound impact on all of our lives.

Back when we were at Notre Dame, if someone had even suggested that someday they were going to come after my son to be a head coach, I would have thought it was such a great honor. I would have been just totally awestruck and dumbfounded. Notre Dame is a place of not only academic excellence, but administrative and athletic excellence as well. It is the pinnacle of success just to be associated with it. It's a first-class operation.

In South Bend, Jon went to Clay High School. There was an older fellow, Jim Derbin, who was mentally challenged and was the biggest Clay fan. Jon really took him under his wing. He was one of those guys who hung around and would help with equipment and do anything they asked him to do. I remember Jon complaining that a lot of the guys made fun of him. My advice has always been the words of Jesus, "Whatever you do unto the least of my brethren, do unto me."

Jon was really into baseball. Jon was a natural right-hander, right-handed batter. His high school coach thought he could make him a switch-hitter and forced him to bat left-handed. My philosophy has always been 'there's a reason for everything.' There was a reason for that. Maybe Jon learned some good lessons from the coach that he can carry through the rest of his life when he deals with players.

A terrible thing happened to Jon at Clay. He broke his neck playing football. When Jon's neck was broken, I saw it, but at the time, we didn't realize there was an **injury**. It was a JV game and was the last play of the game, and he went down, and somebody speared him in the back of the neck. He got up and seemed just to be wobbly. It was just one of those horrible moments in your life when you see something happen, and you're not sure. I didn't know it was broken, and the coaches told him to move his neck and wobble it around. The trainers took him back to the training room and said they thought it was just a strain or something like that. They suggested we go to the hospital just to make sure. I didn't have a clue that it was broken, not a clue because I was listening to the coaches and the trainers. Of course, we found out afterwards that it was broken. I took him to the hospital, and when the doctors in the emergency room told us Jon's neck was broken, I almost fainted. They said he missed being paralyzed by one inch! That was one of those moments where you want to get down on your knees and say "Thank you God that he's all right." Jim was working at Notre Dame at the time and was at a coaches' meeting, and I called him, and he came to the hospital. After that episode, Jon got the nicest letter from Dan Devine. He told Jon to stay with it and get healthy, that he was in good company. Dan wrote Jon that he, Dan, once had a broken neck and told Jon how to deal with it. Dan was always so thoughtful.

It was the same kind of thing with Jay. I was there when he blew out his knee. A mother, when she sees these things, gets physically sick to the point where you just shake and you feel so sick to your stomach. Your own body feels violated and bruised, and that feeling of "Oh, I wish it was me instead," goes through your mind. What hurts our children hurts a parent dreadfully, and every mother and father can relate to that.

It was no different than when Jon was six years old and playing T-Ball. He was at the pitcher's mound. In front of the mound was a little piece of wood embedded in the soil. A batter hit the ball against that piece of wood that in turn hit Jon right in the nose. Of course,

> Among the sixteen most popular college sports, spring football has the highest injury rate.

blood spurted everywhere, and there he is flat on his back on the mound. I'm just worried to death about him. Jim goes out and says, "Jon, wipe your nose. You're going to be fine. Get back up and play." And he did. As soon as you know they're all right, you help them face it, get them back up, and start again, but it's a painful process.

We helped our kids, but they took out student loans. Jay was fortunate to win a scholarship at the University of Louisville, and we really were thankful for that. They all had summer jobs. I can remember our oldest son, Jim, being a telephone solicitor and a short-order cook during the summer to make money. Jon did something in a tomato factory. I can't remember what. Jay was a bagboy at Kash 'n' Karry. When Jon was working at Hooters, shucking oysters, his hands were pretty well cut up, scratches and cuts here and there. But it was a job, and it was one of those things he had to do. It's like one of those things where you have to kiss a lot of frogs before you get to the prince. That's what he was doing. He never complained.

When Jon left to go to Muskingum, our son, Jim, was already gone, but he hadn't gone that far away, and Jay was still at home. We weren't able to go see Jon play at Dayton very often, but I did to go up for Parents' Weekend, and he didn't play. He held the football for the extra kicks. I would ask him if he wanted me to come up, and he'd say, "Mom, I don't think I'm gonna play, so don't come." I only went to two or three games at the most.

All through high school and college, it seemed like Jon had the worst luck, as far as who was ahead of him, and it just ate away at him. What made it so heartbreaking was in the summertime between semesters at University of Dayton, he would come home, and after his job, he would go down to a local football field. He'd take a bag of footballs and throw them all the way down to one end of the field, and then go down to that end and throw them all back. He was working out and practicing and really working hard all the time, and he never really got a shot. It was very frustrating. Jon worked so hard at it. It was just like he was in the wrong place at the wrong time—every time.

While Jim was a coach at Notre Dame, we wanted to refinish the basement, so I did it with "crowd" wallpaper on the top and fake brick on the bottom, just like the Notre Dame Stadium. Then I set benches all the way around the room and painted the little lepre-chaun. The floor was Astroturf with white lines going across, looking like yard lines. When we were moving and trying to sell our house, the would-be buyers fell in love with it. When they came to look at the house, they looked at the upstairs, the downstairs, and just went through lickety-split. Then, they got to the basement and spent a lot of time. Being Notre Dame fans, they bought the house because of the basement.

Jon used to say that his goal was to be the head coach at Michigan. When we were at Indiana, our football teams were struggling. Michigan rolled into town and beat us something like 56-7. We heard that **Michigan fight song** so many times that day, we all memorized it. Jon loved that song, and I think, because there's prestige there, too, he just pulled that out of a hat because Michigan has always been a fine and respected school. He could have just as easily said Notre Dame, Ohio State, Tennessee, or any other well-known university or college where there is a winning football tradition.

When Jon left Tennessee and went to Southeast Missouri, we weren't surprised. Jon has had good advice along the way. If you're going to start, you have to be a graduate assistant. Then you have to go some-place to be an assistant coach. Then, you go from an assistant coach to a head coach or you go another route. It's like a training school for coaches. There are certain steps you take. When he worked for Mike Holmgren with the 49ers, and Jon was absolutely nothing out there, Mike said, "When I get a job, you'll be the first one I call, but this is what you need to do. You need to go get a year under your belt." That was when Paul Hackett called him from Pitt. Jon went to Pitt as the

> Louis Elbel, a South Bend native wrote the Michigan Fight Song in South Bend in a house that is now the site of the College Football Hall of Fame.

> Ricky Nelson and John DeLorean married daughters of 1940 Heisman Trophy Winner Tom Harmon of Michigan.

receivers coach. But there again, Mike had advised him. Coaching is a wonderful fraternity in that coaches give advice and help each other.

Jon got the San Francisco job because of Jim. Mike Holmgren said something to Jim about looking for somebody to do some work, and Jim said, "I've got just the guy for you, my son." I'm sure Jim has gotten other calls about Jon, but I'm not sure that he was influential on any of the other jobs. Jon always saw a purpose in everything. He's always done whatever was necessary to take the next step.

Jon admires so many people and is grateful to them all—Walt Harris, Johnny Majors, Paul Hackett, and a score of others. He admired Mike Holmgren so much. There was just some chemistry there. Mike is a good person, and he is a brilliant man. They had a great relationship. He is fair, and he taught and tutored Jon. If he had told Jon to jump in the lake, Jon would have gone. Mike left one spring and said, "I want you to take this summer and learn how to use a computer. When I get back, I want this, this and this done." Jon went out and got this expert—a computer nerd—and he learned all this technology so he was ready for Mike when he came back. He always wanted to do what was necessary. Jon's a quick study. Now, Jon lives on computers.

By the same token, he loved Bobb McKittrick. He admired him for his work ethic, and for being the person Bobb was. Bobb had a single-track, football-mind, too. He was bound and determined to be the best he could be at what he did. He was an excellent 'X and O' man. He knew so much. Jon just wanted to be a sponge around Bobb and just try to learn from him. Bobb was great with the players. He was just an expert at what he did. If you are learning, you want to be around people like that. You want to learn from the best in the business—from the very best people at what they do. Jon was very upset when he heard that Bobb was about to die. He talked with him at that time, and Jon didn't want to believe him. When they talked, he told Jon that there was more to life than football. When you admire somebody like that, you always want to believe they're invincible. You realize that they aren't after all. Jon just adored that man, and was heartbroken when he passed away.

We love Eddie DeBartolo, the former 49ers owner. He was a great owner, and he has been so kind to us. He was a generous owner. When they won those back-to-back Super Bowls, he took everybody to Kauai, us included, the lowly scouts and wives. He has been good to us through the years. This year, after the Super Bowl, we received a nice big bouquet of flowers from him congratulating us. He sent Jon a big bouquet of flowers and a beautiful letter, just a beautiful letter. Eddie is like that…very thoughtful.

I really think Al Davis liked Jon. I think he loved Jon's fire. I think when he looked at Jon at first, he found somebody that matched his own fire. Jon reminded him of a young Al Davis. That is my own opinion. Jon and his family will always be grateful to Mr. Davis for giving him the opportunity to be the head coach of the Oakland Raiders…for taking a chance on someone so young.

When Jon came to Tampa Bay, he couldn't bring his own coaches. He walked into a situation with a brand new staff, and players who were intensely loyal to Tony Dungy. Dungy was very well liked and respected, and rightfully so. He was the major reason for the success of the franchise.

I was fortunate in teaching in a private school for eighteen years at Berkeley and in Tampa. I loved the parents because they really cared about their children's future. They are paying a high tuition and are doing all the things that are necessary for their children to succeed. They supervise homework. They spend time with them. They go to every conference, every open house. They are actively involved in the child's school life and personal life. They are always there. It was refreshing and reassuring to see some of those parents and their interaction with their children, teaching them values. So, when I arrived at school to teach, a great group of children was already present. The only thing that ever troubled me was children with the poorer work ethic. I would always tell them, "Look, if you don't do your homework, you're not hurting me at all. You're hurting yourself." That's the part that hurt me so much. I absolutely loved teaching—the children motivated me and brightened my world, and I can honestly say that I never taught a child that I didn't love. Living in a child's world was wonderful beyond words. The rewards last forever.

Jon was so good to me when I taught at Berkeley. When he was head coach of the Raiders, he sent a huge box of Raider stuff. Everybody received bumper stickers and their own Oakland Raider hat. You wouldn't believe the pandemonium until you see a classroom of fourth graders going nuts over a big box of items from an NFL team.

Cindy sometimes has a hard time with Jon because he is so finicky about "chewing noise" while eating. When we lived in Dayton, we were very strapped for money. My aunt moved in with us, and she lived with us for two years there. At the dinner table, she sat beside Jon, who was about seven or eight years old. She would sometimes chew loudly and also chew with her mouth open. Jon would sit next to her with his hand up against his ear, the one that was next to her and try to eat with the other hand at the same time. Cindy and Sherry, Jay's wife, say, "Aunt Dutchie really did a number on Jon and Jay." And, God forbid, she chewed gum. Little things like that bothered Jon, and seem to bother Jay now as well.

Cindy was God's gift to Jon. Jon is probably not easy to live with at times, especially when she has to go someplace else just to eat her cereal. She handles everything beautifully. She's a good mother to those little boys, and she's willing to do anything to help anyone else. Jon really, really hit the jackpot with this one! Cindy is one of those people you immediately like. There's something about some people that you like them right away, and she's one of them. She has a special warmth about her.

I feel the same way about Jay's wife, Sherry. She's yet another one of God's gifts. I marvel at her keeping her sanity and being so calm and patient. She's one of those people who is successful at anything she attempts whether it be working in the front office of the Buccaneers, Orlando Predators, or selling real estate. One can only admire a working mother who still finds time, energy, and patience to run three young boys to baseball, basketball, soccer, and football practices and games, all in different directions. She is perpetual motion and never misses a step…or a game! And, she's as sweet as they come.

In the past, every time we were out and someone would ask our name, we'd say Gruden, G-R-U-D-E-N, because everyone would misspell it. Recently I was out with Sherry, and she had to give her name. She said,

"Gruden, G-R-U-D-E-N." Cindy started doing it, and now the grand-children are doing it. Our name was always mispronounced Grud-en or Grunden. For a while, Jim said, "Maybe we ought to change our name to Gru-DEN, like Tony Dor-SETT, but we never did.

There have been a lot of fun things involved with Jon's coaching. I guess I just enjoy being his mother and enjoy watching him. I enjoy watching his interaction with his players. I enjoy watching him work hard. I love to watch him get involved in the strategy of the game. I know that's what he loves. He loves to look for mismatches. I just love to watch him work. I love going to the games with all the grand-children in attendance.

At the Super Bowl, **Phil Mickelson**, sat in front of us. My husband is such an avid golfer, and the TV is always on, and I watch just often enough to be familiar with golfing names. As soon as Phil came down to his seat, I knew who he was. I was just thrilled to be sitting behind him. He was very polite, and I've been an admirer from afar because he's a first class person as well as a golfer. Bob Costas was two rows in front of us, but we didn't say anything to him. While I was there, David Wells, the Yankees pitcher, came over and intro-duced himself to us. Jon met him and really liked him when he was down here last year with the Yankees. It was an honor meeting him, a real privilege. Those experiences made the Super Bowl even more special, because, ordinarily, those things don't happen to us.

At the Super Bowl, after Brooks' **interception**, when I knew we had the game in the bag, I could just sit there and put my head in my lap and cry, overwhelmed by the goodness of God. People say, "Oh,

> Phil Mickelson has never won a golf "major," yet he once held the record for the lowest four-round total in The PGA Championship. A few minutes later, David Toms broke Mickelson's record and won the 2001 PGA Championship.

> Most NFL coaches believe that an interception is twice as valuable as recovering a fumble...Recovering fumbles is largely a matter of luck, while intercepting passes is largely a matter of skill.

you've been such a good parent." It isn't me. God has worked through me. God has considerably blessed our entire family.

Jon knows Jim is gone for a few weeks for draft meetings in San Francisco, and he called me today and said, "Mom, I'm calling to tell you that on Sunday I'm going to pick you up, and we're going to Jay's game together in Orlando." That's my Jon. All the boys have always been very thoughtful and they take good care of mom and dad. My oldest son called last week and said, "Mom, I have a conference in Las Vegas on the twenty-first through the twenty-fourth. I'd like to buy you a plane ticket to come with me." So I am. Jay has called two or three times this week just to see how I'm doing. Cindy and Sherry too.

It's unbelievable to think that Jon is one of thirty-two in the entire world. Actually he's one of one this year—his team won the Super Bowl! As a mother, who'd have ever dreamed this? The Glazer family, as owners of the Buccaneers, certainly has a special place in my heart for bringing Jon here. The Super Bowl was a culmination of hard work and dedication by all those who played a role…the coaches, players, the foundation laid by Tony Dungy, and front office personnel. I really think that the support and enthusiasm of the fans carried us to San Diego. All of Tampa Bay shared the pride and joy of winning Super Bowl XXXVII, and I'm proud to say that I am a member of this fine community.

We like our little house here in the wonderful city of Tampa. We could move to a bigger house, but why would we? We have very caring neighbors and the house is perfect for us. We live just a few minutes from Jon and are close to our other sons. What more could a parent/grandparent want? My only wish would be that my sister, Karen Leber, lived closer than Texas. She just happens to be my best friend as well, always supportive, loving, and caring. She and her husband Terry are big time Bucs fans and attend as many games as they can.

Jon not only loves to coach, but he loves to teach and loves to learn. The success that Jon has achieved—it's just so hard to describe. We are so incredibly proud of him, but we fully realize that a lot of people have had a hand in his success. It's a humbling and overwhelming experience, and I am most grateful—beyond measure—to God for this blessing.